Transatlantic Sport

Transatlantic Sport

The Comparative Economics of North American and European Sports

Edited by

Carlos Pestana Barros

Professor of Economics, Instituto Superior de Economia e Gestao, Technical University of Lisbon, Portugal

Muradali Ibrahímo

Professor of Economics, Instituto Superior de Economia e Gestao, Technical University of Lisbon, Portugal

Stefan Szymanski

Professor of Economics, Imperial College Management School, UK

Edward Elgar
Cheltenham, UK • Northampton, MA, USA

© CIEF, 2002

Published by
Edward Elgar Publishing Limited
Glensanda House
Montpellier Parade
Cheltenham
Glos GL50 1UA
UK

Edward Elgar Publishing, Inc.
136 West Street
Suite 202
Northampton
Massachusetts 01060
USA

A catalogue record for this book
is available from the British Library

Library of Congress Cataloguing in Publication Data
Transatlantic sport : the comparative economics of North American and European sports / edited by Carlos Pestana Barros, Muradali Ibrahímo, Stefan Szymanski.
        p.   cm.
    Includes bibliographical references and index.
        1. Sports — Economic aspects — United States — Cross-cultural studies.
    2. Sports — Economic aspects — Europe — Cross-cultural studies.   I. Barros, Carlos Pestana.   II. Ibrahímo, Muradali.   III. Szymanski, Stefan, 1960–
    GV716.T73   2002
    338.4′7796—dc21   2002070029

ISBN 1 84064 947 X

Printed and bound in Great Britain by Biddles Ltd, *www.biddles.co.uk*

Contents

Figures

Tables

Contributors

Wladimir Andreff, Professor of Economics, University of Paris I, Pantheon Sorbonne, France and Vice President of the International Association of Sports Economists

Robert A. Baade, James D. Vail Professor of Economics, Lake Forest College, Illinois, USA

Carlos Pestana Barros, Department of Economics, Instituto Superior de Economia e Gestao, Technical University of Lisbon, Portugal

J.J. Gouguet, CDES, University of Limoges, General Secretary of International Association of Sports Economists

Muradali Ibrahìmo, Department of Economics, Instituto Superior de Economia e Gestao, Technical University of Lisbon

Stefan Kesenne, Professor of Economics, UFSIA, University of Antwerp, Belgium

Markus Kurscheidt, Lecturer, Department of Sport Management, Ruhr-University. He is assistant of the board of the Arbeitskreis Sportoekonomie and member of the board of directors of the International Association of Sports Economists (IASE)

Jaime Lucas, IDRAM-Instituto do Desporto da Regiao Autonoma da Madeira

Victor Matheson, Assistant Professor of Economics, Lake Forest College, Illinois, USA

H.F. Moorhouse, Director, Research Unit in Football Studies, Department of Sociology, University of Glasgow, UK

Bernd Rahmann, Professor of Economics and Public Finance, University of Paderborn. Former Dean of the Faculty of Economic Sciences and member of the Arbeitskreis Sportoekonomie, the Association of German-speaking Sports Economists

Peter J. Sloane, Jaffrey Professor of Political Economy, Dean and Vice Principal, University of Aberdeen, UK

Ron Smith, professor of Economics at Birkbeck College, University of London, UK

Paul D. Staudohar, Professor of Business Administration, California State University, Hayward, USA

Stefan Szymanski, Professor of Economics, Imperial College Management School, London, UK

Preface

In November 2000 a conference was held in Lisbon organised by CISEP in collaboration with the Department of Economics at ISEG, the Technical University of Lisbon. This conference brought together a group of North American and European researchers (mostly economists) who share an interest in the comparative economics of sports on those two continents. Most of this group have come together under the umbrella of the International Association of Sports Economics (IASE) which is based at the University of Limoges, France,* which is in turn closely connected to the new Journal of Sports Economics.

We hope that this book will demonstrate that our proposed research agenda is both illuminating and worthy of further pursuit. It only remains to thank CISEP and ISEG for their generous support in this venture. In particular, we thank Vitor Martins, the President of CISEP, José Manuel Zorro, Murad Ibrahim, Fernando Tenreiro and Carlos Barros for their enormous efforts in making the Lisbon conference a success.

Stefan Szymanski, 5 November 2001

---

* Contact email: monna@drec.unilim.fr

Transatlantic sport: an introduction

**Carlos Barros, Muradali Ibrahímo and
Stefan Szymanski**

1. THE TRANSATLANTIC DIVIDE

Economics and sports are uneasy companions. Many people, including
many of those involved in running and organising sporting competition,
see little or no role for the application of economic logic to these activities. In this view, sport is something played and watched for the pleasure
of it, often as a release from the daily economic grind. However, wherever
large sums of money change hands, economics must creep in. In particular, the laws of economic competition must inevitably be addressed once
the level of financial interest rises above some minimum level. These laws
take precedence over the rules of sporting competition, and an economic
analysis of sporting rules and organisations from an antitrust perspective
is inescapable.

The minimum level that triggers antitrust involvement was reached first
in the United States, partly because the hurdle of economic significance is
lower and partly because the scale of sporting enterprise grew much faster
in the US than elsewhere. Thus over the last century a coherent body of economic analysis of sport has developed dealing with the organisation of
American sports. Outside of North America the economic dimension of
sport has developed much more slowly. Before 1960 there were few cases
heard, and it is only with the explosion in the value of broadcasting rights
in the 1990s that concentrated antitrust scrutiny has been directed at sport
in the European Union. Almost at once it became apparent that the lessons
of the well developed American model did not necessarily apply to the
context of sporting organisation elsewhere. Indeed, it became apparent that
in many ways the US was a special case that differed significantly in the way
it organised its sports, and therefore in the antitrust analysis of sports.

Many of the chapters in this book highlight both similarities and
differences in the North American and European models of sport. In our
introduction we shall begin by outlining what we see as the key features of
the North American model, and then discussing the ways in which Europe

and much of the rest of the world are different. In our conclusions we relate the issues raised to the contributions in this book.

2.   THE US MODEL

The organisation of sports in North America is distinctive. The dominant sports are professional, and both organisers and participants have no difficulty in embracing purely commercial objectives – they do not shrink from the label 'profit maximisers'. In team sports, which are generally the largest sporting entities in commercial terms, a highly sophisticated structure has developed. Teams are organised into hermetically sealed leagues: both the number of competitors and the identity of those competitors is fixed by the members themselves, so that entry at the level of the individual team is impossible without consent.[1] To be sure, purchase of new franchises, at a price that suits the incumbents, or franchise relocation to exploit taxpayer subsidies are both possible and common, but the degree of turnover of teams in these leagues is much smaller than in leagues where the system of promotion (and relegation) by right operates. Within these hermetically sealed units a number of important economic restrictions operate.

On the labour market, player contracts are now negotiated on the basis of collective bargaining between player unions and team owners (see Rosen and Sanderson, 2001, for a review). Prior to collective bargaining owners imposed significant restraints on player mobility through institutions such as baseball's reserve clause that gave a team the right to renew a contract annually without the player having an opportunity to negotiate an alternative with another team. Once player unions established their right to bargain on behalf of players the reserve clause was diluted, and currently a player becomes a free agent after six years with the same team. However, the scope of player market restraints has expanded over the years to include draft rules (granting exclusive bargaining rights over the best new players entering the league to the poorest performing teams), roster limits (limiting the maximum number of players in the squad), salary caps and restrictions on player trading. All of these mechanisms limit the scope of teams to compete in economic terms against each other to acquire player talent, the essential input for team production.[2]

On the product market side teams have entered into collective agreements that restrict the scope of economic competition. Gate revenue sharing, joint merchandising, and collective sale of broadcasting rights all serve to limit the economic returns to sporting competition.

These kinds of restrictions would clearly not be admissible if competition between teams in the sports leagues were treated in the same way as competition among firms in any other industry. In Walter Neale's famous phrase, team sport has a 'peculiar economics' that renders both the activity and its antitrust treatment unique (Neale, 1964). The three central propositions of sports economics *à la Americaine* can be described as follows:

S1 A sporting contest is uninteresting unless its outcome is uncertain; the more uncertain, the more interesting

S2 In team sports a contest is made more uncertain by establishing an equal distribution of economic resources among the teams

S3 An equal distribution of economic resources is best achieved either by limiting the role of economic power in hiring players (labour market restraints) or equalising economic power through income redistribution

These three propositions, we might call them the three principles of competitive balance, or some variants upon them have been accepted by the US courts in a number of cases, have been used by Congress in justification of the antitrust exemption for collective sale of broadcasting rights, and have recently been used by a Blue Ribbon Committee (Levin et al. 2000) on the future of baseball for the introduction of more labour market restraints and more income redistribution (see for example Ross, 2001). From an economist's perspective one striking feature of these propositions and the antitrust leniency that follows from their acceptance is the lack of robust theoretical or statistical evidence in their support.

Taking each proposition in turn, the idea that outcome uncertainty influences attendance is far less well supported than one might imagine. It is true that interest in a contest whose outcome is known with complete certainty is much less valuable than one whose outcome is even slightly uncertain, and this can be inferred from the significantly lower value of delayed broadcast rights compared to live rights. However, it does not follow from this that there is a monotonic relationship between outcome uncertainty and fan interest, and the balance of statistical evidence does not support this stronger proposition.[3] Partly the problem is that tests are likely to be weak given the difficulty of isolating all the other potential influences on the interest of a match or championship (home team support, regional rivalries, interest in the quality and personality of players, the interest in winning or losing streaks, to name but a few). In practice what fans may want is a *sufficient* degree of uncertainty in a contest, and as the Roman interest in the match between the lions and the Christians demonstrates, the notion of sufficient may vary widely through time and by culture.

To an economic frame of mind it might seem almost axiomatic that an uneven balance of economic resources will lead to uneven outcomes on the field of play, but there remain many who question any such simple relationship is at work, particularly in an American context. The leap of faith that lies at the heart of economic thinking is that over time buyers will tend to pay factors of production according to their economic worth, and that while random errors may enter into the process, spending power will be a systematic component in the explanation of success (see for example Szymanski and Smith, 1997 and Szymanski and Kuypers, 1999). The sceptics, however, can point to a number of potential glitches in the market process that might invalidate this reasoning. First, the emergence of talent is frequently unpredictable, so that when there is competition the winner's curse is likely to operate, while in the absence of competition the player's salary is as likely to depend on the bargaining skills of the agent as on the skills of the player (Krautmann and Oppenheimer, 1994; Marburger, 1994; Carmichael and Thomas, 1993; MacDonald and Reynolds, 1994). Secondly, the market for talent is essentially a thin market, with low player turnover and short careers, and so there are limited opportunities for learning and efficient pricing. Thirdly, coaches responsible for identifying talents also tend to have relatively short careers, and are frequently dismissed for poor performance, so that they have limited opportunities for learning, and may be prone to high risk strategies that will introduce additional noise into the expenditure/performance relationship. Fourthly, team performance may be more than simply the sum of the parts, and so the sum of individual remuneration may be a poor guide to performance.

The third proposition can be questioned on theoretic grounds. It might seem obvious at first blush that *if* there is demand for uncertainty and *if* equal distribution of economic resources increases uncertainty *then* the equal sharing of income will enhance demand for the sport, but this need not be so. Income sharing can have negative effects, particularly when it comes to incentives. For example, when teams share the gate revenue, and if gate revenue also increases when the home team wins, then the visitors acquire an interest in losing the match (for example Fort and Quirk, 1995; Vrooman, 1995). This effect can lead to a general weakening of incentives to field competitive teams, and in the long run this may diminish demand for sport. All forms of sharing can undermine the incentives to field strong teams, and it has been argued that economically weak teams in US leagues have been free-riders on the revenue-generating potential of the strong teams (for example Hausman and Leonard, 1997). In the economics literature it is a longstanding proposition that awarding prizes to the winners of economic contests will tend to sharpen incentives so long as the gap in ability between contestants is not too great.[4] Since in team sports there is no intrinsic gap in ability between the teams (since ability depends simply on the hiring of players), the creation of prize funds for the winners of league competition might be predicted to enhance demand more than equal revenue sharing. The distinction here lies in the difference between equality of opportunity (ex ante), which is desirable, and equality of outcome (ex post) which, if guaranteed by redistribution schemes, penalises effort (Szymanski, 2001b).

Thus, while the generous antitrust treatment of sports in the US has been based on a logically coherent theory of the demand for sporting contests, the economic evidence to support this theory seems in need of some development. This, of course, need not be an issue as long as the products themselves are deemed in practice to be successful, and judged in terms of spectator interest they are indeed successful. But to many commentators there seem to be problems associated with the operation of league rules.

First, the lack of sufficient competitive balance is seen as a problem, certainly in baseball, but possibly also in basketball and ice hockey (see for example Eckard, 1998, 2001; Horowitz, 1997; Ross and Lucke, 1997; Quirk and Fort, 1992). This may be viewed as a consequence of inadequate revenue sharing, but might also be seen as a consequence of inadequate incentives to succeed on the part of the weaker teams. If there is revenue sharing, the teams with weak revenue-generating potential may prefer to remain weak and allow the large market teams to generate income and so maximise league revenues (assuming local market revenues are also increasing in local team success). Even without revenue sharing, the closed nature of the leagues means that small market teams can make more profit from fielding weak teams and relying on the drawing power of visiting talent rather than fielding a competitive (and expensive) home team.

The closed nature of the leagues has also created what is the greatest bugbear of the average fan, the threat of team relocation. Given the limited number of teams, there are usually cities that lack a major league in some sports, so that a given team can threaten to relocate to one of these cities unless the city authority spends taxpayer dollars on new facilities. The adverse effects of this municipal competition have been comprehensively criticised by US economists (see for example Noll and Zimbalist, 1997). However, the search for an antitrust remedy for what seems to an outsider to be a clear abuse of monopoly power has proved elusive. While each of the US major leagues might be considered to be a monopoly, treating the individual team as a monopolist is unappealing. It would be hard to argue that a team is obliged by competition law to remain in the same location any more than a firm could be obliged to maintain its production facilities in the same city.

One solution that has been suggested is the break up of the major leagues into rival leagues (although still permitted to compete for the World Series or the Superbowl) since as independent economic entities (that is with their own independent revenue sharing and player market rules) they would compete to serve all the economically viable cities (Ross, 1989; Quirk and Fort, 1999). The relocation threat would be diminished since rival leagues would be willing to compete to serve all viable markets (and if they did not they would be guilty of conspiracy in restraint of trade under the Sherman Act).

A second solution, suggested by Ross and Szymanski (2002), and Noll (2002) is the adoption of a scheme of automatic promotion and relegation from lesser leagues such as operates in most team sports outside North America. This system would enable all cities to have a team and aspire to the highest level of play. It is clear that such a system seriously undermines the relocation threat, but the imposition of promotion and relegation is problematic as an antitrust remedy. The most plausible approach is to argue that the major leagues are 'essential facilities' and that therefore any team of a reasonable standard should be permitted at least potential access on fair terms. Were this principle to be established, it is likely that the league would voluntarily institute a promotion and relegation system as the most efficient solution to providing reasonable access. However, US courts have been unenthusiastic about the essential facilities doctrine, and therefore an enforced solution seems unlikely in the near future.

3.   THE EUROPEAN MODEL OF SPORT

Until the 1990s sports economics and the antitrust analysis of sports was primarily a North American activity. Europe is dominated by a single sport, soccer, but even this remained a financial minnow until the end of the 1980s. True, competition policy had been used to intervene over the operation of labour market restrictions. Most notably in the UK in 1963, the 75-year-old retain and transfer system, which gave employers the right in perpetuity to determine unilaterally if a player should be allowed to transfer to another team, was ruled illegal (the Eastham case). However, by and large the soccer leagues of Europe engaged in far fewer restrictive practices compared to the North American leagues. Revenue sharing was almost unknown, broadcast income was negligible and thus even when shared had little significance, and joint merchandising was unknown. No attempts were made to use labour market restrictions to equalise access to playing talent: no draft, no roster limits, no salary caps (maximum wages were imposed in some leagues but were mostly withdrawn by the 1960s). Moreover, player trading for cash has long been the norm in European soccer, an institution that, at least in the view of North American league commissioners, is liable to lead low revenue teams to sell their best players to the high revenue teams and hence exacerbate competitive imbalance (although this opinion is widely challenged by US sports economists).

Perhaps not surprisingly, this gives rise to very large differences in income between the top and the bottom clubs, typically much larger than in the US. Does greater income inequality give rise to greater competitive imbalance (S2)? Buzzacchi et al. (2001) show that over time fewer teams share in the top honours in European soccer compared to the North American leagues.[5] This comparison is not straightforward since the promotion and relegation system creates a larger pool of potential winners. They construct a measure of inequality that compares actual entry into the top ranks over time compared to the expected level of entry under the hypothesis of equal team quality. They found that even though the closed US leagues have many fewer potential entrants, a much larger fraction of teams realise this potential, and even the absolute number of entrants is greater for North American leagues. In other words, equality of opportunity (through promotion and relegation) does not in itself ensure equality of outcomes.

Given this one would like to test whether the greater inequality of European outcomes leads to reduced demand for the sports (S1). Such comparisons are, of course, extremely hazardous.[6] All that can be said is that the much greater degree of inequality in Europe has not led to a significant relative decline. Anecdotally European soccer leagues seem every bit as popular as the North American leagues. Is this a product of some other institutional features of European leagues, or simply a reflection of the fact that, within bounds, the degree of outcome uncertainty is not important for demand?

Some important features of the European model are worth commenting on. According to the European Commission (1998), the 'system of promotion and relegation is one of the key features of the European model of sport'. There it was argued that this feature gave European sports an added edge over American style sports: 'Because of the arrival of new competitors the championships are more interesting than closed competitions'. An American might reasonably respond by asking 'more interesting for whom?', but it seems less controversial to argue that the system does significantly alter the incentive structure of the leagues. As well as diminishing the relocation threat, as argued above, the system also ensures that poor performing teams are committed until the end of the season and diminishes the attractiveness of the freerider option. But does it make for more attractive competition overall? The answer to this question may depend on the following unresolved research issue: is there a connection between the existence of promotion and relegation and the failure of European leagues to agree significant income redistribution? To our knowledge no one has yet addressed this issue, either theoretically or empirically. Yet, if we accept S1 for the moment, this would seem to be a critical issue.

Another widely commented on feature of the European model is the claim that team owners and managers are motivated by goals other than profit maximisation. Differences in objective functions can have a significant effect on the implications of activities such as revenue sharing. Sloane (1971) proposed that in the European context clubs are utility maximisers, adopting objectives such as the pursuit of on-the-pitch success subject to a balanced budget constraint, and Kesenne (2000a) has explored some of the implications of this in a more formal model.[7] While American scholars have argued that competitive balance will be unaffected by revenue sharing (for example Vrooman, 1995), it seems clear that if all spare cash is devoted to player spending then redistribution from large to small revenue teams can only improve competitive balance. What seems puzzling, in this context, is the fact that revenue sharing is far less common in Europe, where one might expect it to be far more effective if the utility maximisation hypothesis is correct.

A number of resolutions suggest themselves. First, the hypothesis may simply be incorrect, and recent trends toward the quotation of leading soccer teams in Europe on the stock exchanges seem to point in this direction more and more. Second, if fans in Europe were less interested in competitive balance than North American fans (a point that may also be connected to the structure of competitions) then the value of revenue sharing might be smaller. Third, if the true motivation of revenue sharing was mainly collusive (to limit the extent of economic competition in order simply to raise profits at the expense of consumers and players) then revenue sharing might seem less attractive to large European clubs that have less in common with their smaller rivals in the open leagues than do large US teams with their lesser counterparts in the closed North American leagues.

The final aspect of the European model that is worth commenting upon is the much greater complexity of sporting competition, particularly in soccer. Unlike the North American teams, teams in Europe compete simultaneously in more than one championship, both at home (Cup and League) and abroad (Champions' League or UEFA Cup). This means that a measure that might improve balance in one league might at the same time diminish balance in another. For example, if Bayern Munich were to share all its income with its German rivals, the German league might be more balanced but the Champions' League in which it participates might become less balanced. But this is just one aspect of the greater complexity. Since the teams are obliged to supply players for representative national competitions as well, players are simultaneously engaged in competition of a different kind. Moreover, this kind of competition by its nature is not consistent with balance enhancing measures. Empirically the World Cup does seem like a relatively unbalanced competition, with a small number of teams that repeatedly dominate the competition (Brazil, Germany, Argentina, Italy), but nonetheless the World Cup Final remains the single most popular sporting event in the world measured by TV viewing figures.

Faced with this more complex picture the European competition authorities have adopted a more robust approach to the antitrust analysis of sports. The most famous judgement to date was the celebrated Bosman case,[8] that involved the right of clubs to claim compensation for the transfer of players, even if out of contract, and the right of leagues to agree rules on the composition of teams by nationality. The judgement of the European Court upheld the right of free movement of labour within the European Union, thus outlawing transfer rules that restricted rights of out of contract players and restricted opportunities to move to other parts of the single market. While the leagues raised the defence that restrictive contracts were necessary to ensure that small clubs received adequate compensation for player development, and the Court explicitly recognised the desirability of 'solidarity' – meaning the redistribution of income from rich clubs to poor clubs, the rules at issue were deemed too restrictive.

Since Bosman the European Commission has gone further, and challenged the agreements that enabled clubs to trade players for sums running into tens of millions of dollars. Their reasoning in this case was that excessive transfer fees also served to restrict freedom of movement of labour within the single market. Instead the Commission argued that compensation should be strictly related to economic loss, which is hard to prove in court (the loss of a star player on star wages may impact revenues but also reduces costs). Once again the clubs claimed that the rule would undermine the ability of smaller teams to generate income from developing player talent and then reselling it to large clubs. The Commission accepted this argument in part and in early 2001 a compromise agreement was announced that permitted teams to demand a significant transfer fee for players under contract until the age of 24, but after this gave players almost complete freedom of movement between seasons (while the outline of this deal is public, the precise details have yet to be published).

In other words the market for players has been significantly liberalised by the European competition authorities, giving teams almost no incentives to write long-term contracts with players. Thus the ability of players to move to the highest bidder has never been stronger. The contrast with the restrictive player markets of the US could not be starker. One important factor that has brought about this situation is the absence of collective bargaining between player unions and employers in Europe. Unions have existed in

Europe for some time and in many cases have been instrumental in disman-
tling restrictive practices in the labour market, as in the US. However, since
player unions are fragmented across Europe (one per country), and because
in many member states and at the EU level the unions cannot enforce exclusive bargaining rights, employers have mostly been able to bypass the
unions. A good recent example of this was the walk-out by FIFPRO, the
association of player unions worldwide, from the negotiations over reform
of transfer rules in the EU. Despite this, the European Commission and
UEFA simply concluded a deal, ignoring the views of FIFPRO.
Furthermore, even if a single player union in Europe managed to establish
itself and to win collective bargaining rights with employers, there is still no
equivalent of the antitrust exemption of collective bargaining agreements
in the US – thus any restrictions agreed would still have to be vetted by the
competition authorities.

The other major intervention of the European competition authorities
has been on the broadcasting front. The Commission argues that revenue
sharing by the clubs (solidarity) is an acceptable activity. Solidarity in this
context means not only sharing income with teams in the same division but
also the redistribution of money from the upper levels of the game to the
'grass roots'. Gate revenue sharing and joint merchandising have never
played a significant role in the economics of European soccer. In practice,
the principal form of revenue sharing has been the division of collectively
negotiated broadcast rights. Income from this source was insignificant for
a long time due to the monopoly of publicly owned national broadcast corporations. Facing no competition, these corporations were willing to offer
little to buy the rights, and in many cases the leagues were uninterested in
selling on these terms, fearing that the small amount of extra income would
be outweighed by the loss of live gates.

However, in the 1980s competition on the broadcast front emerged in the
form of satellite and cable companies. This led to a significant growth in the
price of live rights – for example in 1989 the rights for League football in
England cost only £11m per season – by 2001 the price had risen to more
like £700m per season. This huge inflation in rights values was financed in
most cases by the migration of live rights from free-to-air broadcasting to
pay TV. Thus while the number of matches broadcast increased, audience
figures per match tended to decline as only those fanatical enough, or rich
enough subscribed.[9]

Competition authority interest was triggered both by the observation
that consumers were paying so much more to watch their football, and the
desire on the part of some clubs to sell the rights to their own matches independently. In Germany, the Netherlands, Italy and the UK the competition
authorities investigated collective selling. In all cases apart from the UK the

competition authority has upheld the right of clubs to sell their matches individually and has questioned the validity of collective selling,[10] arguing that redistribution could be achieved by other means (see Szymanski, 2002, for a summary). In the UK the Court decided that if collective selling were prohibited under the existing law then any other agreement between the clubs to sell their rights (for example rules scheduling the time at which matches might be broadcast) would also be illegal and therefore chaos would ensue. Since then a new Competition Act has been passed and it is unlikely that the court would face such a stark choice in any future investigation. From an economic perspective, it is reasonable to argue that collective selling is a relatively efficient mechanism for redistributing broadcast income, and that as long as it does not result in significant losses for consumers then it should be permitted. Thus the Sports Broadcasting Act in the US permits collective sales as long as they are made to free-to-air broadcasters. The problem in Europe has been that consumers have suffered from the migration of broadcasting to pay to view. The European Commission has already indicated that it will turn to the consideration of collective selling once the final details of the transfer system have been settled, probably during 2002.

The Commission has already set out its position on another aspect of broadcasting, namely the sale of rights on an exclusive basis to particular broadcasters. It has indicated that it believes exclusivity can be valuable if it encourages the rights holder to invest in the development of the sport, but that exclusivity over a lengthy period can be harmful since it discourages competition in broadcast markets. As a result most sports broadcasting contracts are let for no more than three or four years in the EU.

3. THE CONTRIBUTIONS IN THIS BOOK

We have divided the contributions in this book into three areas: public policy, economic theory and cost–benefit analysis. Part 1 contains three contributions to the public policy debate which largely focus on the applicability of an American framework to the US context. Andreff and Staudohar begin by setting out the clear dichotomy that lay between the traditional North American profit-maximising model and the amateur/not-for-profit traditions of Europe. They consider the fundamental problem as to how teams raise finance for their activities, and stress the revolution that has occurred in Europe. While teams once depended largely on gate income and local subsidies, often from the public sector, as sources of finance, the clubs have increasingly become dependent on television and sponsorship income, a change which has shifted the perspective of the clubs towards a purely commercial framework. They identify corporatisation, as well as globalisation, as a defining characteristic of the new European financing model, which has much in common with the North American model. Moreover, while they argue that this new model is likely to consolidate its hold on European team sports, they see warning signs as well – in relation to issues such as the need to provide inclusive competition and access for all, and the increased incentives for bribery and corruption in a sport where the financial rewards are so much larger.

Sloane adopts a slightly different perspective. He begins by outlining the basic rationale for co-operative activity among teams in a sports league, namely the uncertainty of outcome hypothesis. He then examines this rationale in a European context where teams have traditionally been considered 'utility' rather than profit maximisers and uses this analysis to discuss two antitrust cases from the UK – the Restrictive Practices Court case that challenged the collective sale of broadcasting rights and the Monopolies and Mergers Commission inquiry into the proposed takeover of Manchester United by the satellite broadcaster BSkyB. Finally he considers the Bosman case, pointing out that the kinds of labour market restraints practised in the US have fallen foul of the basic rules of the European Union, particularly in relation to the free movement of labour. Sloane concludes that Europe is in the process of developing its approach to the regulation of team sports, and still has some way to go.

Moorhouse takes as his starting point the Blue Ribbon Report written for the Commissioner of Major League Baseball (Levin et al., 2000) and argues that the same thoroughgoing review of the impact of revenue disparities is required for European soccer. He argues that policymakers in Europe have been too concerned with specific problems (such as the collective selling of broadcasting rights or the free movement of labour) and not enough concerned for the big picture. He considers the proposed format of a European Superleague of Hoehn and Szymanski (1999) which he finds unattractive on the grounds of what he perceives to be its inegalitarian principles. It is also clear that, unlike many economists, he sees the need for a politically driven approach to the governance of European soccer, and hence his call for a more centralised approach. In the end, however, it is not clear exactly what kind of a structure he envisages. Indeed what is clear from all three of these contributions is that there seem at present to be more questions than answers in the European sports policy arena. Each of the contributions sees some connection between current developments in Europe and the established North American model, but all are sceptical of its direct applicability.

Part 2 of the book continues on the theme of contrasting North American and European models of team sports, but is somewhat more theoretical in outlook. Kesenne takes as his starting point the European Court of Justice ruling that struck down the regime of player market restraints (the Bosman case). In that case the defence of the clubs had been that without player market restrictions competitive balance would be undermined. So Kesenne considers other mechanisms to maintain competitive balance that might be suited to the European environment. His model, in line with many of his earlier contributions, starts from the assumption of win maximisation, which he considers the most plausible starting point for the analysis of European soccer clubs. Based on this assumption he shows that competitive balance will be enhanced either with revenue sharing or with a salary cap scheme. He therefore argues that these policies represent credible alternatives to the old system of restraints on player mobility.

Szymanski and Smith consider the issue of measuring competitive balance. They point out that the most popular methods for measuring competitive balance have been static – for example the standard deviation of winning percentages, which describes the variability of outcomes within a season but is silent on the degree of variability within seasons. They then go on to consider a dynamic panel regression approach which generates a measure of the persistence of performance. This measure can then be used to compare the degree of persistence in success or failure across different leagues. They find that while persistence is much greater in North America, the systematic component, measured by the R^2, is much greater in European leagues, the variability of long-run performance (measured by fixed effects), is also greater. One interpretation of this is that North American leagues show much less short-run volatility (since long-term contracts in the labour market ensure that a winning team stays together longer), but in the long run the higher variability of club endowments and lesser incidence of redistributive policies in Europe makes the latter more unequal than the former.

Part 3 turns to basic economic issues in the analysis of sports: do sports events bring benefits to the local economy, and how are such benefits to be measured? Once again it is fair to say that research in this area has been dominated by North American scholarship. Indeed, Robert Baade, who co-authors the first contribution in this section, has been one of the major contributors to the literature. In their joint chapter he and Matheson review the arguments surrounding the economic cost–benefit analysis of the Los Angeles and Atlanta Olympics. They show that, as is so often the case with such events, the true economic impact, once all the potential leakages from the circular flow model have been accounted for, is negligible. The chapter then focuses on the important issue of how municipal authorities, whom they hypothesise will not be deterred from bidding for prestigious sporting events even faced with dismal economic forecasts, can best manage the bidding process to minimise any losses to the local economy. They point out that one of the key problems for the bidding city is the unequal nature of the bargaining relationship. There is a relatively small supply of world class sporting events yet huge numbers of willing hosts. They point out that much of the relative success of the Los Angeles games, which imposed almost no burden on local taxpayers, arose from the fact that the International Olympic Committee had no other realistic options.

In his chapter Gouguet deals head on with the challenge posed by the large number of studies in the vein of Baade and Matheson which show that the *measurable* economic benefits of major sporting events is negligible. He argues that many of the most important effects of sporting events can be characterised as 'externalities' – that is effects that are not mediated directly through market mechanisms but nonetheless have significant economic impacts. For example, 'social cohesion' may be significantly affected in either a positive or a negative way by a sporting event – although this effect will not register directly in any market transaction and therefore cannot be captured directly in a conventional impact study. Gouguet cites as an example of a positive effect on social cohesion (positive externality) the effect that the multiracial French soccer team had on the wider perception of French citizens of their multicultural society by winning the World Cup in 1998. By contrast, he points to hooliganism as an example of a negative externality. He concludes the chapter with a plea for fewer narrow economic impact studies and more attempts to measure the wider social impact of sporting events.

In their chapter Rahmann and Kurscheidt consider the interesting question of how to allocate World Cup matches to cities once a country has won a bid to stage the competition. Their analysis is applied to the case of Germany 2006 where sixteen cities have bid to act as hosts. They present a detailed analysis of the relative attractiveness of each of the candidate locations and the potential economic impact. In general they argue that these impacts are liable to be rather small and are highly uncertain. They argue that in order to generate the maximum economic impact it would be desirable to limit the host cities to ten rather than twelve teams, which currently seem to be planned. They also identify some problems associated with the bidding process. Since the decision to award host status to cities will be awarded some time after the World Cup has been allocated to Germany, this means that municipal authorities have had an incentive to invest in the run up to a decision being made. Potentially this process of competition could be highly costly, not to say wasteful, from the perspective of the local taxpayers.

Finally, Barros and Lucas examine another aspect of sports economics:

the value of contributions made by voluntary sports managers. They show in the Portuguese context that the efforts of these managers have a very high economic value, implying that public subsidies aimed at these voluntary activities is very high. Given that amateur contributions to local sporting activities are significant both in North America and in Europe it may be worth considering whether redirecting public subsidies away from the 'grands projets' of politicians toward more grass-roots based activities would represent a better investment of public funds.

4.   WORLDS APART?

The US model of sport is traditionally a world apart from the European model. North American sports have developed relatively collusive structures on the justification that such collusion is necessary to maintaining a competitive balance, and that without competitive balance consumer interest would die. The four closed professional leagues (baseball, American football, basketball and ice hockey),have many common restrictive features, and relatively equal outcomes, certainly relative to European soccer. These products are undoubtedly very successful.

In Europe, the clubs and the governing bodies may pay lip service to the need for competitive balance, but in practice they have produced a collection of open but highly unbalanced competitions. They have engaged in only limited forms of revenue sharing, and such labour market restrictions as they have established have been struck down by the competition authority. National courts of some member states have struck down collective sale of broadcast rights despite its ability to facilitate revenue sharing, and the European Commission may yet outlaw it completely within the EU. The competition authorities of Europe clearly give little practical weight to the three principles of competitive balance. And yet, the soccer leagues of Europe are undoubtedly very successful.

Maybe this should surprise economists.[11] We are used to thinking that one type of institutional arrangement is likely to dominate another in any given context, rather than co-existing. Could it really be that European consumers are so very different from American consumers that different types of product can succeed in each market? Would European soccer be more successful if it developed a closed Superleague based on American features (see for example Hoehn and Szymanski, 1999), and would US sports be any less successful if they abandoned their restrictions and opened themselves up to promotion and relegation? If competitive balance matters, then we should consider whether the European institutions provide other benefits that act as a counterweight to the relatively low degree of competitive balance in Europe. But perhaps competitive balance is not really very important at all, and so the impressive array of restraints in the US are no more than collusive devices to rob the players and the fans.

In Part 3 of this book we have presented some contributions to the cost–benefit analysis of sports events and activities that show little difference in terms of the fundamental approach on either side of the Atlantic. Yet when it comes to the analysis of team sports, as yet no consensus exists. We hope that this book will be part of the process leading to the emergence of such a consensus, if not by providing the immediate answers, then by the coherent presentation of some of the fundamental questions that remain to be answered.

NOTES

1. Gilbert and Flynn (2001) argue that the appropriate antitrust analogy for a US sports league is a joint venture.
2. Ross (1997) argues that the role of the player unions has been instrumental in creating a number of benefits for the fans.
3. For example, see Demmert (1973), Borland and Lye (1992), Peel and Thomas (1988), Cairns (1987), Jennett (1984), Kuypers (1997), Schmidt and Berri (2001). Note that in some of these papers a careful inspection of the coefficient sign and significance levels is required.
4. There is a surprisingly small subset of papers in the intersection of tournament/contest theory and team sports economics. Relevant contest theory papers include Baik (1994), Baye et al. (1997), Dasgupta and Nti (1998), Dixit (1987), Gradstein and Conrad (1999), Green and Stokey (1983), Harris and Vickers (1985), Higgins et al. (1985), Lazear and Rosen (1981), Nalebuff and Stiglitz (1983), Nitzan (1994), Nti (1997), and Tullock (1980). This is perhaps all the more surprising given the small but significant literature applied to individualistic sports (for example tennis and golf) involving both theory and testing, for example Rosen (1981, 1986), Ehrenberg and Bognanno (1990a, 1990b). Closest in spirit to tournament models are the papers of Atkinson et al. (1988), El-Hodiri and Quirk (1971), and some recent papers including Palomino and Sakovics (2000), and Palomino and Rigotti (2000). Szymanski (2001b) tries to make the connection explicit.
5. Kipker (2000) also performs an interesting comparative analysis.
6. One attempt for English soccer is Szymanski (2001a).
7. Fort and Quirk (2000) is a response to this.
8. This issue has already spawned a sizeable literature, for example Bourg and Gouguet (2001), Ericson (2000), Ross (1999), Szymanski (1999), among others.
9. Szymanski (2000) offers a slightly longer discussion.
10. Ross and Szymanski (2000) offer an interpretation of this judgement.
11. Primault and Rouger (1999) argue that the difference between the US and Europe is so great that Europeans have essentially no lessons to learn; Fort (2000) argues that in reality the differences are not so great. Another interesting perspective on the antitrust differences is Noll (1999).

REFERENCES

Atkinson, S., L. Stanley and J. Tschirhart (1988), 'Revenue sharing as an incentive in an agency problem: an example from the National Football League', *Rand Journal of Economics*, **19**, (1), 27–43.
Baik, K. (1994), 'Effort levels in contests with two asymmetric players', *Southern Economic Journal*, **61**, 367–78.
Baye, M., D. Kovenock and C. de Vries (1997), 'The incidence of overdissipation in rent-seeking contests', mimeo.
Borland, J. and J. Lye (1992), 'Attendance at Australian Rules Football: a panel study', *Applied Economics*, **24**, 1053–8.
Bourg J.F. and J.F. Gouguet (2001), *Economie du Sport*, Paris: Editions La Decouverte.
Buzzacchi, L., S. Szymanski and T. Valletti, (2001), 'Static versus Dynamic Competitive Balance: Do teams win more in Europe or in the US?' Imperial College Management School Discussion paper.
Cairns, J.A. (1987), 'Evaluating changes in league structure: the organisation of the Scottish Football League.', *Applied Economics*, **19** (2), 259–75.
Carmichael, F. and D. Thomas (1993), 'Bargaining in the transfer market: theory and evidence', *Applied Economics*, **25**, 1467–76.
Dasgupta, A. and K. Nti (1998), 'Designing an optimal contest', *European Journal of Political Economy*, **14**, 587–603.
Demmert, H. (1973), *The Economics of Professional Team Sports*, Cambridge, MA: Lexington Books.
Dixit, A. (1987), 'Strategic behavior in contests', *American Economic Review*, **77**, 891–8.
Eckard, E. (1998), 'The NCAA cartel and competitive balance in college football', *Review of Industrial Organization*, **13**, 347–69.
Eckard, E. (2001), 'Baseball's Blue Ribbon Economic Report: solutions in search of a problem', *Journal of Sports Economics*, forthcoming.
Ehrenberg, R. and M. Bognanno (1990a), 'Do tournaments have incentive effects'? *Journal of Political Economy*, **98** (6), 1307–24.
Ehrenberg R. and M. Bognanno (1990b), 'The incentive effects of tournaments revisited: evidence from the European PGA Tour', *Industrial and Labor Relations Review*, **43**, 74S–88S.
El-Hodiri, M. and J. Quirk (1971), 'An economic model of a professional sports league', *Journal of Political Economy*, **79**, 1302–19.
Ericson, T. (2000), 'The Bosman Case: effects of the abolition of the transfer fee', *Journal of Sports Economics*, **1** (3), 203–18.
European Commission (1998), *The European Model of Sport*, Consultation paper of DGX.
Fort, R. (2000), 'European and North American sports differences (?)', *Scottish Journal of Political Economy*, **47** (4), 431–55.
Fort, R. and J. Quirk (1995), 'Cross subsidization, incentives and outcomes in professional team sports leagues', *Journal of Economic Literature*, **XXXIII** (3), 1265–99.
Fort, R. and J. Quirk (2000), 'Sports team behavior and sports policy: the winning percent maximising league', mimeo.
Gilbert, R. and M. Flynn (2001), 'An analysis of professional sports leagues as joint ventures', *Economic Journal*, **111** (469), F27–F46.

Gradstein, M. and K. Konrad (1999), 'Orchestrating rent-seeking contests', *Economic Journal*, **109**, 536–45.

Green, J. and N. Stokey (1983), 'A comparison of tournaments and contests', *Journal of Political Economy*, **91**, 349–64.

Harris, C. and J. Vickers (1985), 'Perfect equilibrium in a model of a race', *Review of Economic Studies*, April, 193–209.

Hausman, J. and G. Leonard (1997), 'Superstars in the NBA: economic value and policy', *Journal of Labor Economics*, **15** (4).

Higgins R., W. Shughart and R. Tollison (1985), 'Free entry and efficient rent-seeking', *Public Choice*, **46**, 247–58.

Hoehn, T. and S. Szymanski (1999), 'The Americanization of European football', *Economic Policy*, **28**, 205–40.

Horowitz, I. (1997), 'The increasing competitive balance in Major League Baseball', *Review of Industrial Organization*, **12**, 373–87.

Jennett, N. (1984), 'Attendances, uncertainty of outcome and policy in the Scottish Football League', *Scottish Journal of Political Economy*, **31** (2), 176–98.

Kesenne, S. (2000a), 'Revenue sharing and competitive balance in professional team sports', *Journal of Sports Economics*, **1** (1), 56–65.

Kesenne, S. and C. Jeanrenaud (1999), *Competition Policy in Professional Sports: Europe after the Bosman Case*, CIES: Standaard Editions Ltd.

Kipker, I. (2000), 'Determinanten der Zuschauernachfrage im professionellen Teamsport: Wie wichtig ist die sportliche Ausgeglichenheit?', Unpublished chapter of PhD dissertation.

Krautmann, A. and M. Oppenheimer (1994), 'Free agency and the allocation of labor in Major League Baseball', *Managerial and Decision Economics*, **15**, 459–69.

Kuypers, T. (1997), Unpublished PhD Thesis, University College London.

Lazear, E. and S. Rosen (1981), 'Rank order tournaments as optimal labour contracts', *Journal of Political Economy*, **89**, 841–64.

Levin, R.C., G.J. Mitchell, P.A. Volcker and G.F. Will (2000), *The Report of the Independent Members of the Commissioner's Blue Ribbon Panel on Baseball Economics*, Major League Baseball.

MacDonald, D. and M. Reynolds (1994), 'Are baseball players paid their marginal products?', *Managerial and Decision Economics*, **15**, 443–57.

Marburger, D. (1994), 'Bargaining power and the structure of salaries in Major League Baseball', *Managerial and Decision Economics*, **15**, 433–41.

Nalebuff, B. and J. Stiglitz (1983), 'Prizes and incentives: Towards a general theory of compensation and competition', *Bell Journal of Economics*, **14**, 21–43.

Neale, W. (1964), 'The peculiar economics of professional sport', *Quarterly Journal of Economics*, **78** (1), 1–14.

Nitzan, S. (1994), 'Modelling rent seeking contests', *European Journal of Political Economy*, **10**, 41–60.

Noll, R. (1999), 'Competition Policy in European Sports after the Bosman Case' in Kesenne and Jeanrenaud (eds).

Noll, R. (2000), 'The economics of promotion and relegation in sports leagues: the case of English football', *Journal of Sports Economics*, **3** (2), 169–203.

Noll, R. and A. Zimbalist (1997), *Sports, Jobs and Taxes*, Brookings Institution Press.

Nti, K. (1997), 'Comparative statics of contests and rent-seeking games', *International Economic Review*, **38** (1), 43–59.

Palomino, F. and L. Rigotti (2000), 'The sport league's dilemma: competitive balance versus incentives to win', mimeo.

Palomino, F. and J. Sakovics (2000), 'Revenue sharing in professional sports leagues: for the sake of competitive balance or as a result of monopsony power?', mimeo.

Peel D. and D. Thomas (1988), 'Outcome uncertainty and the demand for football: an analysis of match attendances in the English football league', *Scottish Journal of Political Economy*, **35** (3), 242–9.

Primault, D. and A. Rouger (1999), 'How Relevant is North American Experience for Professional Team Sports in Europe', in Kesenne and Jeanrenaud (eds).

Quirk, J. and R. Fort (1992), *Pay Dirt: The Business of Professional Team Sports*, Princeton, NJ: Princeton University Press.

Quirk J. and R. Fort (1999), *Hard Ball: The Abuse of Power in Pro Team Sports*, Princeton, NJ: Princeton University Press.

Rosen, S. (1981), 'The economics of superstars', *American Economic Review*, **71**, 845–58.

Rosen, S. (1986), 'Prizes and incentives in elimination tournaments', *American Economic Review*, **76**, 701–15.

Rosen, S. and A. Sanderson (2001), 'Labour markets in professional sports', *Economic Journal*, **111** (469), F47–F68.

Ross, S. (1989), 'Monopoly sports leagues', *University of Minnesota Law Review*, **73**, 643.

Ross, S. (1997), 'The misunderstood alliance between sports fans, players, and the antitrust laws' *University of Illinois Law Review*, 1997, 519.

Ross, S. (1999), 'Restraints on Player Competition that Facilitate Competitive Balance and Player Development and their Legality in the United States and in Europe', in Kesenne and Jeanrenaud (eds).

Ross, S. (2001), 'Antitrust Options to Redress Anticompetitive Restraints and Monopolistic Practices By Professional Sports Leagues', paper delivered to the 2nd Annual American Antitrust Institute Conference.

Ross S. and R. Lucke (1997), 'Why highly paid athletes deserve more antitrust protection than unionized factory workers', *Antitrust Bulletin*, **42** (3), 641–79.

Ross, S. and S. Szymanski (2000), 'Necessary restraints and inefficient monopoly sports leagues', *International Sports Law Review*, **1** (1), 27–8.

Ross, S. and S. Szymanski (2002), 'Open Competition in League Sports', *Wisconsin Law Review*, **2002** (3), 625–56.

Schmidt, M. and D. Berri (2001), 'Competitive balance and attendance: the case of Major League Baseball', *Journal of Sports Economics*, **2** (2), 145–167.

Sloane, P.J. (1971), 'The economics of professional football: the football club as a utility maximizer', *Scottish Journal of Political Economy*, **17** (2), 121–46.

Szymanski, S. (1999), 'The Market for Soccer Players in England after Bosman: Winners and Losers', in Kesenne and Jeanrenaud (eds).

Szymanski, S. (2000), 'Sport and Broadcasting', Paper presented at the Institute of Economic Affairs, London, 18 October.

Szymanski, S. (2001a), 'Income inequality, competitive balance and the attractiveness of team sports: some evidence and a natural experiment from English soccer', *Economic Journal*, **111**, F69–F84.

Szymanski, S. (2001b), 'Competitive Balance and Income Redistribution in Team Sports', Imperial College Management School discussion paper.

Szymanski, S. (2002), 'Collective selling of broadcast rights to sporting events', *International Sports Law Review*, **2** (February), 3–7.

Szymanski, S. and T. Kuypers (1999), *Winners and Losers: The Business Strategy of Football*, London: Viking Books.

Szymanski, S. and R. Smith (1997), 'The English football industry, profit, performance and industrial structure', *International Review of Applied Economics*, **11** (1), 135–53.

Tullock, G. (1980), 'Efficient Rent Seeking', in J. Buchanan, R. Tollison and G. Tullock, (eds), *Toward a Theory of Rent Seeking Society*, Texas A&M University Press, pp. 97–112.

Vrooman, J. (1995), 'A general theory of professional sports leagues', *Southern Economic Journal*, **61** (4), 971–90.

PART 1

Public Policy and Sports Economics

1. European and US sports business models

Wladimir Andreff and Paul D. Staudohar

The sports business in Europe continues to evolve in interesting and important ways, not always to the satisfaction of interested parties. In some cases European paradigms closely resemble those in the United States, while in other ways the European situation is unique. This chapter examines three models of European sports: (1) amateur sports model, (2) traditional professional sports model, and (3) contemporary professional sports model. Key aspects of the sports business are reviewed in the models, including operation of club finances, access to capital markets, role of the media and influence of the labour market.

We find that the contemporary professional sports model is prominent at the highest levels of competition in Europe, and is expected to play an even greater role in the future. We then compare key features of this model with the contemporary professional sports model in the US. There is a somewhat different mix of sports in the two areas. Football (soccer) dominates in Europe, with basketball, rugby, and ice hockey occupying crucial market niches. In the US the top four team sports are baseball, football (American style), basketball, and ice hockey. Thus, the primacy of certain sports and their potential appeal to spectator audiences are different. Nonetheless, at the top or major league level there are numerous similarities in the nature of leagues, labour relations, finance, marketing and government regulation. Indeed, at least at the top level, there appears to be a convergence on several characteristics of the models.

1. AMATEUR SPORTS MODEL

Transformation of club operation has been less radical at the amateur level in Europe. An amateur club's financial receipts reflect its basic aim of gathering members who are interested in the practice of sport. The club's purpose is for recreation and development of young players. Economic viability is sustained largely through subscriptions and private

Table 1.1   The structure of amateur sports clubs' finance in 1976–77

Receipts from (in %)	Club A	Club B	Club C
Gate receipts (spectators)	19.3	27.2	62.4
Subsidies, cash donations and redistribution[a]	42.8	9.8	24.3
Bar, etc. (commercial receipts)	17.9	14.6	[b]
Sponsors, advertising	0	0	4.4
TV rights	0	0	0
Other (of which subscriptions)	20.5	48.4	8.9
Total	100	100	100

Notes:
[a] Subsidies from local authorities (municipalities), private donations and redistribution from the sport federation.
[b] Included in gate receipts:
  Club A: football, 77 subscribers, 1976–77.
  Club B: multisports with a core football activity, 1976–77.
  Club C: multisports, with a core rugby activity (CA Brive, Nationale 1), 1976–77.

Source: Andreff (1980).

cash donations, as illustrated historically for clubs A and B in France in 1976–77 (see Table 1.1).

Depending on the level of sporting events in which it is involved, an amateur club may also derive revenue from gate receipts. This share could become extensive if the club's first team participates at the highest level of competition, such as the rugby club in Table 1.1. With as much as two-thirds of revenue from gate receipts, a few amateur clubs have a financial structure that is closer to that of a professional club. Funds also come to the typical amateur club from concession stands at games, parking, fairs, dances and sale of club merchandise. For those amateur clubs at high competitive levels, income may also derive from advertising and sponsorship from outside business.

The financial structure of European amateur sports is little changed from a generation ago. For example, one can compare Table 1.1 with data for 1997–98 for all sports clubs in Switzerland. On average, the Swiss clubs show financing from subscriptions at 28 per cent, donations at 5 per cent, gate receipts at 5 per cent, commercial revenues at 16 per cent, sponsoring at 13 per cent, and other sources (including subsidies), at 33 per cent.[1] Moreover, in an amateur club, the major sources of finance (that is, subscriptions, donations, subsidies, and spectators) continue to be derived from local sources.[2]

2. THE PROFESSIONAL SPORTS MODEL: TRADITIONAL

Throughout the first half of the twentieth century, the primary source of revenue to European professional sports was gate receipts. In some countries (France, Germany, Italy) there were subsidies from national and local governments and industrial patrons such as Fiat, Bayer, Philips and Peugeot.[3] Advertising revenues became more important, and in the 1960s and 1970s corporate sponsorship increased significantly as firms sought more direct identification in terms of audience, image, notoriety and sales. Even in cases where a club received subsidies from local authorities, usually municipalities, there was corporate sponsorship (but not ownership), typically in situations where companies were geographically located close to the club (for example Fiat and Juventus, both in Torino, Italy; Philips and PSV, both in Eindhoven, Holland; Peugeot and FC Sochaux, both in Sochaux-Montbéliard, France).

In the 1970s, revenues from gate receipts of professional teams were far greater, absolutely and proportionately, than for amateur clubs. Also, professional clubs received less from advertising, patrons, and sponsorships. For instance, Table 1.2 shows that in Division 1 French football clubs in 1970–71, 81 per cent of revenues were from spectators, and just 1 per cent from sponsors and advertising. During 1966–68, football clubs like Saint-Etienne, Lille and Paris received two-thirds to nine-tenths of their revenues from gate receipts (see Table 1.3). France was unique in that 18 per cent of Division 1 football revenues came from municipal government subsidies. But similar to other countries, the lion's share of the gate receipts were from local or national French residents.

The above model of finance can thus be referred to as *Spectators–Subsidies–Sponsors–Local* or SSSL. It has existed for a long time in all European countries. In countries where public subsidies to professional clubs are forbidden, most of the difference is made up by private donations, subscriptions, and membership fees. This is illustrated by 1978 data from two British cricket clubs in Kent and Sussex (see Table 1.4). Cricket was not profitable at this time because clubs were unable to attract enough spectators and thus had to depend on corporate sponsors (for example Schweppes, Benson & Hedges, and Gillette) to finance major events.

Although television rights sales appeared in the financing of the British cricket clubs in 1978 and in French football in 1980–81, television was not an important source of funds to clubs. In 1967, for instance, the British Football Premier League rejected a BBC proposal of a million pounds for live broadcast of championship matches. In France, the Stade Rennais football club refused a 50000 franc proposal in 1965 for televising a single

Table 1.2   The evolving structure of French football professional clubs' finance Division 1 (1970–98) and Division 2 (1993–98)

Receipts from	Division 1								Division 2			
(in %)	1970–71	1974–75	1980–81	1985–86	1990–91	1993–94	1996–97	1997–98	1993–94	1994–95	1996–97	1997–98
Spectators	81	62	65	50	29.4	25.4	21.9	19.9	15.3	15.9	15.3	12.8
Subsidies	18	29	20	21	23.8	19.4	14.7	11.8	35.7	27.0	23.1	20.6
Sponsors and advertising	1	9	14	22	25.6	24.7	26.3	20.5	17.3	20.4	25.6	21.9
TV rights	0	0	1	7	21.1	22.7	32.4	42.5	24.5	25.7	30.7	34.4
Other (merchandising, etc.)	0	0	0	0	0	7.8	4.7	5.3	7.2	0	5.3	10.3
Total[a]	100	100	100	100	100	100	100	100	100	100	100	100

Notes:
Average finance calculated for all clubs in Division 1 and Division 2.
[a] Excluding allowances for players' transfers which are accounted for in a separate balance sheet by professional clubs in other European countries (in order to facilitate comparisons with Table 1.3).

Sources: National Football League and Bourg and Nys (1996).

Table 1.3 *The finance of some French football professional clubs*

Receipts from (%)	ASSE	SP	LOSC	Paris-Saint-Germain			Girondins	Bordeaux	O.M.	Nantes
	1966–67	1966–67	1967–68	1982–83	1986–87	1994–95	1986–87	1997–98	1986–87	1994–95
Spectators	68.1	95.8	88.2	75.1	60.0	39.8	56.8	19.9	40.7	30.3
of which European Cup		4.1[b]		25.1	5.7	19.0	11.9	0.8	0	
Subsidies	18.9		5.6	11.4	11.4	14.6	18.5	11.6	20.9	10.6
Sponsors and advertising	13.0[a]		6.2	4.9	27.1	35.0	22.2	24.5	26.7	20.5
TV rights						5.3		33.3		32.6
By-products (merchand., etc.)				2.9	1.4	5.3	2.5	10.7	11.6	2.3
Total	100	100	100	100	100	100	100	100	100	100

Notes:
LOSC: Lille Olympique Sporting Club; SP: Stade de Paris; ASSE: Association Sportive de Saint Etienne; O.M.: Olympique de Marseille.
[a] Including subscriptions by the members of an Honour Committee.
[b] Including cash donations and subscriptions.

Sources: National Football League.

Table 1.4 *The structure of finance in European basketball, cricket, ice hockey and rugby*

Receipts from (%)	Limoges	Basketball	Pro A,	France	Pro B	Kent[b]	Sussex[d]	Hockey[d]	ST[c]	RCN[c]
	1988–89	1988–89	1993–94	1997–98	1993–94	1978	1978	1992–93	1997–98	1997–98
Spectators	71.1	25	17.2	17	12.2	25.6	9.5	13.9	18.5	22.0
Subsidies	18.4	42	40.4	28	49.0	38.5[b]	32.5[d]	54.4		
Sponsors and advertising	10.5	20	32.3	36	28.6	23.4	30.3	13.1	43.5	56.5
TV rights			8.1		7.1				19.5	17.0
By-products		13[a]	2.0	19[a]	3.1	12.5[a]	20.6[a]	18.6[a]	18.5	4.5
Total	100	100	100	100	100	100	100	100	100	100

Notes:
[a] Including TV rights.
[b] Kent County Cricket Club; subscriptions; source: Sloane (1980).
[c] Stade Toulousain, rugby and Racing Club de Narbonne, rugby; source: press.
[d] Sussex County Cricket Club; here "subsidies" refer in fact to cash donations and Hockey: ice hockey, France, 1992–93; source: Bourg and Nys (1996).

match. The leagues and clubs were fearful that live television broadcasting would decrease attendance at the stadium, thus shrinking their major source of revenue. Given the lack of competition among broadcasters – there was only one public television station at the time – the monopsony rights fee would not be sufficient to compensate for lost gate receipts.

3. THE CONTEMPORARY PROFESSIONAL SPORTS MODEL

Most top-level European professional clubs no longer have the financial structure of the old SSSL model. During the 1980s, and even more so in the 1990s, new sources of revenue emerged and old ones declined. For example, gate receipts in Division 1 French football fell from 81 per cent in 1970–71 to 50 per cent in 1985–86 and 19.9 per cent in 1997–98 (see Table 1.2). In Italian Division 1 football a similar trend is evident, as spectators brought in 71 per cent of revenue in 1988, but only 36 per cent in 1998 (see Table 1.5). An exception to the trend is Spanish football, which remains more dependent on spectators due to the important system of season ticket buyers ('socios') in that country.

In the contemporary professional sports model, subsidies have declined in countries where they are not already banned. The share of revenues from advertising and sponsorships has held steady for the past 15 years in the range of 20-25 per cent in football. The advertising-sponsor share is some-what higher in basketball, which more recently became a professional sport in Europe, and higher still in rugby, whose 'professionalization' only dates back to 1994.

If the SSSL model has declined, what are the new sources of funds to professional sports? In 1997–98, television rights took the first rank in the finance of French professional football and the second rank in the finance of several big European clubs (see Tables 1.2 and 1.5). The relative impor-tance of television is increasing in other sports as well. Television has become, or is destined to be, the main source of professional sports finance.

A media takeover is evidenced by the current strategy of firms in the broadcast industry, such as BSkyB, CLT-UFA, AB Sports, Canal Plus, and Pathé (Bourg, 1999), which consists of buying up shares in a professional club's stock. Involvement of the media is not entirely new. For instance, the French newspaper *L'Equipe* (and its ancestor *L'Auto*) has provided decisive financial support to European professional cycling and motor racing events (Bourg, 1989). Also, public television channels have long been contributors to football revenues (RAI to Italian Calcio, ARD-ZDF to German

Table 1.5 The structure of European professional football finance

Receipts from (in %)	Italy D1,1988	Italy D1,1998	Spain D1,1998	England D1,1998	MU[b] 1997–98
Spectators	71.2	36	45	36	34
Sponsors and advertising	6.6	25[a]	17[a]	37[a]	13
TV rights	15.1	39	38	27	19
By-products	7.1				34
Total	100	100	100	100	100

Commercial receipts[c]	Newcastle 1995–96	Newcastle 1996–97	Manchester United 1995–96	Manchester United 1996–97	Tottenham 1995–96	Tottenham 1996–97	Milan AC 1995–96	Milan AC 1996–97	Juventus de Turin 1995–96	Juventus de Turin 1996–97	A[e] 1997–98	B[d] 1997–98
Gate receipts	46.4	42.6	39.4	36.5	54.9	51.3	44.4	40.7	53.7	37.0	23.7	25.6
Sponsors and advertising	17.1	16.0	11.6	13.4	19.6	18.6	15.5	15.2	29.2	28.0	24.8	46.2
TV rights	12.2	19.4	11.5	15.3	10.2	16.8	29.6	34.2	17.1	35.0	51.5	28.2
Merchandising	24.3	22.0	37.5	34.2	15.3	13.3	10.5	9.9	0	0	0	0
Total	100	100	100	100	100	100	100	100	100	100	100	100

Notes:
[a] Including merchandising, according to Deloitte & Touche. *Sources*: Caselli (1990), Deloitte & Touche (1998).
[b] Manchester United.
[c] From the study achieved for Olympique de Marseille by the Centre de Droit et d'Economie du Sport, Limoges (excluding allowances for players' transfers and subsidies).
[d] B = Average of group 4 French clubs (PSG, Monaco, Olympique de Marseille, Lyon, Bordeaux).
[e] A = Average of French clubs in Division 1.

Bundesliga, BBC to British Premier League, and ORTF to the French National Football League). However, their support has been a subsidiary source of funds compared to spectators, patrons and sponsors.

A major reason explaining the rise of television and participation by media companies is increased competition in the industry. Whereas once there was one public television station, now there are many public and private channels to choose from (Andreff et al. 1987; Bourg and Gouguet, 1998). Professional leagues and clubs can make use of this competition by negotiating more lavish television rights deals. This is a consequence of privatization and deregulation of the media industry in Europe, particularly television channels, and the phasing out of the monopsonistic position of a single public channel on the market for sports broadcasting in each European country.

Television is increasingly taking a bigger part in financing professional sports in Europe, and there is far more growth to come. This tendency is strengthened by the relatively unsaturated European market and the internationalization of sport (Andreff, 1989). The sports that are most conducive to television are those in which European or world events attract widespread interest.

Another interesting aspect of the revised model is the emergence of a new generation of entrepreneurs onto the scene. These corporate titans are no longer the unselfish, financially disinterested businessmen of the past, but investors bent on improving financial results of the clubs through ownership and control. There are numerous examples, a few of which are Jean-Luc Lagardère (Matra into Racing Paris), Silvio Berlusconi (Fininvest into Milano AC), Joe Lewis (ENIC into Glasgow Rangers), Mark McCormack (IMG into RC Strasbourg), and Rupert Murdoch (BSkyB's bid for Manchester United).

The penetration of entrepreneurs and corporations into the sports business has triggered two significant changes. One is that the club's administration is taken over by professional managers, usually but not always resulting in financial stability. The other change is that the club's finances benefit from the ability of these new investors to mobilize additional funds for further growth and competitive edge. The new owners are eager to establish vertical integration in the industry through promotion of sporting events, control of stadium facilities, ownership of television rights, merchandising and facilitating other aspects of a corporate empire.

A synergism can develop as a result of the interaction between sport and business. Merchandising, for example, has long been a practice of clubs. But they lacked the resources for full-scale marketing. Specialists are now doing a better job of promoting a larger variety of team merchandise to greater numbers of people across broader geographic areas. Merchandising reached 10 per cent of football club Milano AC's revenue in 1997, 13 per cent of Tottenham Hotspur's, 22 per cent of Newcastle's and 34 per cent of Manchester United's. For the latter, in 1998, merchandising revenues provided as great a share as gate receipts. Merchandising is currently the main by-product of football clubs' operations, providing a whole catalogue of items – apparel, linen, toys, schoolbags, watches, perfumes and so forth.

Another feature of the new model is a magnified distinction between clubs as demanders and suppliers of talent. Some clubs concentrate more on seeking to increase revenue and return on investment by issuing securities (stocks, bonds) on financial markets and borrowing funds from banks. Other clubs are more conservative in their finances, but seek to take advantage of richer clubs' desire for talent by becoming net suppliers of players. The French football clubs at Nantes and Auxerre are well known as breeding grounds for talented players whose sale to other clubs is a major revenue source.

This strategy of supplying the market with new players has been pursued more because the Bosman case allowed any club to recruit an unlimited number of players from other European Union countries. For instance, French football has been a net supplier to the European market for professional players after Bosman, and this has contributed to a flourishing financial state for French clubs.[4] Numerous British, Spanish and Italian clubs, net buyers in the market, are in the red (Szymanski, 1999).

European professional clubs are leading the world in selling stock to the public. In the 1998–99 season, 33 football clubs from six countries were quoted on a stock exchange: 22 in the United Kingdom, 6 in Denmark, 2 in Portugal, and 1 each in Italy, the Netherlands, and Switzerland. The stock value of the 22 British clubs is in the range of $1.8 billion. Funds collected from stock sales are used to modernize or extend stadium capacity, repay debts, train young players, or recruit 'stars'. The latter strategy is risky because poor performance or injuries to star recruits can trigger a collapse in stock price, as happened to the Newcastle football club shares on the London Stock Exchange in 1997. Although the trend toward initial public offerings of stock has continued – one German team (Bayer Leverkusen) recently issued stock, and another (Borussia Dortmund) plans to do so in 2000 – stock prices have not held up well. After reaching a high at the beginning of 1997, the Kick-Index of 20 UK soccer stocks has fallen 35 per cent, and excluding the success of Manchester United, which has outperformed the market, they have fallen even more.

To conclude, this model is based on four pillars: *Media–Corporations–Merchandising–Markets*. Moreover, there is no longer a necessary link between the nationality of the professional club and the television broadcaster, or the company that has an investment stake, or the stock underwriter, or the players on the field. Thus, at least on a European scale, professional sport finance is globalized. We thus refer to this model as MCMMG.

4. FINANCING STRATEGIES IN THE TWO PROFESSIONAL MODELS

The evolution from the SSSL model to the MCMMG model is, in the first analysis, a shift from focus on quantitative variables to emphasis on qualitative variables. When the objective is to maximize gate receipts, clubs rely on influencing fairly simple decision variables in the SSSL model, such as improving attendance density by spectators, attracting a larger group of season ticket holders, and increasing the number of games (through qualification for domestic and European cup events). This is so because ticket prices cannot be raised too much without affecting attendance. A strategy of decreasing prices to attract more spectators has not proved to be successful due to a low price elasticity for sporting events (Andreff, 1981). Qualitative variables such as stadium comfort and access to the stadium and parking appear to influence attendance more than ticket prices. If the stadium is owned by a municipality, the club must negotiate a subsidy to improve the facility, and if the club owns the stadium, it must engage in an investment strategy to be financed in the capital market. The latter case is facilitated through the MCMMG model.

The MCMMG model rests more on price and quality variables than on quantitative approach to the management of a professional club. Television contracts attract sponsors who inflate revenues to the stations and thus justify more generous rights fees to the club or league. This amount is a function of the broadcast market (Bourg and Gouguet, 1998). For instance, in the case of a supply monopoly of a professional league selling its events to several competing television channels, broadcast rights fees are far higher than in the case of a monopsony by a single channel negotiating rights with several competing leagues or clubs. The latter situation applied to all professional sports in Europe until the early 1980s, under the SSSL model.

The entry of entrepreneurs and corporate managers into the market has made the value of assets a strategic variable. Under the MCMMG model, the club seeks to maximize its return from not only the stadium but also television, merchandising and capital markets. This model enables the club to take advantage of economies of scale through a wider range of services and products. Quantitative variables such as number of issued shares or number of stockholders do not matter as much to a club as qualitative variables such as stock value and the value of dividends distributed to shareholders, which are determined by the profitability of the club, winning percentage and reputation.

5.   THE TRANSITION BETWEEN THE TWO MODELS

Prior to the 1980s, European economies were much more government administered and regulated, so that intervention of public authorities into the sports business was common. European economies were less internationalized and less open to competition. With the emergence of globalization and more open markets, no sector, including sports, can now escape the logic of the market (Andreff, 1996b). The transformation of some professional clubs into joint stock equity corporations and the impetus toward profitability are logical outcomes of applying the MCMMG model to the deregulated market structure.

The SSSL model is necessarily running out. Under this model, the wage bill was spinning out of control. In French professional football in 1966–67, wages (including mandatory social security payments) were 56 per cent of overall expenses and caused a deficit of 6.5 million francs. By 1974–75, wages reached 72 per cent of expenses and about 84 per cent in 1982–83. Only after a financial stabilization programme was launched by the auditing body of the French National Football League in 1990–91 did the wage bill decline, to 48 per cent in 1993–94 and 45 per cent in 1997–98. This is compared to wage bills in 1997–98 of 43 per cent in Germany, 46 per cent in Spain, 52 per cent in England, and 68 per cent in Italy (Deloitte & Touche, 1998). As noted above, deficits have existed in the United Kingdom, Italy and Spain. This creates a need for new sources of finance.

In clubs that behave as win maximizers (Kesenne, 1996), the demand for acquiring star players is very high, and this demand is exacerbated by the absence of restraints in the player labour market, as, for example, the draft of players and salary caps in American professional sports. The only restriction prior to the Bosman case was a limitation on the number of foreign players on European teams. Thus, the high demand for star players could not be satisfied, which placed strains on the domestic market, the relevant market for the SSSL model. The value of the best domestic players was correspondingly overrated, fixed above the equilibrium price by excess demand. This was incompatible with the hard budget constraints of clubs hemmed in by the limited sources of finance in the SSSL model. It is not surprising that a number of European clubs have lost money.

The conventional solution to financial troubles under the SSSL model is to increase the number of games to increase gate receipts and attract more subsidies and sponsors. But in the long run, this solution is detrimental to quality of play and, in any event, the supply of public subsidies and private donations is not infinite. One way out of the crisis is a drastic financial stabilization programme prohibiting the acquisition of star players. Another is for a professional league to regress the clubs in the red into a lesser division of competition. Perhaps most important is to resort to new methods of finance. This is the way of the MCMMG model and the route taken by many clubs. Fresh money from new sources of finance has alleviated the budget crunch for some clubs, whereas deregulation of the player market in the Bosman case has facilitated international mobility of stars toward clubs that have adopted the revised model.

For clubs that cling to the SSSL model, the threat is to sink deeper in the red or to be marginalized from the most profitable sporting events. It seems that such a trade-off was at stake in the aborted proposal of a European football superleague, which was imagined by and for big clubs already converted to the MCMMG model.[5] Should a superleague come into fruition, second rank clubs would have their own national championships. These clubs would include those with a financial structure close to the SSSL model or who are in transition to the MCMMG model. It may be, given the growing international demand for sport, that the system of national premier leagues will give way to a system where the most important form of competition is international (Noll, 1999).

6. SHORTCOMINGS OF THE CONTEMPORARY MODEL

Although we foresee more widespread adoption of the MCMMG model in coming years, it is not without its problems.[6] One is a problem of domination by the rich clubs. In Europe, the outcomes of games, especially in the major sport of football, are increasingly determined by the financial capacity of clubs. In the absence of a player draft, the wealthiest clubs can skim off the exceptionally talented players so as to become even more competitive. They then earn more money, which in turn enables recruitment of even more top players. These powerful clubs have a higher probability of qualifying for and winning European cup events. The aforementioned superleague project was an attempt to institutionalize the domination of the wealthiest clubs, allowing the others to more realistically compete for prestigious national events.

A second problem is the determination of competition calendars and rules of the game on financial criteria, and the television taking over greater control of events to maximize exposure. There has been discussion, for instance, of changing a European football game into four quarters rather than two halves to leave more room for advertising screens.

Another issue is what appears to be growing corruption in European professional sports, especially football. The directors of four prominent French football clubs, for instance, have been sued for various financial misdoings. The Saint-Etienne club was found to have engaged in embezzlement and hiding funds in 1982; the Bordeaux club embezzled and illegally acquired real estate in 1990; the Marseille club misappropriated 101 million francs between 1987 and 1993 including through illegal transfer of funds to Switzerland; and the Paris-Saint-Germain club was recently found to have embezzled 22 million francs.

There have also been increased revelations of doping by football players to enhance performance and relieve the fatigue from playing two or three matches a week, due to the overall increase in the number of matches (a solution sought for solving the crisis of the SSSL model). This work overburden is less striking in those clubs that have adopted the MCMMG model insofar as their extended financial resources enable them to recruit more players. Two years ago, some managers of the Italian Calcio were sued for having facilitated players' doping by hiding the whole issue. In July 1998, the share of the budget of the French ministry for sports devoted to the fight against doping was doubled.

A last shortcoming of the MCMMG financing model is a number of purely illegal behaviours. Fixing the outcome of a 1994 football game sent Bernard Tapie of the Olympique de Marseille to jail for eight months. In 1996, a football referee from Switzerland was accused of corruption for proposing an 'arrangement' to Grasshopper Zurich before one of its European cup matches. In 1997, a Belgian football club, Anderlecht, was sanctioned by the European football federation (UEFA) for fixing several games in the European cup. Illegal gambling operations have sprung up in various countries: in the Italian Totonero which is much more profitable than the official Totocalcio; with the former goalkeeper of Liverpool and Southampton who was accused of organizing a worldwide gambling network based on rigged football matches. The Russian mafia is well known for money laundering through western European professional sports.

These examples appear to be only the tip of an iceberg, suggesting that the MCMMG model has gone adrift and that more regulation should come from government. European professional sports are discovering the down side of big money inflow. The rich get richer and the purity of the institutional arrangements and games themselves may be sullied. The trade-off, of course, is that fans receive more games, fancier stadiums, greater exposure to the television, and enhanced merchandise amenities associated with team identification. On the other hand, both traditionalists and advocates of sporting ethics resist the internationalization and 'monetization' of sport, and would like to return to the old days of local control and involvement by genteel sportsmen. However, 'the cat seems to be out of the bag', concerning top-level competition.

7. US SPORTS MODEL

Figure 1.1 illustrates the main components of the US sports industry model. The three principal institutions shown are government, management and labour, with government's role that of regulating the other participants.

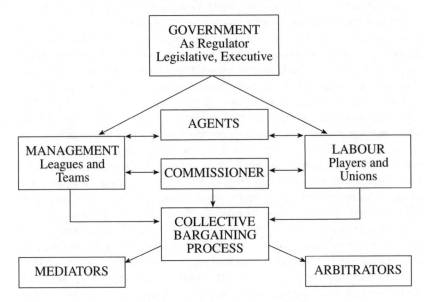

Source: Staudohar (1996, p. 7)

Figure 1.1   US sports industry model

In the US the federal government regulates sports under its legislative, executive and judicial branches. Although the European Commission has broad powers under the Treaty of Rome to assume jurisdiction over sports issues, the individual countries retain some control on legal matters. This is analogous to the American states exercising legal authority under the separation of powers found in the US Constitution. Governments in European nations have greater control over sports than states do in America. The EC and federal government, however, exercise hegemony on matters involving commerce across national or state boundaries, such as antitrust, player movement and television broadcasts.

Management of major team sports is undertaken in both the US and Europe through the league structure and individual team ownership. This provides for the planning, supervision and control of decisions affecting club operations. Leagues are regulated by government but retain substantial autonomy. In Europe the leagues consist of teams from single countries, such as the French National Football League, English Premier League and the German Bundesliga. There is international competition between teams from these leagues, especially for the annual European Cup, but each league is a separate entity.

Labour refers to players and their unions. In European soccer and American baseball unions were established as far back as the late nineteenth century and it is common today for players to belong to unions or associations in their sports. Unions in the US, however, have been more active. This is due to the influence of collective bargaining, in which negotiations occur over the division of revenue between owners and players.

Figure 1.1 shows a commissioner, whose role varies among sports. In a sense the commissioner is a public spokesman and ambassador for the sport, who promotes its interests generally. But as a practical matter, commissioners are selected and paid by team owners to represent league interests. Thus commissioners are typically involved in negotiations with unions and with television networks over the sale of rights to broadcast games. The commissioner is the most powerful league representative but is acting on behalf of the owners and can be removed from office at their discretion.

Europe does not have commissioners of sports in the same way the US does, but it does have UEFA, a soccer federation that establishes policies that are followed by leagues, teams and players. Overseeing UEFA is FIFA, the international soccer group which regulates the sport and organizes events such as the Olympic Games and World Cup.

Agents are depicted in Figure 1.1. Their basic role is similar in the US and Europe. They represent players in individual salary negotiations and sometimes also in investment programmes. By providing players with professional representation, agents have been a strong force in raising levels of player compensation.

Mediators and arbitrators, also shown in Figure 1.1, are available to resolve disputes between owners and players. Mediators attempt to broker agreements through persuasion, while leaving the final decision up to the parties. Arbitrators, on the other hand, issue a final and binding decision on the dispute. Mediation has been used for collective bargaining in American baseball and football, but with little success.

Arbitration, performed by private individuals, is used for player grievances in all American sports and has proved to be a successful method of resolving these disputes. Workplace disputes in Europe are commonly handled by a labour court in an individual country or by the European Court of Justice.

8. PRODUCTION AND DISTRIBUTION OF SPORTING EVENTS

In both Europe and the United States, sports leagues are joint ventures that can be viewed as a single entity or cartel. The clubs are separately owned with discretion to fix prices, market the games and adopt strategies to compete with other clubs. (An exception to this arrangement is the US major soccer league in which ownership is pooled into a syndicate that allocates players to teams to accomplish competitive balance.) The rookie draft of new players is a characteristic of the American system. The team with the worst record drafts first, and so on through the team with the best record, which picks last in successive selection rounds.

Besides the draft, joint determination on franchise locations and marketing of national television rights through the league are found in the American system. Another key aspect of league marketing is selling licenses to manufacturers and vendors. There is a high value market in the United States for a variety of products such as trading cards, clothing and memorabilia. The 'official' soft drink, credit card, airline and so forth of the leagues are powerful marketing tools that sponsors pay dearly to own. The European market is similar in this regard except that licensing is typically handled by individual teams.

American sports leagues have essentially domestic competition, with regular seasons and then playoffs to determine a champion. The only international aspect of this is that baseball, basketball and hockey leagues all have Canadian franchises. In European leagues, the top teams compete both domestically and internationally (Hoehn and Szymanski, 1999). Unique to European leagues is promotion or demotion of teams based on win–loss records. That is, teams may advance to a higher division if they win a high percentage of their games or drop to a lower division if they are habitual losers. Changes in American leagues, on the other hand, come from adding new franchises and relocation of a franchise to another city. If franchises are added, existing teams share the fees paid by the new entrants. There is also the possibility of bankruptcy removing a team from a city or a league and entire leagues may cease operation for financial reasons. Bankruptcies have occurred fairly often historically but have been rare in recent years (Quirk and Fort, 1992).

A potential advantage of the closed American-style league is that revenue can be distributed equally among teams to provide for greater balance of financial strength. The best example of this is American football, where all television revenues from national broadcasts are divided equally among teams. Gate receipts are divided into 60 per cent for the home team and 40 per cent for the visiting team. As a result, there is less economic disparity and a team like the New York Jets (in a big market) has about the same revenue as the Green Bay Packers (in a small market).

In the other American sports – baseball, basketball and hockey – there are separate national and local broadcast agreements. Although the national revenues are shared equally among teams, similar to what occurs in Europe, there is significant variability in local broadcast revenues. A big-market team, the New York Yankees in baseball, gets $60 million a year from sale of its local broadcast rights, whereas small-market teams receive as little as $4–$6 million. This leads to disparity in competing for players and puts the big-market teams in a better position to win games, which can lead to competitive imbalance. There is a limited sharing of local broadcast revenues among baseball teams, but not enough to help small-market teams compete effectively. Gate receipts are retained 100 per cent by the home team in basketball and hockey, which is also the norm in Europe. Because teams in big markets can be expected to attract more spectators and corporate money for luxury boxes, this also contributes to financial imbalance.

Empirical evidence from North America indicates support for profit-seeking (if not maximizing) behaviour, whereas there is less emphasis on profits according to studies of European examples (Cairns et al., 1986). Salary caps, not common in Europe, have developed in the United States as a quid pro quo for free agency in the labour market. Basketball implemented the first team salary cap in the 1984–85 season and football followed suit in 1994. There was a salary cap for rookies in hockey established in 1995 (Staudohar, 1999). Basketball imposed a cap on individual player salaries in 1999–2000.

In recent years, the North American labour market has become more internationalized. The players in football remain almost entirely American, but baseball, basketball and hockey now have more players from foreign countries. This is most apparent in hockey. Until about the early 1970s, nearly all the players in the National Hockey League (NHL), were Canadian born. Currently, about 60 per cent of NHL players are Canadian, 18 per cent American, 10 per cent from countries of the former Soviet Union and the remainder from other European countries such as Sweden, Finland, the Czech Republic and Slovakia.

Similar to Europe, the United States has a heavily regulated workplace. There are numerous laws pertaining to labour relations and antitrust that have a significant impact on sports. A number of decisions have been made by US administrative agencies, such as the National Labor Relations Board and by the federal courts that determine a web of rules and regulations. There has been a greater tendency in the United States for examining issues of public policy in the courts, especially antitrust, although governments in both Europe and the United States have generally adopted a 'hands off' approach, giving sports cartels specific or de facto immunity under competition policy (Cairns et al., 1986).

It might be supposed that in America, the land of free enterprise, sports teams would not receive subsidies. Although there are no direct payments from government to teams, there are generous tax concessions. Sports teams are the only kind of business that can depreciate human assets to reduce income taxes. Even more important are in-kind subsidies in the form of stadiums built at the expense of local governments to induce teams to stay in an area or attract teams from other communities (Noll and Zimbalist, 1997). Not only do teams get free or low-cost use of publicly financed stadium facilities, but they often receive revenues from concessions, parking, luxury boxes and other amenities available at these stadiums. The high intensity of fan interest and fans' fear of losing their teams leads owners to say, 'Build us a new stadium or we will move to another city.' Imagine a multimillionaire owner looking for a handout.

9. SPORTS LABOUR MARKET

A significant characteristic of the US model, which thus far has not been much in evidence in Europe, is collective bargaining. The players in the team sports are organized into unions that negotiate the terms applicable to all players in a multiemployer bargaining unit that encompasses the league. This process of dividing the revenue of the industry has led to numerous strikes and lockouts, many of which have interrupted play during the regular season.

In 1995 the European Court of Justice ruled in the Bosman case that the player transfer system and restrictions on the maximum number of foreign players on teams were illegal violations of the Treaty of Rome. Prior to this decision, players were not free to move from one team to another because transfer could occur only if two clubs agreed on a transfer fee to the club losing the player. This limitation on mobility kept player salaries low. Also changed in Bosman was the 3 + 2 rule, a quota system allowing only three foreign players on a team in a national league, plus two other foreigners if they played for five years without a break in the host country.

This decision has caused dramatic changes in the European sports business, particularly football (soccer), ice hockey, basketball and rugby. The Bosman case is akin to the 1975 arbitration ruling in the United States that allowed free agency for baseball players who played with their clubs for one year without a contract and which was later extended to American football, basketball and hockey.

The Bosman case outlawed payment of transfer fees for players whose contracts with their clubs had expired. It did not prevent payment of transfer fees for players under contract, which has been a more common practice. The European Commission has objected to transfer fees under any circumstances, perceiving little difference between professional athletes and other workers. This political opposition led to a decision by FIFA to bow to the EC's wishes. Thus, on 31 August, 2000, FIFA president Sepp Blatter announced that clubs could no longer demand fees for their players.

There is also individual salary negotiation between a player and his club, with the player usually represented by an agent. The process of individual negotiations is similar to that in Europe, although the player contracts are usually more detailed and for longer durations (Hoehn and Szymanski, 1999). The role of player agents in British soccer is similar to that in the US. In both countries agents' negotiating skills have produced dramatic increases in player earnings. The problem of agents improperly signing up players while in amateur status is more characteristic of the US than in Britain. But agents on both sides of the Atlantic have occasionally engaged in ill-advised investment programmes on behalf of players, which have cost them dearly.

Agents in Britain are prohibited by Football League rules from arranging transfers from one club to another or renegotiating existing contracts (Flynn and Guest, 1994). These restrictions do not apply in the US. While solicitors and accountants may represent players in Britain, agents are more likely to be former players. In the US the role of attorney and agent is commonly combined in one person. Fees for agents who negotiate player contracts are about 4 per cent of the total deal in the US. In Britain, fixed negotiation fees are more common. These arrangements are gaining some acceptance in the US in the National Basketball Association (NBA), as a result of the 1999 collective bargaining agreement which imposed limits on individual player salary increases.

Licensing of agents has been proposed by UEFA. Agents in the US are licensed and regulated by the players' unions, although the unions do not have the resources to engage in close monitoring. Several state laws in America have provisions that regulate agents, requiring posting of bonds and stipulating proper behaviour.

Although collective bargaining may take place in Europe over wages, hours and working conditions applicable to all players, these negotiations have rarely if ever resulted in work stoppages. Consequently, there has been less need in Europe for mediators and arbitrators to provide dispute settlement functions. As the size of the economic pie grows in Europe, however, one might expect the system to become more adversarial than it is now.

A major reason for the adversarial nature of American professional team sports is the free agency system that began about 20 years prior to the Bosman case in Europe. Free agency has provided an enormous financial windfall to players in US leagues, who have the opportunity to have their salaries determined by market conditions rather than what a single monopsonist employer might be willing to pay. But it has placed an added financial burden on clubs, especially in small-market cities, to compete for players and win games.

As noted above, European free agency has been extended beyond the ruling in the Bosman case as a result of FIFA's intention to drop transfer fees in 2000. Perhaps this result was inevitable, given the pressure for a free labour market from the EC. But the result has been despair for club owners who found themselves with formerly prime assets that were now worthless on the balance sheet. Table 1.6 shows the transfer fees for the ten most expensive soccer players in history. The magnitude of the fees that Real Madrid paid to acquire Luis Figo, and that Lazio paid to get Hernan Crespo hastened the end of the transfer system. In 2001 a record transfer fee of $64.5 million was paid for French star Zinedine Zidane. He moved

Table 1.6   Ten highest European transfer fees as of 2000

Rank	Name	Country	From	To	Transfer Fee	Year
1.	Luis Figo	Portugal	Barcelona	Real Madrid	$56.1 million	2000
2.	Hernan Crespo	Argentina	Parma	Lazio	$54.1 million	2000
3.	Christian Vieri	Italy	Lazio	Inter Milan	$50.0 million	1999
4.	Nicolas Anelka	France	Arsenal	Real Madrid	$35.7 million	1999
5.	Denilson	Brazil	Sao Paulo	Real Betis	$35.0 million	1997
6.	Gabriel Batistuta	Argentina	Fiorentina	AS Roma	$33.8 million	2000
7.	Amoroso	Brazil	Udinese	Parma	$33.1 million	1999
8.	Ronaldo	Brazil	Barcelona	Inter Milan	$27.9 million	1997
9.	Rivaldo	Brazil	Deportivo	Barcelona	$26.7 million	1997
10.	Andriy Shevchenko	Ukraine	Dynamo Kiev	AC Milan	$25.0 million	1999

Source: *Los Angeles Times*, 3 August, 2000, p. B2

Table 1.7   Ten highest paid soccer players, 2000

Rank player (nationality)	Club (Country)	Annual earnings
1. Alessandro Del Piero (Italian)	Juventus (Italy)	$11 million
2. Ronaldo (Brazilian)	Inter Milan (Italy)	$9.2 million
3. Christain Veiri (Italian)	Inter Milan (Italy)	$6.5 million
4. David Beckham (English)	Manchester United (England)	$6 million
5. Gabriel Batistuta (Argentine)	Fiorentina (Italy)	$5.9 million
6. Alan Shearer (English)	Newcastle United (England)	$5.8 million
7. Nicolas Anelka (French)	Real Madrid (Spain)	$5.7 million
8. Steve McManaman (English)	Real Madrid (Spain)	$5.36 million
9. Hidetoshi Nakata (Japanese)	AS Roma (Italy)	$5.33 million
10. Zinedine Zidane (French)	Juventus (Italy)	$5.2 million

Source: Los Angeles Times, 24 May, 2000, p. B2.

from Juventus to Real Madrid. Although FIFA's new rules on transfers were officially approved shortly before the Zidane deal, these rules did not apply because they do not take effect until 2002.

It remains to be seen how FIFA's decision will work out. Following the announcement that it would bow to the EC's desires for a free labour market, there were negotiations as to the details of such an arrangement. Participants included the EC, FIFA, UEFA and FIFPro. FIFPro is an international federation of soccer groups, including French, Scottish, English, Italian and Dutch players' associations, plus several South American and Eastern European groups. FIFPro's position was akin to that of the EC – completely free labour markets – but the practical application of this idea created problems, particularly for small clubs that train and develop young players.

A compromise situation was reached in which training compensation is due on transfers up to the age of 23. Each time a young player moves to a higher level team, clubs that were involved in his training will receive a transfer fee. Contract lengths are specified for all players, with a minimum of one year and a maximum of five years. An arbitration system is established to handle disputes, which may also be submitted to the civil court in individual countries. This new system was ratified at a special FIFA conference in Buenos Aires in July 2001. Meanwhile, FIFPro filed a lawsuit in a Belgian court to nullify the application of transfer fees. As a group, US major league athletes are by far the highest paid in the world. In 2000 the highest average salary was in the NBA, about $3.2 million. Next highest were baseball players at about a $2 million average, followed by hockey at

Table 1.8   Ten highest paid baseball players, 2000

Rank	Player	Club	Salary[a]
1.	Kevin Brown	Los Angeles	$15.7 million
2.	Randy Johnson	Arizona	$13.4 million
3.	Albert Belle	Baltimore	$12.9 million
4.	Bernie Williams	NY Yankees	$12.4 million
5.	Larry Walker	Colorado	$12.1 million
6.	Mike Piazza	NY Mets	$12.1 million
7.	David Cone	NY Yankees	$12.0 million
8.	Pedro Martinez	Boston	$11.5 million
9.	Mo Vaughn	Anaheim	$11.2 million
10.	Greg Maddux	Atlanta	$11.1 million

Note: [a]Salaries are rounded to the nearest tenth of a million.

Source: *San Francisco Chronicle*, 6 April, 2000, p. D4.

$1.35 million and football at about $1.1 million. The highest paid American team athlete ever was the now-retired Michael Jordan, who in 1997–98 was paid $33 million by the Chicago Bulls. (Heavyweight boxer Mike Tyson was paid $75 million for three fights in 1996, the most ever by an individual athlete.)

Tables 1.7 and 1.8 show the salaries of the ten highest paid players in European soccer and American baseball. Although the top baseball players make more money, the soccer players are also rewarded at astronomical levels. As a result of the elimination of transfer fees in Europe, which will allow players to move more freely among teams, one would expect the gap between baseball and soccer salaries to narrow in the future.

10.   REVENUE SOURCES

One of the most important aspects of convergence between the American and European models is media involvement. Revenues to American sports from sale of television rights have skyrocketed. Table 1.9 shows these increases over the years in American football and the resulting rise in player salaries. Free agency has been the engine for driving player salaries upward, but it is television that provides the fuel.

Several US television networks have positioned themselves or are seeking access to take advantage of the emerging European market, including NBC, CBS, ESPN and Fox. Fox is owned by Rupert Murdoch (News Corp.) who also owns the Los Angeles Dodgers baseball team and has

Public policy and sports economics

Table 1.9   The NFL's television contract history

Years	Total	Annual TV income per team	Average player salary
1960–1961	$600,000[a]	$45,000	$15,000
1962–1963	$4.65 million[b]	$330,000	$20,000
1964–1965	$28.2 million[b]	$1 million	$21,000
1966–1969	$75.2 million[c]	$1.6 million	$22,000
1970–1973	$185 million[c]	$1.8 million	$23,000
1974–1977	$269 million	$2.6 million	$30,000
1978–1981	$6416 million	$5.8 million	$60,000
1982–1986	$2.1 billion	$13.6 million	$100,000
1987–1989	$1.428 billion[d]	$16.7 million	$211,000
1990–1993	$3.65 billion[e]	$32.6 million	$355,000
1994–1997	$4.4 billion	$39.2 million	$700,000
1998–2005	$17.6 billion	$73.0 million	$1,400,000

Notes:
[a] Fee paid to the league for the NFL Championship Game, aired by NBC.
[b] CBS is the only network broadcasting NFC games.
[c] With NFL and AFL merger, CBS broadcasts NFC games, NBC broadcasts AFC games. ABC begins Monday Night Football telecasts.
[d] ESPN begins broadcasting preseason and Sunday night games in eight weeks of season.
[e] TNT begins broadcasting Sunday night games in first eight weeks of season.

Sources: *Sports Illustrated*, 27 December 1993, p. 19; *Wall Street Journal*, 24 December 1993, p. A4; and author's estimated average player salary for 1994–1997 and 1998–2005. Cited in Staudohar (1996, p. 60).

significant television and soccer interests in Europe. In 1999 and 2000, British Premier League games were shown in the United States on the Fox Network. ESPN has a one-third ownership in the Eurosport Consortium, which broadcasts in English, German and Dutch to 40 million homes.

US sports leagues are also interested in placing teams in the European market. The World Football League, a minor league established by the National Football League, already has a successful operation in Europe. The National Basketball Association (NBA) is involved in an international tournament called the McDonald's Basketball Open, in which NBA and European teams compete. Both the NBA and the NFL have contemplated regular season expansion to Europe, although there are no immediate plans in that direction. Travel and time zone problems present a substantial barrier to international expansion, as do nationalism, self-determination, language barriers and entrenched foreign commercial interests that are wary of encroachment on their turf.

Although European clubs were the first to issue stock on a widespread basis, this idea is catching on some in America. The Green Bay Packers football team is owned by numerous stockholders in that Wisconsin city, although there are few market transactions. More recent examples of listed and actively traded stocks are those of the Boston Celtics (basketball), Cleveland Indians (baseball) and Florida Panthers (hockey).

11. CONCLUSION

We have examined and compared three models of sports finance in Europe: amateur, professional (traditional) and contemporary. The model of European amateur sports has remained fairly stable over the years and is not expected to change much in the future. It represents an important part of the overall picture of European finances because amateur clubs occasionally compete in top-level events. Also, funding from local sports enthusiasts keeps this 'grass-roots' activity and serves as a source of healthy recreation for participants.

A major theme of this chapter is the transition from the traditional to the contemporary professional sports model. We see that the contemporary or MCMMG model places less emphasis on gate receipts, subsidies and sponsors and more emphasis on vertical integration through a corporate structure that pursues a strategy of maximizing merchandising and television revenues and the value of the team's shares of stock. Clubs using what we call the SSSL or traditional model will be under increased financial pressure and less able to compete with top-level teams.

There has been a recent convergence between the US and European sports industry models. Perhaps the most important evidence of this is the Bosman decision in 1995 and the elimination by FIFA in 2002 of transfer fees for players under contract. These developments provide players with freedom to move from one club to another, breaking the monopsonistic hold that kept salaries low in the past. They are similar to the effect of the 1975 arbitration decision in the US, allowing baseball players to become free agents for the first time. The result of free agency was later modified in a collective bargaining agreement between the baseball owners and players' union, so that a player must wait six years before becoming a free agent. Similar agreement provisions are in effect in American football, basketball and hockey. The financial impact of free agency in American professional sports was immediate and dramatic, as salaries escalated to unimagined levels.

Another key area of convergence is media involvement. Deregulation of television in Europe has created several new networks that are competing to acquire television rights to games. This is driving rights fees skyward and providing more money to teams. Player salaries have seen a corresponding escalation. Thus, television, which has fuelled the rapid rise of revenues to sports in the US, is doing much the same now in Europe.

As the size of the pie grows larger, as it inevitably will in years to come, elite European teams, especially in football, will become even more dominant financially and on the field. This gives rise to proposals for a European superleague which would likely surpass in size and strength any single sports league in the United States. Even if the superleague does not materialize, there will be more international competition between top-level European teams in the future. This is likely to attract television viewers to the highest level of competition. It will cause more greed and corruption problems that will be dealt with through government regulation. Also, we expect that salary caps and methods for dealing with labour disputes will get greater attention in Europe.

NOTES

1. For a comparative analysis of sports finance in 12 European countries, see Andreff (1994 and 1996a).
2. Subsidies are understood here *lato sensu* so as to encompass public subsidies by local authorities, private donations and funds redistributed to clubs by the sports federations.
3. In some European countries, national legislation forbids government support to professional clubs, as is currently the case in Austria, Finland, the Netherlands, Sweden and the United Kingdom.
4. French Division 1 clubs had a cumulative deficit of 619 million francs in 1989–90. After a financial stabilization plan implemented by the DNCG (the auditing body of France's National Football League), the deficit was turned into a financial surplus of 60 million francs in 1994–95. After the Bosman case, the surplus grew to 483 million francs in 1997–98.
5. The economic rationale for a superleague of international competition is discussed in Hoehn and Szymanski (1999).
6. For more details, see Andreff (1999 and 2000).

REFERENCES

Andreff, W. (1980), 'La gestion de l'association sportive: des principes à la pratique', *Sports et Sciences*, Paris: Vigot.
Andreff, W. (1981), 'Le Prix du Spectacle Sportif et le Comportement du Spectateur', in *Le Spectacle Sportif*, Paris: Presses Universitaires de France.
Andreff, W. (1989), 'L'internationalisation Économique du Sport, in W. Andreff, (ed.), *Economie Politique du Sport*, Paris: Dalloz.
Andreff, W. (ed.) (1994), *The economic importance of sport in Europe: financing and economic impact*, Background document to the 14th Meeting of European Sports Ministers, Council of Europe, Strasbourg, April.
Andreff, W. (1996a), 'Economic environment of sport: a comparison between Western Europe and Hungary', *European Journal of Sport Management*, (4).

Andreff, W. (1996b), *Les Multinationales Globales*, Paris: La Découverte.
Andreff, W. (2000a), 'Les finances du sport et l'éthique sportive', *Revue d'Economie Financière* (55).
Andreff, W. (2000), 'Sport finance versus sport ethics', *European Journal of Sport Management*, 7 (1), November.
Andreff, W. and P.D. Staudohar (2000), 'The evolving European model of professional sports finance', *Journal of Sports Economics*, 1 (3).
Andreff, W., J.F. Nys and J.F. Bourg (1987), *Le Sport et la Télévision. Relations Économiques*, Paris: Dalloz.
Bourg, J.F. (1989), 'Le marché de la presse sportive', *Revue Juridique et Economique du Sport*, (10).
Bourg, J.F. (1999), 'Le sport à l'épreuve du marché', *Géopolitique*, (66).
Bourg, J.F. and J.J. Gouguet (1998), *Analyse Économique du Sport*, Paris: Presses Universitaires de France.
Bourg, J.F. and J.F. Nys (1996), 'Le financement des clubs sportifs', *La Lettre du Cadre Territorial*, June.
Cairns, J., N. Jennett and P.J. Sloane (1986), 'The economics of professional team sports: a survey of theory and evidence', *Journal of Economic Studies*, (13).
Caselli, G.P. (1990), 'Which way for the Italian football industry?', Colloquium Paper no. 122, 'Le football et l'Europe', European University Institute, Florence.
Deloitte and Touche (1998), *Annual Review of Football Finance*, August.
Flynn, A. and L. Guest (1994), *Out of Time: Why Football Isn't Working*, London: Simon and Schuster.
Hoehn, T. and S. Szymanski (1999), 'The Americanization of European football', *Economic Policy*, (28), April.
Kesenne, S. (1996), 'League and management in professional team sports with win maximizing clubs', *European Journal of Sport Management*, (4).
Noll, R.G. (1999), 'Competition Policy in European Sports after the Bosman Case', in C. Jeanrenaud and S. Kesenne (eds), *Competition Policy in Professional Sports. Europe after the Bosman case*, Antwerp: Standaard Editions.
Noll, R.G. and A. Zimbalist (1997), S*ports, Jobs and Taxes: The Economic Impact of Sports Teams and Stadiums*, Washington, DC: Brookings Institution.
Quirk, J. and R. Fort (1992), *Pay Dirt: The Business of Professional Team Sports*, Princeton, NJ: Princeton University Press.
Sloane, P.J. (1980), 'Sport in the Market?', Hobat Paper No. 85, The Institute of Economic Affairs, London.
Staudohar, P.D. (1996), *Playing for Dollars: Labor Relations and the Sports Business*, Ithaca, NY: Cornell University Press.
Staudohar, P.D. (1999), 'Salary Caps in Professional Team Sports', in C. Jeanrenaud and S. Kesenne (eds), *Competition Policy in Professional Sports: Europe After the Bosman Case* Antwerp: Standaard Editions Ltd.
Szymanski, S. (1999), 'The Market for Soccer Players in England after Bosman: Winners and losers', in C. Jeanrenaud and S. Kesenne (eds), *Competition Policy in Professional Sports. Europe after the Bosman case*, Antwerp: Standaard Editions.

2. The regulation of professional team sports

Peter J. Sloane

---

1. INTRODUCTION

Professional sports leagues pose particular problems for competition policy because of their special nature. Nowhere has this been more evident than in the US where the National Football League alone has had to defend over sixty antitrust suits since 1966 and the National Basketball Association and National Hockey League have likewise been affected. Only baseball of the four major team sports has escaped because of its broad antitrust immunity granted by the Supreme Court in 1922 (Roberts, 1991). Increasingly in Europe the clash between professional team sports and European competition law has become apparent following the Bosman case and recent alterations to the post-Bosman transfer arrangements for within-contract players.

The purpose of this chapter is to identify what might be an appropriate stance for competition law in relation to professional team sports. We focus on three recent decisions relating to professional football – namely the Bosman case, the UK Monopoly and Mergers Commission's investigation into the attempted takeover of Manchester United by BSkyB and the UK Restrictive Practices Court investigation into the collective sale of rights to television live games on television by the FA Premier League (FAPL) also involving BSkyB. Before going on to consider these it is necessary to place all of this into context by outlining the nature of professional sport leagues, an issue on which there is a considerable divergence of views among sports economists.

2. THE NATURE OF PROFESSIONAL SPORTS LEAGUES

The economics of team sports are unusual because it is not possible to produce output without the assistance of other producers or teams. Mutual inter-dependence is an essential element. Whilst in a competitive industry competition will eliminate inefficient producers in professional team sports, individual producers (clubs) have a vested interest in the economic viability of other clubs in order to maximise the interest of spectators and hence revenues from the sale of the product (the joint game). The nature of the product thus creates the requirement for uncertainty of outcome. There is an additional element in so far as spectators are interested in the position of teams in the league (the league standing effect). That is individuals who rarely attend games follow the outcome of the championship in the media (newspapers, television, and so on) and clubs can capture the economic rents of this by selling games on television and marketing club products. This poses an immediate problem for competition policy. Monopoly power is normally opposed on the grounds that restriction of output forces up prices and eliminates consumer surplus through the deadweight loss. The primary purpose of a league organisation is, however, to ensure that there is a viable product (thereby creating consumer surplus), though monopoly power also provides the possibility of forms of conduct which may not be in the public interest. It is also possible that the market is inherently unstable. Since it is not possible for all clubs to be successful in the sporting sense in any given season, it follows it may not be possible for all clubs to be profitable, given a positive relationship between playing success and profitability. The question is then whether the sports industry should be exempted either fully or partially from the requirements of competition policy or antitrust laws.[1]

The relationship between uncertainty of outcome, instability and mutual interdependence is illustrated in Figure 2.1, which compares a large city team L with a small city team S in a two-team league. It is assumed that the costs of producing a winning team rise linearly and are identical for both clubs. The returns to winning rise initially at an increasing rate, but then at a decreasing rate as interest wanes if teams win too often. The total returns to winning schedule for the large city team (TRL) lies above that of the small city team (TRS) as the larger population means the former will attract more spectators for any given winning percentage. There will be a unique profit maximisation percentage of wins for each team and it is realistic to suppose that it will pay the large city team to win more often (OWL) than the small city team (OWS). Instability arises from the zero sum nature of the league. If the large city team wins more often denoted by L', this means that the small city team will win less often, denoted by S'. Thus the success of one club will drive the other into the shaded area of loss-making. The small city club is more vulnerable than the large city club as it has a smaller range of winning percentages over which it is profitable, BC as opposed to AD for the large city club. Further, the pursuit of the maximisation of playing success subject to a break even constraint, OW'S for the small city club and OW'L for the large city club, will increase the likelihood of losses. Mutual interdependence is also illustrated by the fact that if the large city team population grows indicated by L" this may induce the belief in the small city that it can never hope to win the championship and its own total revenue schedule will shift down as indicated by S". It is clear that successful leagues need to minimise local population size differences among the constituent member clubs.

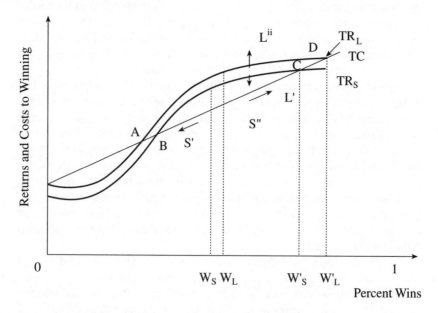

Figure 2.1   Uncertainty of outcome, instability and mutual interdependence

In an early paper Walter C. Neale (1964) argued that professional team sports were natural monopolies and it is the league and not the individual club which is to be regarded as the firm of economic theory. The clubs can be compared to the establishments of multi-plant firms, even though they have an independent existence, set prices and take profits (or losses). In defining the league as a natural monopoly he does not mean that there are necessarily economies of scale (declining long-run average costs), but merely the situation in which one league has lower long-run average costs than where there are competing leagues because of diseconomies which are external to the firm (club) though internal to the industry (league). This explains why there is a strong tendency towards a single league. One aspect of this is that there can only be one world champion (though in some sports it is not unknown for even this to be disputed).

It is more usual, however, to characterise professional team sports leagues as cartels, which impose various organisation rules on their members. Sporting rules are essential to determine how the game is played. Thus the league must be able to establish a fixture list and a set of playing rules. It must be able to impose some rules concerning the selection and employment of players by individual clubs. It may require determination of both the number of clubs in the league and their geographical location.

There will be a limit on the number of clubs because within a season there will be a finite number of available dates and too many games will overtax players as well as spectators. The league must also ensure public confidence in the honesty of contests, so that limitations may be placed on individuals having controlling interests in more than one club.[2] It is also necessary to determine rules for the allocation of gate revenue. It is doubtful if competition authorities would object to any of these in their purest form.

Other rules are designed to influence market structure and/or conduct and these do raise issues for competition policy. In the former case there are, for instance, rules relating to controls on league size, controls on the distribution of league franchises and conservative constitutions and voting rules. In the latter case there are labour market controls relating to recruitment (for example the player draft) and retention or movement of players and other controls on club behaviour including the freedom to negotiate their own broadcasting contracts.

The objectives of controls on market structures are to regulate potential competition to those currently in league membership. According to cartel theory output limitation and the erection of effective barriers to entry are a sine qua non for joint profit maximisation (see for instance, Davis, 1974 for baseball and Schofield, 1982 for cricket). Exclusion from the league may, however, in itself be insufficient and an effective cartel must additionally prevent the appearance of competing leagues. The defence against rival leagues in North America has usually operated through the labour market. In Europe control by supra-national governing bodies means that recognition may not be given to new leagues, so that it is difficult for them to become established.

In addition to the control of league members, leagues also conventionally determine the geographic location of members. In Europe the geographic transfer of clubs is rare but in North America franchise movements are very common and must be sanctioned by franchise owners acting as a group. Indeed, in the US, cities without major league franchises have engaged in competitive bidding in order to persuade teams in the major sports to relocate. Noll and Zimbalist (1997) report that both state and local governments have frequently contributed to the capital costs of stadium construction and have also provided tax concessions. According to Siegfried and Zimbalist (2000) 46 major league stadia were built or refurbished for teams in the four majors between 1990 and 1998, and a further 49 are under construction or planned. This covers the vast majority of the 115 professional teams. Of the $21.7 billion expended, two-thirds will be provided from public funds. Yet independent analysis of the economic impact of stadium development has uniformly found that there is no statistically significant positive relationship between stadium construction and economic development once appropriate allowance has been made for substitution effects, leakages and negative effects on local government budgets. League clubs are able to exert such pressure according to the above authors because the monopoly power of the leagues has left a shortage of teams relative to the demand of various cities which could support additional clubs. They recommend dividing up existing clubs into competing leagues in order to inject elements of competition into each sport, thereby reducing the bargaining advantage that the clubs currently possess. They implicitly deny, therefore, that clubs are natural monopolies. That remedy would not appear to be relevant in the European context where major teams are located in relatively small towns. For example, there are 92 teams in the English football leagues alone, and the use of promotion and relegation, together with feeder leagues, allows for a limited degree of entry. If the natural monopoly argument holds then the appropriate policy response could be some form of regulation and this is reinforced by the fact that many clubs have local monopolies. Regulation has recently been proposed by a Football Task Force in England which was set up by the Minister of Sport.[3]

Conduct rules centre around labour market activities and the sharing of gate receipts and other revenues among the competing clubs. The objectives of labour market controls are ostensibly the promotion of uncertainty of outcome through attempts to balance clubs' playing strengths, and this has been a contentious area. El-Hodiri and Quirk (1971), for example, concluded that only a system of player drafting and the prevention of transfers of players between clubs for cash will tend to equalise playing strengths. However, empirical work has foundered because of an inability to capture uncertainty of outcome by a suitable proxy. There are two approaches to measuring this concept. The first looks at the standard deviation of winning percentages. Thus Scully (1989) utilised the measure below

$$\sigma = \sqrt{\frac{\sum_{i=1}^{n}(I_i - \bar{I})^2}{n}}$$

where I_i represents team I's talent level and talent is the primary component in determining each game's outcome. Thus I_i can also be viewed as team i's performance in terms of winning percentage over the season. $\bar{I}$ is the league average winning percentage (which is always 0.5) and n is the number of teams in the league. If the optimal level of competitive balance within a league existed when every team had an equal chance of winning every game, joint league revenues would be maximised if $I_i = \bar{I}$ for every team. However, where the market catchment area (P_i) differs in size across teams the optimal level of competitive balance will require that large city teams win more often. Thus, the optimal level of league competitive balance would be given by

$$\sigma' = \sqrt{\frac{\Sigma[I_i - \bar{I} + \lambda(P_i)]^2}{n}}$$

where λ represents the weight attached to the league's market population.

However, this does not take into account the dynamics of uncertainty of outcome in terms of the league championship. Thus, the fact that a team has a large lead at the beginning of the season may not depress attendances very much because fans believe the team concerned may eventually be caught, whilst late in the season fans may believe the contest is virtually over.

The second approach is to include an uncertainty of outcome variable in a model explaining attendances, though many such models have excluded such a variable altogether. A wide variety of such measures have been used including league positions of home and away teams prior to a match, average lead of the first division leader over the season, betting odds offered prior to a match and number of games required to win the title. To varying degrees these all suffer from the problem referred to above. In addition, there are three types of uncertainty of outcome – uncertainty of match outcome, seasonal uncertainty of outcome and long run domination or lack of it. Few, if any, studies have included all three measures, let alone interacted them. This may explain why rather mixed results have been obtained in terms of the significance of the variable. Finding an appropriate measure of uncertainty of outcome remains a major research issue in the economics of professional team sports but would seem at the minimum to require the identification of the proportion of meaningless games over the season.

The question of whether more equal-sharing of gate and other revenue will assist in achieving competition balance has been no less contentious. There are considerable variations in the extent to which revenues are shared: the NFL currently splits non-luxury box gate revenues 60/40; baseball is 80/20; but in basketball, ice hockey and European football the home team does not share any revenue with the away team in league competition. Most US sports economists hold that more equal gate revenue sharing has no effect on competitive balance (El-Hodiri and Quirk, 1971; Fort and Quirk, 1995; Vrooman, 1995). This assumes the simplified case of a two-team league with no local TV revenues. Fort and Quirk (1995) argue that gate sharing will lower the value of an additional win percentage to a team because it only captures a fraction of any increased revenue at home games. But the demand for a winning schedule will reduce equally for both teams and the intersection point will occur at the same winning percentage as before. Kesenne (2000) has attempted to clarify what he refers to as a confusion in the literature. He shows that if one assumes that the objective of clubs is to maximise games won subject to a break-even constraint, revenue sharing will unambiguously result in a more even distribution of playing talent. He also shows that even if the clubs are profit maximisers revenue sharing can improve competitive balance if absolute quality of the teams is an important determinant of revenues.

There is, however, a basic flaw in the Fort and Quirk argument even in the assumptions of their own model. Home and away winning percentages are not separable in the context of a league championship. Even where a home club retains all the revenues the marginal returns to winning will not be zero for the away team in the context of a league competition in which fans are interested in which team wins the title and prefer this to be the team they support. This effect would be even stronger if the sharing mechanism was such that a fixed percentage of each club's annual revenue was taken by the league and shared at the end of the season on the basis of the league performance of each club. The financial incentive to reach a particular position in the league table would be relatively higher for smaller teams than for bigger teams. League points accrue equally whether games are won at home or away and it is the overall performance that keeps clubs in contention.[4] Let us assume that the large clubs have larger stadia (and possibly charge more per seat). Under plausible assumptions it will always pay the small club to win more often and the large club less often under revenue sharing compared to 100/0 allocation. In the English Premier League the ground capacity of the smallest club (Southampton), in 2000 was only 15000 compared to 67000 for the largest (Manchester United) and in Scotland the ground capacity of St Johnstone was 10000 compared to 60000 for Celtic. With a substantial degree of gate sharing there must be an increase in the returns to winning of the small clubs relative to the large assuming supporters value away wins as highly as home wins. Under plausible assumptions it would seem, therefore, that more equal gate sharing must increase competitive balance.

Szymanski (2001), however, suggests that if sharing takes the form of, say, the visiting team getting 20 per cent of the home gate and the home gate is increasing in match (as well as championship) success then sharing may reduce the incentives of small teams by more than those large teams. Using a tournament theory approach, his model suggests that revenue sharing of the conventional kind actually reduces competitive balance. However, since match success is only known after the event, it is not clear how sharing of revenues would reduce the incentive for a small club to win a particular match. While the same argument could be applied to championship success, the likelihood of winning the championship for a team in a particular position in the league table can be estimated with a greater degree of certainty than the probability of winning a particular match. All of this points to the need for more research in this area.

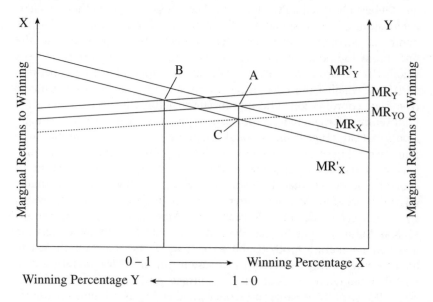

Figure 2.2   Gate sharing and a competitive balance

This fact is illustrated in Figure 2.2. A represents the starting point with no revenue sharing and team X has a much higher winning percentage than team Y. According to Fort and Quirk, with revenue sharing the marginal returns to winning schedules will shift downwards by the same amount, depending on the new gate sharing formula, and the teams end up at C with the same winning percentages as before. However, if we assume that the marginal returns curves represent the returns to winning with home and away attendances combined, then for Y the schedule will rise to, say, MR'_Y and the club will end up at B with a higher winning percentage than before, whilst X wins fewer games than before.[5]

From the point of view of competition policy it is not the existence of the league cartel per se that is the issue, but whether its actions are in the public interest or not.

Recently a third approach to the classification of sports leagues has become apparent – the joint venture. Roberts (1991) argues that not every type of cooperative action between separate persons can possibly be illegal. Thus, different divisions of the same company may agree jointly the prices they charge for their products with impunity. A sports league deciding on the location of its teams is no different than General Motors deciding where to locate its plants. The sports league is more appropriately regarded as a joint venture which produces sporting competition. Flynn and Gilbert (2001) came to an identical conclusion, arguing that the characterisation of professional sports leagues as single entities on the one hand and associations of independent competitors on the other is a false one. From the point of view of competition policy the central issue is whether the coordination of professional team sports harms competition and, if so, whether this effect is more than offset by benefits to consumers from such coordination. The appropriate structure for this question is the joint venture. This includes a broad spectrum of possible business arrangements that can range from informal collaborations to share information to joint ownership of existing assets or new products. For conventional antitrust analysis they suggest the most important organisational feature of sports leagues is whether the teams comprising the league are individually owned by separate economic interests or whether they are jointly owned by a single economic entity. Recent North American league new entrants such as Major League Soccer, Women's National Basketball Association and new competing football and basketball leagues have all chosen to adopt a single entity ownership structure in which the league rather than its individual teams owns all player contracts and negotiates player salaries collectively. It remains to be seen whether this is a long-run equilibrium structure which can maintain spectators' trust in the honesty of the competition. It may, however, be able to avoid the antitrust problems that have beset the established sports. When in April 2000 the soccer players brought a class action lawsuit against Major League Soccer the federal judge ruled that the single entity was both proper and lawful and did not violate the antitrust laws. Such issues have yet to be addressed in Europe where the Commission is still feeling its way in relation to sporting activity. The European Commissioner for competition policy has stated (Monti, 2000) that one of the principles adopted by the Commission is that policy should take account of the special characteristics of sport and that competition rules should be applied in a manner which does not question the regulatory authority of sporting organisations to implement genuine 'sporting rules'. What this means in practice, however, has yet to be determined.

3. SOME CASES

The above discussion suggests that there are many problems in attempting to apply standard competition policy rules to professional team sports and three cases below illustrate the sorts of issues that are likely to arise in practice.

The Monopolies and Mergers Commission Investigation into the Attempted Takeover of Manchester United by BskyB

One important development in professional football is the increasing tendency for clubs to be listed on the Stock Exchange (see Appendix 1). This has left clubs open to the possibility of takeover. The attempt by BSkyB, a vertically integrated broadcaster, to take over Manchester United led to a high degree of public debate and ultimately investigation by the Monopolies and Mergers Commission (MMC, 1999). This proposed merger qualified under the 1973 Fair Trading Act as the value of the assets to be taken over exceeded £70 million, but at that time it was the only club which would have qualified for investigation. This merger also represented a change of ownership, but no reduction in the number of providers. Much hinged on the definition of the market, which the MMC interpreted narrowly as being no wider than the matches of the Premier League Clubs rather than the player market as a whole, while the broadcasting market was similarly narrowly defined as sports premium pay TV channels, with pay TV considered as a separate market. This was done on the basis of perceived substitutability, though no attempt was made to estimate cross price elasticity of demand. Indeed, one might argue that these two markets are themselves close substitutes for one another and should therefore be considered as a single market. The test used was one commonly used by the competition authorities, namely whether a supplier serving 100 per cent of a particular market would be able to maintain prices at 5–10 per cent above competitive levels. The MMC thought so, but given that football clubs are local monopolies a competitive price has no meaning. Profit maximising prices will not be influenced by a change of ownership. Indeed a more crucial factor is stadium capacity constraints. It will always pay to price such that the ground is filled, given that ancillary sales and sponsorship which depend on this are substantial and Manchester United had, indeed, been increasing its ground capacity.

The broadcasting market is perhaps more problematical, given BSkyB's control of the market at that time, though subsequent events suggest that potential entry to this market is not as limited as the MMC implied.[6] Of concern to the MMC was the prediction of auction theory that when a bidder in an auction has an ownership stake in an asset being sold (in this case one-twentieth), or a toehold, it is more likely to win the auction than competitors without the toehold. This arises for two reasons. First, part of the value of any bid will return to the bidder with the toehold, enabling a higher bid to be put in. Second, the winner's curse may operate given the uncertainty of the value of the asset and the probability of others over-bidding, knowing the concern with the toehold can afford to pay more. The winner's curse is likely to operate more strongly in an ascending price (English) auction, where each bidder can observe the behaviour of rivals in the bidding process. This problem could, however, have been reduced if the MMC had made sealed bid options a requirement for allowing the merger and if toeholds are important this should, as George Yarrow argued for the defendants, have encouraged other broadcasters to obtain toeholds by buying other clubs. The MMC concluded that the proposed merger was against the public interest on the grounds that it would harm football by reinforcing the tendency towards greater imbalance among clubs, in terms of financial resources, and by providing BSkyB with greater power to influence decisions relating to the organisation of football, which did not reflect the long-term interests of the game. It also argued that the adverse effects on the quality of football would be even more marked if the merger precipitated other mergers between broadcasters and other clubs. However, it is not clear how making decisions which are not in the long-run interests of the game would be beneficial to a broadcaster. Further, the allegation that the scope for innovation would be reduced runs counter to the facts.

The conclusions of the MMC seem to have been overtaken by events, including not only the contrary decision of the RPC and the subsequent new collectively negotiated TV contract, outlined below, but also by the sub-sequent purchase of minority shares in football clubs by a number of broad-casters. Because of a potential conflict of interest if a single individual controlled more than one club in the same division, English Premier League regulations forbid any single individual or organisation from holding more than 10 per cent of the assets of any one club, though it may be possible to circumvent this by purchasing shares in a holding company.[7] At the time of writing media companies held shares in no fewer than 11 of the 20 English Premier League Clubs and one Scottish Premier League club (see Appendix 2). Frequently these deals include additional payments for acting as the club's exclusive media agent, thereby likely improving the quality of the product in the long run. Further, no less than four media companies have toehold effects, thereby threatening BSkyB's dominant position. The market now looks very different from the one investigated by the MMC. However, from the point of view of competition policy a situation in which a single company holds 10 per cent of several clubs appears more problematical than a situation in which a single company has 100 per cent control of a single club. In the latter case the interest of the owner will be to win games, but in the former case there may be an incentive to manipulate results to ensure more uncertainty of outcome. It is the former case that may be seen as a greater threat to the perceived honesty of the competition.

The Restrictive Practices Court Investigation into Collective Selling of TV Rights by the English Premier League

The Restrictive Practices Court (RPC, 1999) took a somewhat different stance to the MMC on a number of issues when considering whether the exclusive right of the Premier League (PL) to negotiate on behalf of all its member clubs and the exclusive right of BSkyB to show live matches up to the end of the 2000–2001 season was a restrictive practice which was against the public interest.[8] Whilst finding that the PL was a cartel in the meaning of the legislation it qualified this by stating in paragraph 277 that

> some aspects of economic theory dealing with competition cannot readily be applied in this case. If products or services in the market place are homogeneous it may be possible to identify a competitive level of price, and so determine whether competition in the market place is extracting excess profits by its strength in the market or by a monopoly position. In a market place where products are differentiated and thus heterogeneous both in nature and price, such conclusions cannot be reliably drawn.

Like the MMC the Court accepted the importance of the maintenance of competitive balance. It found that collective selling assisted this process because of the relatively equal sharing of broadcasting income within the PL,[9] the parachute arrangements for relegated clubs and substantial payments to the Nationwide Football League for ground improvements. Whilst, however, the Office of Fair Trading (OFT) had argued that the relevant market was the market for TV rights for live PL matches, the Court accepted a much wider definition stating that the relevant market was on the one hand the TV rights relating to sporting events and on the other hand the supply of broadcasting services.

In putting forward the OFT case an expert witness argued that the PL acted as a cartel in restricting output and raising price. Broad exclusivity where only one broadcaster has the right to broadcast particular matches, and no other broadcaster has the right to broadcast any other league match, denied the public opportunities for choice and distorted competition. An expert witness for the defendants argued that collective licensing arrangements were very different from the ordinary business cartel. The latter produces no output that is distinct and additional to the outputs of the cartel numbers. But the League Championship is a joint product which cannot be produced in the absence of a cartel arrangement. The value of a particular match depends on the fact that it is part of the PL competition. One might add that the broadcaster requires a contract for the league as a whole because he wants to show the best games and these cannot be firmly established until the season unfolds. Second, broadcasting of games can have detrimental effects on live attendances. Therefore the seller has a vested interest in the timing of broadcasts, a feature not relevant in other markets.

The court found the views of the expert witness for the defendants much more persuasive than those of the expert witness for the OFT. It noted that the main product of 580 PL games per season was not in any way limited by the exclusivity restrictions. The arrangements did not represent a straightforward example of restriction of output to raise price and a factor which weighed with the court was that PL clubs did not on the whole make large profits. For these reasons the court found in favour of the defendants.

The European Commission has suggested that exclusive broadcasting contracts for one season do not normally pose any problem for competition policy. However, exclusivity for a long duration and for a wide range of rights would be unacceptable because of the likelihood that it would lead to market foreclosure (Monti, 2000). The Commission has noted that the RPC did not base its decision on Community competition law and may consider an exemption. However, it is the preliminary view of the Commission that a joint selling agreement restricts competition because it is a price-fixing mechanism, it limits the availability of rights to football events and it strengthens the market position of the strongest broadcasters because they are the only ones who can bid for all the rights in a package (Pons, 1999).

In negotiating a revised TV deal to operate from the season 2001–2002 the PL had to make a sealed-bid process as open as possible in order to satisfy the competition authorities by publication of an official tender document, an unbundling of categories of games to be sold and a shortening of contract duration to three years. BSkyB won a new contract for 66 live games with first pick of premiership games at a price of £1.15 billion. NTL paid £328 million for 40 live matches in a season with a second pick of fixtures defeating other bids from ON-digital and Telewest[10] and ITV paid £61 million for the right to show recorded highlights, defeating a rival bid from the BBC worth £41 million.[11] No one broadcaster was allowed to win a contract for more than one category, so much more competition has emerged in the broadcasting market than the MMC in particular seemed to have envisaged.

The Bosman Case

At the European level the Bosman case has had a significant impact and its long-run implications are still to be fully worked through. The European Court of Justice ruling (ECJ, 1995), was made after written submissions in favour of the status quo by the French and Italian governments and oral submissions by the Danish and German governments. The existing rules were, however, found to be incompatible with article 34 of the Treaty of Rome, as were the limitations placed on the number of players employed by individual clubs. The rules laid down by the football authorities under which a professional footballer who is a national of one Member State may not, on the expiry of his contract with a club, be employed by a club of another Member State unless the latter club has paid the former a transfer fee, restricted the free movement of labour. Similarly the rules laid down by the authorities under which clubs may field only a limited number of professional players who were nationals of other member states was contrary to the prohibition of discrimination based on nationality. The Advocate-General did accept the argument that uncertainty of outcome was important, but proposed two alternatives to the retain and transfer system as then operated – salary caps and a more equal distribution of gate receipts and television income. He also concluded that transfer fees might be justified if they were limited to the amount expended by the previous club on the player's training and development. More recently however, the commission has taken the view that requiring a fee for the transfer of a player within a contract period represents a violation of Article 81 of the Treaty of Rome as it constrains free mobility of labour.[12] This issue caused the intervention of Tony Blair and other EC leaders and seemed to cast doubt on the ability of employers to form long-term contracts, though a compromise formula has now been agreed.[13] The Commission claims to be well aware of the need to ensure that smaller clubs are not deprived of rewards from their training of young players (Pons, 1999). Pons also suggests that he would not be surprised if the future application of competition rules to sport were to reach the conclusion that the following were beyond the scope of article 81(1) of the Treaty – nationality clauses for national teams, quotas governing the number of teams participating in international competitions, rules for the selection of individuals on the basis of objective and non-discriminatory criteria, rules setting fixed transfer periods for the transfer of players and rules needed to ensure uncertainty of results, where less restrictive methods are not available. This, however, leaves a large number of issues linked to the organisation of sports about which considerable uncertainty remains.

4.   CONCLUSIONS

There is considerable confusion about what the appropriate stance towards professional team sports should be as far as competition policy is concerned. Should professional team sports leagues be treated as natural monopolies, cartels or joint ventures? Should there be special exemptions from the standard provisions of competition law? What is the appropriate definition of the market? The judgements of the Monopolies and Mergers Commission and the Restrictive Practices Court, for example, diverge in important respects. The European Union has yet to develop coherent policies.

Given the special features of professional team sports, treating them as just like any other industry seems unlikely to maximise consumer welfare. At the same time a carte-blanche exemption would leave open the possibility of abuse of monopoly power. Partial exemption conditional on certain safeguards would appear to be much more appropriate than either of the above. A US style player draft would likely fall foul of the free mobility of labour provisions of the Treaty of Rome; likewise salary cap provisions which, in any event, would be difficult to implement in the context of European sport, though they have been applied in rugby league and rugby union. More equal revenue sharing would have the advantage not only of helping to increase uncertainty of outcome, but also of controlling labour costs. Its disadvantage is that it would be resisted by the larger clubs as reducing their ability to compete in lucrative European club competitions. That is why European-wide solutions are required to restore stability.

APPENDIX 1: LISTED BRITISH FOOTBALL CLUBS (1999/2000)

London Stock Exchange

Premier League	Aston Villa
	Leeds United (Leeds Sporting)
	Leicester City
	Manchester United
	Newcastle United
	Southampton
	Sunderland
	Tottenham Hotspur

Nationwide I	Bolton Wanderers (Burden Leisure)
	Sheffield United
Nationwide II	Millwall
Scottish Premier	Celtic

AIM

Premier League	Charlton Athletic
	Chelsea Village
Nationwide I	Birmingham City
	Preston North End
	Queens Park Rangers (Loftus Road)
	Nottingham Forest
	West Bromwich Albion

OFEX

Premier League	Arsenal
	Bradford City
	Manchester City
Scottish Premier	Aberdeen
	Hearts
	Rangers

APPENDIX 2: MEDIA INTERESTS IN FOOTBALL CLUBS (1999/2000)

	Club	Media Company	Share
Premier League	Arsenal	Granada	5% (with further 4.9% if planning permission for new ground)
	Aston Villa	NTL	9.9% (five year convertible loan certificate)
	Chelsea	BSkyB	9.9%
	Leeds United	BSkyB	9.1% of Leeds Sporting
	Leicester City	NTL	9.9% (five year convertible loan certificate)
	Liverpool	Granada	9.9%
	Manchester City	BSkyB	9.9%
	Manchester United	BskyB	9.9% (originally 11%)
	Middlesborough	NTL	5.5%
	Newcastle United	NTL	9.8%
	Sunderland	BSkyB	5%
Scottish	Hearts	SMG	37.4%

Note: BskyB also has an agreement with Tottenham Hotspur as an internet-only partner.

NOTES

1. Whitney (1993) argues that unrestricted competition in the market for athletics talent will result in destructive competition and in consequence sub-optimal social welfare.
2. Periodically rules may be changed in order to increase spectator interest. Thus Schofield (1982) notes a series of rule changes in first class cricket to reduce the likelihood of draws, to increase scoring rates and to reduce time wastage during games. In football Newson (1984) examined the effect of the introduction of three points (instead of two) for a win in the English Football League in 1981–82. Subsequently rule changes have limited pass-backs to goalkeepers, changed the offside law and other aspects designed to make the product more entertaining.
3. Its recommendations included a Football Audit Commission to ensure greater account-ability of clubs, an 'Ombudsfan' to investigate individual complaints by fans and a Financial Compliance Unit. A Code of Practice includes detailed proposals on pricing policies, merchandising and supporter representation in the running of clubs. The Government has recently announced that it is to set up an Independent Football Commission.
4. The minimum requirement for modelling a league with a play-off and incorporating an 'in contention' variable where each team determines its own actions in the light of the expected actions of every other team is a three-team league. This is much more difficult to model than the conventional two-team league.
5. For a similar diagram see Kesenne (1999).
6. The MMC considered four scenarios:

   (i)   the continuation of collective selling of TV rights and no other mergers;
   (ii) individual selling of TV rights and no other mergers;
   (iii) collective selling of TV rights and other mergers;
   (iv) individual selling of TV rights and other mergers.

   In every case it felt the situation would be inferior to the status quo in terms of price, choice and innovation.
7. UEFA rules also prohibit clubs owned by the same company (with control defined as a stake of 51 per cent or more) taking part in the same competition. This rule was chal-lenged by ENIC which held majority shares in Vicenza and Slavia Prague and minority shares in Glasgow Rangers, FC Basle and AEK Athens. In August 1999 The Court of Arbitration for Sport (CAS) ruled in favour of UEFA on the grounds that this rule was necessary and proportionate.
8. The exclusive rights offered to the BBC to show edited highlights of Premier League games was also part of the case. However, the Nationwide Football League's exclusive deal was not so referred.
9. TV income is shared on the basis of 50 per cent equally shared among the 20 Premier League clubs, 25 per cent according to league position (positively) and 25 per cent according to TV appearances. After the new deal was signed the less wealthy clubs argued that the larger sums involved under this formula would widen income inequality in the league and proposed that the additional income involved should be shared equally among all clubs. This proposal was narrowly defeated.
10. In October 2000 NTL announced that it was withdrawing from the contract, which it had not signed, without giving any substantive explanations. Thus the Premier League was faced with need to engage in a new auction.
11. In addition the BBC in partnership with BSkyB won the rights to the FA Cup with a bid of £400 million.
12. The Commission takes the view that the player should pay compensation for his breach of contract and then be allowed to move without a transfer fee being payable. The Commission claims, however, to be aware of the need to ensure that the smaller clubs are not deprived of compensation for the training of young players and suggests that the

creation of a common solidarity pool allowing for a redistribution of a share of revenues from sporting competitors may also be acceptable (Pons, 1999).

13. After considerable debate, the FIFA, UEFA and EU in March 2001 finally agreed on reforms to the existing transfer system. The essence of the new arrangements, which will not affect existing contracts and initially will apply only to cross-border transfers, is that:

- Players' contracts will range from one year to five with transfers involving fees possible at two windows in summer and midwinter of each season, subject to the agreement of the player and both clubs.
- Where a club and player are not in agreement to a transfer, movement in the first three years of a contract would be subject to league sanctions, as well as civil remedies.
- For players aged 18–23, compensation for the costs of training and player development will be provided based on a fixed formula.
- In all cases, independent arbitration will be available.

The net effect of these changes will be to increase the bargaining power of the players relative to the clubs.

REFERENCES

Davis, L.E. (1974), Self Regulation in Baseball, 1990–71, in R.G. Noll (ed.), *Government and the Sports Business*, Washington, DC: Brookings Institute.

El-Hodiri, M. and J. Quirk (1971), 'An economic model of a professional sports league', *Journal of Political Economy*, **79**, 1302–19.

European Court of Justice, Case C-415/93 *Union Royale Belge des Sociétés de Football Association ASBL and others v Jean Marc Bosman and Others*, (1995) ECR 1-4921 (1996) 1 CMLR 645: (1996) CEC 38.

Flynn, M.A. and R.J. Gilbert (1999), 'The Analysis of Professional Team Sports as Joint Ventures', unpublished manuscript, University of California at Berkeley, December.

Flynn, M.A. and R.J. Gilbert (2001), 'An analysis of professional sports leagues as joint ventures', *Economic Journal*, **111** (469), F27–F46.

Fort, R. and J. Quirk (1995), 'Cross-subsidisation, incentives and outcomes in professional team sports', *Journal of Economic Literature*, **33** (3), September, 1265–99.

Kesenne, S. (1999), 'Player Market Regulation and Competitive Balance in a Win Maximising Scenario', in C. Jeanrenaud and S. Kesenne (eds), *Competition Policy in Professional Sports: Europe After the Bosman Case*, Antwerp: Standaard Editions Ltd, 117–32.

Kesenne, S. (2000), 'Revenue sharing and competitive balance in professional team sports', *Journal of Sports Economics*, **1** (1), February, 56–65.

Monopolies and Mergers Commission (1999), *British Sky Broadcasting Group Plc and Manchester United Plc, A Report on the Proposed Merger*, CM 4305, HMSO, April 1999.

Monti, M. (2000), 'Sport and Competition', Excerpts of a Speech Given at a Commission Organised Conference on Sports, Brussels, 17 April, 2000.

Neale, W.C. (1964), 'The peculiar economics of professional sports', *Quarterly Journal of Economics*, **78** (1), 1–14.

68 *Public policy and sports economics*

Newson, G. (1984), 'Three points for a win: has it made any difference?', *The Mathematical Gazette*, **68** (444), 87–91.

Noll, R.G. and A. Zimbalist (eds) (1997), *Sports, Jobs and Taxes: The Economic Impact of Sports Teams and Stadiums*, Washington, DC: Brookings Institution Press.

Pons, J.F. (1999), 'Sports and European Competition Policy', Fordham Corporate Law Institute, 26th Annual Conference on International Anti-trust Law and Policy, New York, 14–15, October 1999.

Restrictive Practices Court (RPC) (1999), Restrictive Trade Practices Act, Judgement of the Court on the Agreement, Relating to the Supply of Services Facilitating the Broadcasting on Television of Premier League Football Matches and the Supply of Services Consisting in the Broadcasting on Television of such Matches.

Roberts, G.R. (1991), 'Professional Sports and the Anti-Trust Laws', in P.D. Staudohar and J.A. Mangan (eds), *The Business of Professional Team Sports*, Urbana and Chicago: University of Illinois Press.

Schofield, J.A. (1982), The development of first class cricket in England: an economic analysis, *Journal of Industrial Economics*, **XXX** (4), 337–60.

Scully, G.W. (1989), *The Business of Major League Baseball*, Chicago: University of Chicago Press.

Siegfried, J. and A. Zimbalist (2000), 'The economics of sports facilities and their communities, *Journal of Economic Perspectives*, **14** (3), Summer, 95–114.

Szymanski, S. (2001), 'Competitive balance and income distribution in team sports', Unpublished Manuscript, Imperial College Management School, London, February 2001.

Vrooman, J. (1995), 'A general theory of professional sports leagues, *Southern Economic Journal*, **61** (4), April, 971–90.

Whitney, J.D. (1993), 'Bidding till bankrupt; destructive competition in professional team sports, *Economic Inquiry*, **XXXI** (1), January, 110–15.

3. The distribution of income in European football: big clubs, small countries, major problems

H.F. Moorhouse

THE AMERICAN CHALLENGE

> Measured simply in terms of gross revenues, which almost doubled during the five complete seasons (1995–1999) since 1994, Major League Baseball is prospering. But that simple measurement is a highly inadequate gauge of MLB's economic health. Because of anachronistic aspects of MLB's economic arrangements, the prosperity of some clubs is having perverse effects that pose a threat to the game's long-term vitality. (Report of the Commissioners Blue Ribbon Panel on Baseball Economics, 2000, p. 2)

The Report of the Panel on Baseball Economics published in July 2000 is a salutary document viewed by anyone interested in the well-being of European football. I will come to its diagnosis of the problems posed by prosperity soon, but we should note immediately how this major American sport:

- established a committee of experienced football outsiders (an academic, ex-Senator, ex-Governor of the Board of the Federal Reserve System, and so on) to examine the economic and sporting problems of the game;
- made the report easily available – it can, for example, be downloaded on the internet – as an aid to general discussion;
- set out a wide-ranging and rational appraisal of the problems and possibilities a changing situation had created – it did not spend time harking back to how some 'traditional situation' was so much better;
- is seeking to plan for the future rather than being driven by the tide of events.

Whatever happens to the detailed recommendations of this report, whatever its precise motivations, such energy, such rationality, such appraisal, such perspective, such transparency, is in stark contrast to the activities and mind-set of those who supposedly govern European football. These authorities are enclosed, secretive, unwilling to discuss, backward looking, seemingly impotent in the face of the new forces shaping soccer, while covertly making many easy compromises with such forces. The football authorities' constant moaning about 'Bosman', agents, incursions of the law, the European Commission, their hundred and one futile attempts to 'turn things round', the endless, usually pointless, lobbying, the reiteration of assertions and assumptions not hard evidence, and so on, all reveal not just plain ignorance (empirically, many of the benefits they claim for past arrangements can be shown to be false) but also a state of mind which is negative, undynamic and lacking the vision to protect European football from the problems steadily engulfing it. We have, for example, rapidly entered a stage where economic competition between clubs on a European level is a vital element in their sporting rivalry without any official attempt to create standardised knowledge about football finances. The plain truth is that nobody can honestly say which of Europe's elite clubs is truly the richest and by how much. European football exists in a state of ignorance. Europe's major sport does not have the basic statistics to carry out anything like the analysis of problems and possibilities attempted for Major League Baseball in America. Now, it is possible to regard this state of affairs as endearing, charming, the way things have always been, an opportunity for dubious econometrics, and so on, but it is highly dangerous for the future well-being of football in Europe.

For the last decade, FIFA, UEFA, the national associations, the national leagues, insofar as they have facilitated any discussion at all, have encouraged a low level of debate in which the solution to almost any problem in football is said to be the maintenance of, even a return to, traditional labour market restrictions. Let me state plainly, what is blatantly obvious, that is not going to happen. The negative mind-set, the wasteful lobbying, the failure to analyse, the abdication of sophisticated leadership, the lack of honest, open, analysis, means, in the main, that in most current discussion about European football:

- the wrong problems are being addressed;
- the wrong 'solutions' are being touted;
- truly crucial issues are being neglected.

I will endeavour to expand on this assessment throughout the rest of my chapter.

BASEBALL'S PROBLEMS

We also begin with the assumption that it is clearly in the best interests of MLB and its fans to have franchises located in viable markets throughout North America rather than concentrated in a few major markets. This report also assumes that a reasonable degree of competitive balance is an essential foundation for the continued popularity and growth of the game, and that mechanisms must be in place to ensure long-term competitive balance despite the inevitable inequalities in size, local market conditions and demographics of the communities in which MLB franchises are located (Report of the Commissioners Blue Ribbon Panel on Baseball Economics, 2000, p. 13).

The Report on Baseball Economics sees 'the heart of the problem' facing contemporary baseball as a large and growing disparity in 'local revenues' (gate receipts; fees for local TV, radio, and cable rights; advertising and publications; parking; suite rentals; and so on) between clubs in the leagues. Such local revenues make up the largest single element in the income of most clubs, and the ratio between the highest and the lowest club has more than doubled in the last five years. The report frankly recognises that such local revenues flow far more readily to clubs located in large media markets. In 1999 the New York Yankees took $176 million in local revenues, the Montreal Expos just $12 million. This new and growing imbalance between clubs has undermined previously established mechanisms designed to redistribute revenue and maintain competitive balance: 'Although Central Fund revenues, which historically have been distributed evenly among all clubs, have more than doubled since 1995, they are now a smaller percentage of most clubs revenue than in 1995' (Report, p. 2). We should note that this American sport already practises *more* redistribution of revenues than is done at an equivalent level of European football, but does not consider it nearly enough to sustain competitive balance. Either American sport has totally misunderstood the potential problems or European sport needs to discuss all the issues involved openly and rationally.

The report argues that this economic imbalance between clubs in the same league has led to widening payroll disparities, which is tending to mean that only a few clubs in MLB have any real chance of sporting success. Its judgement is: 'The goal of a well-designed league is to produce adequate competitive balance. By this standard, MLB is not now well-designed' (p. 5). Despite immediate prosperity, inherent structural factors have strong potential to tarnish baseball's future: 'To ensure baseball's broad and enduring popularity, and to guarantee its future growth, MLB needs a structure under which clubs in smaller markets can have regularly recurring chances to contend for championships' (p. 6).

The solutions the report offers are to:

- convert more of these 'local revenues' into central industry revenues;
- allocate these augmented central funds disproportionately to the lower revenue clubs (especially to help with payroll costs);
- introduce a competitive balance tax designed to force club payrolls into a narrower band by compressing those at the top and raising those at the bottom;
- make various changes to the drafting of players to the benefit of smaller clubs;
- enable more franchise relocations to take place so that clubs can move to more economically hospitable 'home towns'.

For what the report believes is that: 'A reasonably level playing field, on which clubs representing markets which are quite diverse geographically, demographically and economically can compete with at least periodic opportunities for success, is fundamental to MLB's continued growth and popular appeal' (p. 12).

BOSMANIA AND THE REAL PROBLEMS OF FOOTBALL

I hope the outline of my argument is becoming clear. The problems this recent report on American baseball identifies are very close to those that are the really crucial ones inherent in contemporary European football:

- the effects of great disparities of income between supposedly comparable clubs;
- how competitive balance is to be maintained;
- the desirability of maintaining and increasing spectator interest in football in all geographic regions (markets);
- not allowing unregulated market forces to decide the competitive patterning of the sport.

Yet such issues are little discussed in Europe. Instead almost all officials, the media and the majority of academics are afflicted with virulent Bosmania. There is scarcely an analysis or discussion of the current state of European football which does not start from a, usually misunderstood, 'Bosman' or 'Bosman ruling', and such a starting point limits the breadth and depth of analysis. It almost enforces nostalgia for past stability and a policy desire for a 'return to normality'. So, for example, Mr Champagne, an advisor to the President of FIFA, offered his opinion that: 'The Bosman ruling ended up sparking off an era of wild capitalism as players cashed in financially by virtue of their increased bargaining powers with clubs' (Reuters, 12.4.2000).

So, apparently, the basis of current problems is 'greedy players'. In contrast, let me suggest something that sounds heretical – if Bosman had never occurred then most of the problems endemic in contemporary European football would still exist in something like their present forms. Yes, footballers' wages would be a little bit lower, but not that much. Transfer fees would have spiralled even higher. But these are not the crucial issues. The truth is that the real drivers of the fundamental changes in train in European football do not have much to do with Bosman, but rather concern:

- the increasing significance of relatively new income streams and the fact that these are mainly being treated, in American terms, as 'local revenues',
- the continuing expansion of the TV and other electronic communication industries, desperate for the exciting content that sport provides.

What has Bosman to do with these? I have argued elsewhere (Moorhouse, 1993, 1995, 1999a, 1999b, 2000) that:

- the traditional transfer system never performed the redistribution functions that UEFA claim – not much money ever did 'trickle down the pyramid of football' or substantiate all the rest of the clichés regularly deployed;
- in England, anyway, very little income was ever redistributed between clubs through other mechanisms, and these mechanisms have been in steady decline since the mid-1980s;
- the crucial issue that needs to be addressed with the greatest of urgency in Europe is that of the redistribution of income between clubs.

Such evidence, such arguments, have little effect on the football authorities. They are obsessed with labour market restrictions and in none too imaginative ways at that. In recent years their energies have been expended on trying to reinstate former restrictions in some new way or, at the least, to limit the impetus of these changes. Since 1995 both UEFA and FIFA have lobbied to get what they like to refer to as the 'disruptive Bosman ruling' changed, and to get sport declared to be a 'special case' to insulate it from the scope of European Commission directives on freedom of movement of labour and on competition. They have singularly failed in these aims and, in 2001, had to concede more changes to the traditional transfer system as a result of pressure from the European Commission.

'Bosman' has become a misleading proxy for the manifold ills of European soccer, and the fevered attention devoted to it has hindered a fuller analysis and open discussion of the game's vital problems in a new era, where its economics have changed fundamentally. FIFA and UEFA like to declaim about the 'specificity of sport' but are quite unspecific about just what this means. The real problems facing European football are being neglected and appropriate solutions are not being devised or even discussed.

UEFA AND THE REDISTRIBUTION OF INCOME

> Domestic leagues are only a means to an end; Europe is where you promote clubs as a business and as a product. (Alex Fynn, *The Sunday Herald*, 26.3.2000)

In a previous paper I demonstrated that, in the post war period, there does not seem to have been that much redistribution of income in national leagues in Europe, and such as there was has been curtailed in recent decades (Moorhouse, 2000). So if many of the domestic leagues do not carry out much significant redistribution, what happens at the highest level of pan-European club competition, a level controlled directly by UEFA? The Champions League is the main pan-European tournament and clubs participating in it keep virtually all the gate money from their home matches. In the various qualifying rounds clubs can also strike their own TV and merchandising deals, but in the Champions League proper (that is from the last 32 clubs onwards) UEFA controls the TV rights and advertising opportunities centrally (UEFA, 2000). In season 1999/2000 the gross income UEFA obtained from these sources amounted to 828 million Swiss francs (around £330,000,000). This was distributed as follows:

- 30 million went to UEFA for its general purposes;
- 96 million went to the running costs of the competition;
- 110 million went in various unequal 'solidarity payments' to the associations, leagues and clubs of the 51 member associations of UEFA;
- 592 million went in unequal shares to the 32 clubs in the Champions League (of which 5 per cent of each club's payment went to their national leagues).

The first two elements speak for themselves. While they may be thought to be too high or too low they have little to do with any attempt to redistribute income. UEFA explains the distribution of the third element as:

Each of the 51 UEFA member associations will receive Swiss francs 300,000, and each club which has participated in the 1999/2000 campaign will receive 80,000 per round if they do not qualify for the UEFA Champions League group-match stage, or if they were eliminated in the second round or earlier in the UEFA Cup. In addition, each domestic champion who failed to reach the group-match stages in the UEFA Champions League will receive a bonus of Swiss francs 150,000. (UEFA, 2000, p. 3)

Clearly, there is some attempt at redistribution here but it is to national associations rather than to clubs, and at a low level. A former General Secretary of the English FA noted that Real Madrid received about £15 million from UEFA while the whole of Welsh football got just £300,000 (*The Independent*, 2.10.2000).

The fourth element in UEFA's distribution is divided into:

- 332 million Swiss francs as 'fixed payments';
- 260 million Swiss Francs as 'market share payments'.

'Fixed payments' are, in fact, based on appearance and success in the Champions League. Each of the 32 clubs got 1.5 million francs just for being in the first group-match stage (which many big clubs enter automatically) plus 500,000 francs per match, plus a performance bonus of 500,000 francs for a win and 250,000 for a draw. So a totally unsuccessful club eliminated at the end of the first group stage was guaranteed 4.5 million Swiss francs. All clubs who entered the second group-match stage (that is the last 16) got another half a million per match plus the performance bonuses, and so picked up at least another 3 million. The quarter-finalists all got 4 million each, the semi-finalists 5 million, the runners-up 6 million and the winners 10 million Swiss francs. UEFA indicated that a club which won all its matches and so the whole competition would obtain 32.5 million Swiss francs from this stream of income and, as UEFA helpfully points out: 'This sum does not include a club's gate receipts from their home UEFA Champions League matches or its proportion of the market share' (UEFA, 2000, p. 6).

'Market share' is the amount 'distributed according to the proportion of the value of each TV market represented by clubs which participate in the UEFA Champions League' (UEFA, 2000, p. 3). Nominating clubs as 'representing' media markets is a very unusual way of thinking about European football, and one whose logic, as I will indicate, UEFA seems unwilling to follow on all occasions. UEFA notes that it is impossible to detail the 'market share' aspect before the relevant clubs are known but: 'UEFA believes that the five strongest markets will receive a share of between Swiss francs 35 and 55 million each, depending on the television contracts signed with each market' (UEFA, 2000, p. 7). Which, taking the mid-point of 45 million and multiplying by 5, leaves very little to be shared out among clubs from all the remaining, weaker, media markets. The exact amount flowing to each club from this element depends on four, rather odd, factors:

- the number of clubs from each market in the competition;
- the league standing of the club;
- their performance in the Champions League;
- the performance of other clubs from the same country.

'Depending on all these factors, in the best possible scenario, a club can be allocated approximately Swiss francs 30 million' (UEFA, 2000, p. 7).

Well, what my summary shows is that in the main football competition that UEFA directly controls:

- it does not practise much redistribution of income between even the elite clubs of Europe;
- the principles it operates are those which *reinforce* market advantage and playing success.

The comparison with sports in the USA could hardly be starker. This is the more so because, through various mechanisms recently introduced, for example the seeding of clubs in the Champions League, UEFA seeks to smooth the path of the very biggest clubs in reaching the later rounds of its competition. UEFA's summary of the distribution of Champions League revenue for season 2000–2001 reveals that clubs from the 'Big 5' leagues of Italy, Spain, England, Germany and France gained over 75 per cent of the money in principle available to clubs from all over Europe. In many cases 'market share' payments were much greater than what clubs earned via sporting success – especially for the clubs from Germany and France (UEFA.com 21.8.2001). Of course, it is well known that, in recent years, UEFA has been engaged in giving way to the demands of the very biggest clubs in Europe in order to forestall the threat of a breakaway 'super league'. It has not been able to organise the distribution of rewards from the Champions League just as it pleases. But my charges are that it never did carry out much redistribution, that it has not been ready to raise this as a problematic issue, or to put it on the agenda of European political bodies, and that it is not well prepared to face the consequences the play of market forces are producing. Rather, in its rhetoric, UEFA tends to pretend that it is carrying out some significant redistribution from the proceeds of this competition, which is plainly untrue.

The failure to attend to the redistribution of income as a problematic issue in either the domestic or trans-national levels of competition is leading to all manner of strains and stresses in European football. To underline the consequences of these tensions, I want focus on one specific outcome of the growing imbalances of income between clubs in Europe: the new difficulties posed for traditionally big clubs based in small countries (markets).

THE SIXTH BIG LEAGUE?

In recent years the involvement of clubs from smaller countries has sharply contracted. Great names such as Ajax, Anderlecht, Benfica and Celtic are being reduced to occasional players on the European stage dominated by the big five leagues . . . These clubs are no longer able to generate the income required to compete. Compare three clubs each of whom regularly have 60,000 crowds, having a world-wide brand name, with supporters all over the globe. By 2003, Barcelona's television income from domestic sources and the Champions League will be £60 million a year. Manchester United is expected to be upwards of £35 million, Celtic will be just £4 million. The mathematics are simple. To establish a squad capable of competing in Europe you now need to spend £150 to £160 million. After 2003 some clubs will be able to generate that in four years – a period in which we will only have earned £16 million . . . The Scottish Premier League generates one and a half times the combined revenue of the Austrian, Danish and Greek leagues yet its clubs lost £20 million in the last six years. If a league which has been shown to have the best financial leverage in Europe is technically bankrupt and a club the size of Celtic cannot compete, the situation must be addressed. Otherwise the top level will become, in effect, an American-style closed shop franchise. (Celtic spokesman at the Football Expo 2000 conference, reported in *The Independent*, 1.3.2000).

In the last two years the big clubs from some of Europe's smaller countries have been discussing and promoting the idea of creating a new cross-national league – initially named the Atlantic, later called the Euro, League. The principle behind the proposal was that European club football is more and more dominated by teams from what are called 'the Big 5' leagues – those of Italy, Spain, England, Germany and France. In these countries large and wealthy populations facilitate major TV contracts which provide important new income streams to their biggest clubs. By joining forces, the major clubs from a number of small countries aimed to form a sixth European league spanning a population comparable to the big nations, with the same kind of wealth, and so, potentially, TV and related income. For it is not simply TV revenue that is at issue, for the lack of exposure has a knock-on effect onto other vibrant new streams of income like sponsorship and merchandising. The new league would allow them to match the 'Big 5'. And the new league would make them more attractive to the best players who are unwilling to join these clubs, not just because of finance but because their domestic leagues are perceived to be less glamorous, less exciting, and as offering less opportunity for lucrative personal spin-offs.

According to a director of Rangers, eight clubs – Porto, Benfica (of Portugal), Feyenoord, Ajax, PSV (Holland), Anderlecht (Belgium), Celtic, Rangers (Scotland) – were the main discussants and they, and a few other clubs, put their plan to UEFA in late 2000. The proposal was designed to try to align these clubs' future financial position with their traditional sporting status. Their basic belief was that the top teams from smaller leagues can only continue to compete at the highest levels in Europe through the creation of new, trans-national, forms of competition. Their concern seems to be justified. A study of Belgian football by KBC Bank indicated that:

> The average $5.4 million available to each first division club was just one eighth of the average budget of an English Premier League side. Anderlecht, Belgium's richest club would have been fourteenth in terms of budget in the English league in the 1997–98 season.

and argued:

> If Belgian clubs want to compete at the highest European level in the future, they will have to achieve a very considerable expansion in their income base. (Reuters, 24.5.2000).

And such financial inequalities seem to be having sporting consequences for big clubs from smaller countries. The chief executive of Celtic commented about the Champions League: 'If you look at the clubs who have qualified for the later stages in the last three years, the smaller countries have had two representatives, one, and one again' (*The Herald*, 19.9.2000). Moreover, in Scotland it has been suggested that Atlantic/Euro League proposals emanate from the Dutch members of the G14 grouping of clubs who believe that the richest clubs in Europe are unhappy with the present structure of European club competition and that: 'Changes proposed by the Italian clubs and others from the Big 5 leagues may result in a future structure that effectively excludes, for example, the Dutch' (*Celtic View*, 19.1.2000).

So big and famous clubs from smaller media markets face a problem of potential economic or organisational exclusion from effective elite competition in Europe, and a new trans-national league was their solution. As it developed, the suggested format for the new league was that it would contain four teams from Holland and Portugal, three from Scotland, two from Belgium and one each from Norway, Sweden and Denmark. The proposers hoped that the new league would have the same rights of entry to the Champions League as the 'Big 5', so that a fairly large number of clubs from this new league would be guaranteed access to UEFA's riches. The proponents also aimed to forge an organic link between the new league and their respective national leagues, so that there would be a system of promotion and relegation between them. One suggested format was for the national champions of those countries involved to play off with the bottom club from their country in the Euro League to decide which one would take part in the trans-national league the next season. If this format had been accepted, the number of teams from Holland, Portugal and Scotland anyway, had been neatly calibrated to mean that the truly big clubs from these small countries would normally be insulated from any consequences of the organic link.

This initiative was much misrepresented. It was, for example, argued to be only a tactic by 'second string clubs' designed to pressure UEFA into restructuring its secondary competition – the UEFA Cup – into a league format like the Champions League, thus guaranteeing participating clubs more games. Such responses suggest that the real situation of big clubs in small countries has not been grasped by many people in 'the family of football'. And these clubs insist their plight is extreme. As the chairman of Ajax put it: 'It is in no-one's interest to have a situation where only five countries dominate the football market. If you consider Europe to be one country, which is what we are heading for, why not have competition within that country?' (*The Sunday Herald*, 26.3.2000), while the chairman of PSV argued:

> We're sinking slowly. Its not a question of wanting to join a European league. We have to. The Dutch first division in its current form is out of date. (Reuters, 7.1.2000)

and:

> We want to compete with the best in Europe and to do that we need to improve our budgets. We need more money to invest, we need more cash to buy players and we cannot get that at the level we are operating in at this moment. Rangers cannot do it in Scotland, PSV and Ajax cannot do it in Holland and the same goes for the others. Where do we get the money from? From TV and commercial partnerships. The spin-off from TV and commercial sponsorships in our own countries are too limited. The players that Rangers, Ajax and PSV are buying at the moment are not big enough to bring us to a higher level. Players can get wage packets triple or four times the amount they can get in Holland and Scotland and we need to change that . . . The chairman of Rangers, Celtic, Ajax, myself, we do not want to be part any longer in a competition that cannot lift us to a higher level in financial terms and in football terms. (*The Sunday Times*, 13.8.2000)

The chief executive of Celtic, explaining that while Celtic were the fifth best attended football club in the world, they could not afford the wages of the top players in Europe, declared:

> You need to place our ambitions in the context of the market environment in which we operate. By this I mean the Scottish Premier League . . . in the long term, i.e. five years, we have to ensure Celtic is part of a football environment that will not ultimately bankrupt us when we attempt to compete with big clubs in the large leagues of Europe. (*Celtic View*, 19. 1.2000)

And the owner of Rangers agreed with his fellow executives: 'Financially, Rangers and Celtic have an expenditure that is not being met by our income. Both of us have a set-up which is not set up for Scottish football. Unless we address the problem, we are going to run out of money.' (*The Scotsman*, 16.8.2000). While the chairman of Celtic added in his annual report for 2000:

> I believe it is accepted that the Scottish football structure is not succeeding in its present form. We face the prospect of a steady downward spiral in which both the strongest and the weakest clubs sides will see a deterioration in their ability to supply attractive competitive football. It cannot be healthy for domestic competitions to be dominated by a very few teams while our top clubs enjoy only limited success in Europe. The European pie gets bigger year by year, but shared by a diminishing number of teams from the select few countries, while the smaller countries and clubs scramble for the crumbs. (*The Herald*, 12.8.2000)

The chief executive of the Scottish Premier League put plainly the issue facing all Europe: 'Clubs cannot be paralysed because they come from a small television market like Scotland. We have to try to change that' (www.scotprem.com, 26.7.2000).

Well, on the face of it, the formation of a new trans-national league would seem a way to let these clubs get onto a level playing field with those from 'the Big 5', so increasing sporting competition and expanding the appeal of elite competition into more geographical areas (markets) of Europe. But UEFA's response indicated an unwillingness to recognise this economic and sporting problem. Reacting to stories about the Atlantic League the chief executive of UEFA said (with no evidence and little logic): 'Domestic leagues are the base of our entire system. If the national championships are eclipsed everything disappears' (Agence France Presse, 15.2.2000) and again: 'Simply the bread and butter of any club comes from its national league. If a national championship becomes a second string event everything disappears. We mustn't turn our backs on national competitions in the pursuit of money, otherwise we are heading for disaster' (Agence France Presse, 16.2.2000).

The president of UEFA was just as cool: 'such a trans-national league is not part of European sporting culture' (Agence France Presse, 23.2.2000), while later in the year the chief executive told *L'Equipe*: 'I believe we have reached the limit of what the public can take in terms of international games. Priority must be given to the national leagues.' He saw European football as full of risks with all these strange plans and rumours of break-away leagues, and quickly linked them to UEFA's ruling obsession: 'As long as we don't abolish the consequences of the Bosman ruling – that freedom to rule, buy at any time, to give up solidarity – there will be a risk' (*L'Equipe*, 3.4.2000). In Scotland Celtic have claimed that UEFA's obsession with Bosman meant they were not prepared to give the proposal for a new league the attention it deserved.

In late September 2000 when the clubs finally submitted their proposal for consideration, UEFA said it had 'major concerns' and their spokesman added: 'The proposals are unlikely to be acceptable. They raise more questions than answers . . . We are committed to maintaining the domestic leagues and current European club competitions' (*The Guardian*, 21.9.2000). In response the Scots clubs reiterated that change was necessary, and that UEFA would, in the end, sanction such a league. In any case, as a director of Rangers put it: 'Whatever the outcome, there is a bigger issue – the problems surrounding the bigger clubs in the smaller countries – and that is something that should never be overlooked' (*The Herald*, 22.9.2000). In December 2000 UEFA flatly rejected the proposal, blaming the problems these clubs faced on the Bosman ruling and freedom of movement (Reuters, 15.12.2000). At the same time, UEFA issued what it refers to as 'Ten Commandments' on the development of club football in Europe, principles that reiterate the importance of national leagues and seek to place new restrictions on any grouping trying to find new solutions to the problems of big clubs in small countries (*The Times*, 16.12.2000). The only carrot UEFA offered were changes to the UEFA Cup to guarantee clubs in that competition more European games, though a later reference by a UEFA spokesman about the need to help: 'clubs who are traditionally competing in the UEFA Cup' (Reuters, 20.4.2001) sounded ominous for the ambitions of big clubs in small countries. This 'solution' was welcomed by some club spokesmen but rejected as irrelevant to 'lack of competitiveness' by others. A director of PSV Eindhoven, for example, argued: 'UEFA have listened to the problem, and say they understand it but they do not seem ready to want to listen to our solution', and indicated the continuing problems of these kind of clubs in the current set up: 'Not only are the best players moving away from the smaller countries, but the next best players are leaving as well' (*The Guardian*; *The Independent*, 1.2.2001).

The war of words continued throughout 2001, and it was suggested that, if UEFA blocked the development of the Euro League, Celtic might be prepared to challenge the football body at law, as acting in restraint of trade (*The Financial Times*, 24.7.2001). But later a change of emphasis started to occur – in Scotland at least. In mid-July 2001, Dermot Desmond, a director and chief shareholder in Celtic told an Irish business journal that he believed that it was 'inevitable' that Celtic would join the Premier League in England. This in a context where the top five teams in Division 1 of the English Nationwide League (that is in effect, the English *second* division) earned more than Celtic and Rangers from their domestic TV contract (*Daily Record*, 13.7.2001). The chairman of Celtic added: 'the League structures are archaic, put together in a different age, with different priorities, and, naturally, no perception of public limited companies and modern economics' (*The Scotsman*, 13.7.2001).

Later in July Desmond was interviewed about his belief that Celtic and Rangers would be joining the English Premier League. He pointed out that, while Celtic and Rangers received something like £2.5 million from their domestic football contract, Bradford City – just relegated from the English Premier League – had earned four times this amount. But he was at pains to promote a positive economic rationale. Speaking of the need to 'improve the product', that it made 'economic sense', and suggesting that 'the English football bubble' might burst, he argued:

> Its very simple, there's no mystery to it. Commercially it would work because the audiences would increase – in Ireland, Scotland, globally – then the advertising revenue would increase. Second, from a football standpoint would the Premier League be better with Celtic and Rangers in it? I'd like to think so. That's progress – for everybody.

And went on:

> This is not an anti-Scottish agenda. It is a question of whether Scottish clubs fly the Scottish flag in their own backyard or farther afield. I believe you should go for a market that creates a greater football challenge and remunerates you at a level that means you can compete with the best. Because money determines whether you can retain players – not even buy them, retain them. (*The Guardian*, 28.7.2001)

Such a view was backed, slightly less emphatically, by spokesmen for Rangers. Celtic were involved in a share issue at the time, and some commentators interpreted this new 'proposal' as a ploy to influence possible investors, but it was much more warmly received in Scotland than the Euro-League proposals.

However, this new tack to try to solve the problem of big clubs in small countries in Europe was, again, not well received by the football authorities. A spokesman for FIFA said:

> Given that there is a viable national league in existence, it would appear most unlikely that Rangers and Celtic would be allowed to play in an English league. There is no compelling sporting reason for them to do so. (*The Scotsman*, 31.7.2001).

UEFA was slightly more ambiguous, with its chief executive citing the example of Welsh clubs playing in the English leagues as a precedent, and saying: 'I don't think we would stand in anyone's way if everybody agreed, but I think that is something which needs to be achieved' (*The Sunday Herald*, 26.8.2001). But he was quoted in a more opaque style on UEFA's own website:

> The idea of these two clubs joining the Premier League was brought up by the clubs themselves but UEFA's position is that it believes in the national structures for the basis of our competitions. We do not, as such, support teams moving from one country to another. In this specific case, if both associations and the league wish to change this principle they must make a proposal to the international bodies. (UEFA.com, August 2001)

UEFA's slightly more conciliatory tone was probably because of the floating possibility of a restraint of trade legal action, because such simple cross-border switches could be seen as a less fundamental threat to its basic framework of national associations than any Euro League, and probably because of a shrewd suspicion that the two Scottish clubs had a lot of work still to do to convince a majority of top English clubs that such a change would be mutually beneficial. For while the Scots like to dwell on the large crowds the Rangers and Celtic can attract and their brand's 'global appeal', English officials have tended to pour cold water on the idea. A Premier League spokesman said at the outset of this 'proposal':

> Celtic and Rangers are not joining the FA Premier League. There are no plans to change the current structure and no discussions are taking place. We haven't even contemplated it to be honest. (*The Scotsman*, 31.7.2001)

And, amidst continuing speculation, the chief executive of the English Premier League reiterated:

> We are so successful anyway that it would be arguable if it even made a marginal difference to the Premier League should Celtic and Rangers join. It's not going to increase gate revenues when there are 18 other clubs with full houses

most weeks. You have to say its by far to the advantage of Celtic and Rangers, more than it is to the Premier League which is why I can't think we will be racing to make it happen. (*The Scotsman*, 11.8.2001)

A recent proposal for a two-tier English Premier League, designed to share out TV revenues amongst more clubs, only envisaged incorporating most clubs in Division 1 of the Football League in England into the existing Premier League (Agence France Presse, 17.9.2001), while in October 2001, the Scottish vice president of FIFA spoke of a UEFA executive committee meeting he had attended as an observer in September, where he had raised the issue: 'Though there was no vote the feeling was unanimous. UEFA will not accept that clubs can be situated in one country but play in a league located in another' (*The Sunday Times*, 7.10.2001). What appeared to be precedents were not. The apparently conciliatory words of UEFA's chief executive had been 'misconstrued'. And: 'There is an expectation, a fear, that the whole set-up of football would fall apart if, for example, Austrian clubs played in Italy or Dutch clubs in the Bundesliga' (*The Scotsman*, 8.10.2001).

Whatever the official reaction, Celtic and Rangers' hopes of joining the English Premier League, often with attendant suggestions that Portuguese clubs could join the Spanish league, the Dutch, the German, and so on, are insecurely based. They allude to their global appeal, suggest that the English competition may soon need 'spicing up' and that the TV companies would welcome the change, but all these arguments lack substance. This 'proposal' – largely played out in the Scottish media – panders to the historic concerns of Scottish fans (Moorhouse, 1987) but lacks the fundamental logic of the Euro League plans. Instead of banding together with a number of clubs who have a similar structural, economic, and sporting problem around Europe, the two big Scottish clubs seem to be pinning their faith on the hope that they will, for vague reasons, be granted a slice of the burgeoning TV and ancillary revenues in England, when there is no compelling economic motive for most English clubs to agree to this. But, despite inherent implausibility, this is the preferred option for future developments in Scotland as of late 2001.

For, in early August 2001 *The Sunday Times* announced 'The Euro-League Lies Dead' and went on:

> The Old Firms' desire to join the English Premiership is poised to become desperation after it emerged their alternative way out of the Scottish game, forming a Euro League, has been all but abandoned by key players involved in the plan, most notably Ajax.

In May a majority of the clubs involved in the Euro League proposal had concluded that they could not bring it into being. The factors precipitating their loss of confidence were UEFA's rejection of the plan, the opposition of the G14 group of clubs, the proposed alterations to the format of the UEFA Cup competition by 2003, doubts about the projected economic benefits, and Celtic and Rangers' interest in joining the English Premier League. According to van Eijden, the managing director of Ajax:

> The Euro League is about making the market for TV rights bigger, but by bringing the six countries together, you don't make one TV market. It'd still just be Dutch TV, Belgian TV, Scottish TV. Only when you have a common European market can you do something like that. Football is a local business and Celtic belong in the Scottish market. Their potential is how many people live near the stadium, how many local companies give them sponsorship. Clubs are not international teams. Barcelona versus Alaves is much more important than Barcelona v. Ajax. Bayern Munich v. Bayer Leverkusen is a full stadium, Bayern Munich v. Porto a half-full one. There must also be a sporting criteria to any league. Football in Europe should not be like sport in America.

Regardless even of his defeatist tone and old-fashioned appreciation of clubs as 'brands', van Eijden offered no solution to the problems of big clubs in small countries which had spawned the Euro League proposals in the first place, especially as he seemed to dismiss other possible solutions: 'everybody has to be honest with themselves. Celtic can say "we want to join the Premiership", but the Premiership doesn't want them.' Rather, he seemed to have fallen back on magical, rather than rational, thinking: 'History shows that every ten years we can be in the final of the Champions League. Ajax are coming back again.' (*The Sunday Times*, 5.8.2001).

The crucial point is that the big clubs in the small countries of Europe see themselves as on a downward spiral. If they keep falling financially behind the big clubs located in big media markets, they will not be sporting competitors with, but dependents of, a tiny handful of really wealthy clubs in the continent. Especially this will be so if the very biggest clubs of Europe do organise themselves into an exclusive club, either within UEFA or outside. If their vision is correct, and it seems accurate to me, then vast areas of the continent will be culturally excluded from any direct participation in Europe's premier sport at its highest level. Centralisation has its place, but surely we should expect sport, and football in particular, to reflect the diversity of Europe and span the European continent? But this will not happen 'naturally'.

However, the plans for a Euro League, eminently sensible as they appear to be, are fraught with problems around the themes that I have tried to raise in this chapter.

To begin with, even if the Euro League came into being, vast geographical areas (and markets) of Europe would still be effectively excluded from elite competition. Eastern Europe, of course – no one really bothers about it – but also Austria, Finland, Greece, Ireland, Switzerland and Turkey. The crucial question posed here for all policy makers is what is 'Europe' to be in sporting terms?

Then, the truth is that there is not really a 'Big 5' of football leagues in Europe but a big four, maybe only a big three. It is not difficult to find statements that French and German clubs are not at the same financial level as those from Italy, Spain and England. So, commenting on the fate of AS Monaco, which had just won the French league and lost four star players – two to Italy and one each to Germany and England, *Le Monde* summed up: 'Faced with the economic muscle of their English, Spanish and Italian adversaries, the better off French clubs have to exist condemned to part with their best players' (*Le Monde*, 27.7.2000, my translation). And when the President of Olympique Lyonnais was asked how he planned to pursue that club's economic development he replied:

> The National Football League must change its strategy for sharing the fees for television broadcasting. No other team has been the subject of so many broadcasts as ours this season. The distribution of income must be calculated, among other things, pro rata to televised exposure. We must accept the inequality of elitism, otherwise we will all be small-fry. French exceptionalism is not a good thing. The Europe club, a grouping of twelve clubs, which I organise, is going to put its claims to Noel Le Graet, who happens to be in the seat of President of the League . . . We hope both to set up exploitation of the internet and to have detailed negotiations with local stations. We can also develop by making better use of stadiums. Take as a starting point the 100 francs price of a ticket. English fans spend 300 francs at the venue on associated products. Here, fans stick at the initial 100 francs. (*Le Monde*, 29.2.2000, my translation)

In July 2000 Monsieur Le Graet was voted out of office in favour of a candidate thought to be more willing to allow the big clubs in France to get more from the TV deal. At the moment, then, the perceived solution to the problems the top clubs in France and Germany have in competing economically with the others in the 'Big 5' tends to be a truncation or subversion of such mechanisms of income redistribution that operate currently within their domestic leagues.

Thirdly, it seems clear that one price of UEFA's agreement to clubs moving out of their domestic leagues, will be that they will have to make 'solidarity' payments to the smaller clubs left behind in national leagues. So, unlike the richest clubs in the biggest leagues, steadily consolidating their sporting grasp over their own domestic competitions, big clubs from smaller leagues will be burdened with extra costs to enable national competitions to stay afloat in something like their current forms. Once more, this reveals how UEFA refuses to plan rationally for the future of

Europe's game but reacts, and seeks to maintain, where it can, traditional structures.

Finally, what the proposed Euro League offers is the equal right to become unequal. As far as I can ascertain the plan provides no discussion of the merits of income redistribution, nor can it really, as the clubs involved are trying to match the very biggest European clubs who are driving along on a largely unchecked, individualistic, basis. The proposed new league would contain non-commensurate clubs from countries that vary in terms of average wealth, and profound inequalities already exist between these clubs. The development of yet another league mainly driven by market forces may add a couple more competitors from other countries to the handful of clubs threatening to dominate Europe, which would be a very good thing, but it will not solve the underlying issues of competitive balance and geographical exclusion right across Europe.

BIG CLUBS AND EVEN MORE MONEY

> Sanz (The President of G14) added that each of the fourteen clubs would be given voting rights in the new organisation according to a formula based on successes in European competition. Half of the group's finance would be funded equally by all clubs, with the other half in proportion to the members to the number of votes each one receives. (Reuters, 9.6.2000)

It is the big clubs from the big leagues which can pay the massive transfer fees, with Italy and Spain totally eclipsing all the other '3 big leagues' in the purchase of players over £10 million in the summers of 2000 and 2001. Of 21 such moves in 2000, 13 were to clubs in Italy and 4 to clubs in Spain. It is these clubs that can sign teenage talent from around the world. It is these clubs that are developing a worldwide network of nursery, co-operating, and 'interim' clubs so they can sift through youngsters from all points of the compass and cope with the problem of 'naturalising' non-European Union talent in an easy fashion (*The Independent*, 14.3.2000). Their money, the exposure, glamour and allure it gives, hands these clubs massive advantages in the search and competition for new football talent, worldwide.

Moreover, it is these clubs that are racing to exploit new sources of income. It has recently been decided that pay per view income belongs to the home club. As the chief executive of Manchester United put it: 'Pay per view will be an extension of our gate, which is a critically important element because supporters are buying into your club. Ultimately we will sell television season tickets' (*The Sunday Telegraph*, 23.7.2000). Then, the new television contract signed by the English Premier League in 2000 contained the innovations that individual clubs will:

- own the highlight and archive rights to their home matches after a delay of three days or even less;
- be allowed to keep the revenues from selling their home matches after this delay on their own TV channels and websites.

Without much discussion, it has been decided that what could have been thought to be a collective asset will now be an individual one. This is set fair to widen the already huge gap in wealth between the few rich clubs in Europe and the rest. One expert told UEFA that internet revenues could contribute as much as $2.3 billion to football in the next decade, of which around $1billion would be new money via merchandising, betting and new income streams, most of which would go to the biggest clubs (Reuters 16.2.2000). So Europe will soon get a potentially huge extension of 'local revenues', to use the American term, and one ushered in almost without discussion. To repeat, the roots of the problem in American baseball are assumed to be the growth of just these local revenues, and the fact that they are outside existing schemes of income redistribution.

There have been two recent plans to create a European Super League of the big clubs outside UEFA structures. When Media Partners produced a plan in mid-1998 for a breakaway league *The Financial Times* (15.5.1998) stated: 'The radical principle at the heart of the concept is that a group of founder clubs will enjoy permanent membership of the league by virtue of their size and wealth.' This abstract idea was greeted with much horror, but the truth is that this is precisely what is happening *de facto* at the highest level of European competition. A small, highly geographically concentrated, group, is coming to dominate European club competition. Allowing market forces to operate more or less unchecked will lead to this.

The G14 grouping is, supposedly, a grouping of the big clubs of Europe that acts as a lobbying group with UEFA and European authorities. The group has established an office in Brussels and principles based on success and market power order its inner workings. At first it contained only economically dominant clubs, but a few more were added as a gesture to sporting inclusion. Thus we have the anomalous situation that three clubs within the G14 are amongst those who were trying to establish the new transnational Euro League so that they could stay in economic touch with their fellow members!

This concentration of big clubs and big money has not gone unnoticed. There have been a number of English language publications on 'the new football business' including Morrow (1999), Hamil et al. (1999, 2000) and Garland et al. (2000). In general, however, they have not dealt in great detail with revenue sharing or related issues, and have been mainly concerned with the preservation of traditional structures. This is especially the case with the contribution of Bell (2000) who, as 'legal adviser on EU affairs to UEFA', can hardly be described as an impartial observer. The contributions of Hamil and Garland contain very little on either revenue sharing, the problems of big clubs in small nations, small media markets, UEFA's practices with its own income streams or the possibility of a new European League, all of which are dealt with in this chapter.

Hoehn and Szymanski (1999) certainly do directly confront many of the issues I have been emphasising but argue against revenue sharing on the grounds that, theoretically, it has perverse effects, though they are moved to note:

> Given the theoretical prediction that revenue sharing will adversely affect competitive balance and investment opportunities, it is perhaps surprising that the National Football League in the USA manages to maintain both a relatively balanced competition and a high level of playing investment. One explanation might have to do with the objectives of owners. (Hoehn and Szymanski, 1999, p.221)

Which is to say that controllers of clubs might actually be utility maximisers, which would profoundly disturb Hoehn and Szymanski's basic theoretical assumption. Since Real Madrid (hugely influential in the G14) admit to being around $250 million in debt, it does, indeed, seem likely that many big clubs are not after some simple profit maximisation.

Hoehn and Szymanski are intent on a policy intervention, and advocate a closed USA-style franchise system as the way forward for European football. Their paper focuses on the issue of income redistribution only to dismiss it as a relevant mechanism for Europe, they concentrate on a few possible labour market restrictions. But it seems to me there are many difficulties with the analysis of the problems of European football and in the solutions Hoehn and Szymanski offer. Among the most crucial are:

- they do not follow the full logic of American systems of the organisation of sports but pick and choose the elements they want;
- they accept current economic imbalances between clubs as given and do not consider whether historical accident or market advantage may need curbing if clubs from all parts of Europe are to have the chance to participate meaningfully in elite competition.

In brief, what Hoehn and Szymanski offer, based on debatable theoretical assumptions, is a mainly unregulated future for European football where market forces will decide patterns of sporting competition. They seem to assume that:

- somehow this will still allow more than a tiny handful of European clubs to compete meaningfully for the major prizes;
- all of Europe does not need (or deserve) to be drawn together through its paramount sport. In this cold appraisal, small markets should expect to have less fun.

CONCLUSIONS

> Galatasary needs its own stadium, it must have some form of public listing as a company, it must organise its fans all over the world, and it must establish the financial support for all these plans. Milan, Barcelona, Manchester United – these are the clubs we have taken as examples. When we can match them in terms of tactics, management and business, then we will have joined their ranks. If success is limited to the field then its just a surprise, a one-off. You have to carry the success off the field. (Coach of UEFA Cup winners Galatasary of Turkey, later the coach of Milan. Reuters, 10.5.2000)

Traditionally, football in Europe has been organised vertically, through a series of national leagues, but it now needs to be organised horizontally, so that clubs of equivalent capabilities and status meet each other on a regular basis. And it should be arranged such that all clubs have an opportunity for ultimate success. This requires current arrangements to be critically examined; it needs creative thinking, and the willingness to argue for, and then create, new economic mechanisms and platforms so that clubs from much of Europe are not excluded from meaningful competition by an almost undiscussed adherence to market forces which, as I have tried to suggest, would put American sports to shame. In marked contrast to America, what we have in Europe is a gold-rush football economy where those already in favoured positions are busy grabbing all the pay-dirt they can.

I have argued throughout this chapter that neither the football authorities nor European politicians, nor most academics have grasped the real roots of the problems inherent in contemporary European football. Along with their proposal for a Euro League the interested clubs, representing six small nations in Europe, asked UEFA to initiate a review of the quality, competitiveness and economics of European club soccer (Reuters, 12.12.2000). Of course, UEFA did not act on this, but such an analysis is just what is required, and very soon. Europe needs its own research on its own sports and has to stop relying on findings from America to substantiate arguments and validate proposed structures. Those concerned about the future of football in Europe need to create a well-founded discussion about the benefits and limits of income redistribution between clubs, and to examine the net of relations between revenue sharing and feasible labour market restrictions. To facilitate this I make three final suggestions:

- The European Commission and European politicians have to be made aware that the adherence to market forces and advantage is driving European football into a situation where success in pan-European competition will soon be the prerogative of only four or five clubs in the continent, and that UEFA is doing very little to combat this.
- Studies of the efficacy of the redistribution of income should not just concentrate on new revenues from TV and telecommunications, as is the tendency even when the issue is raised. *All revenue streams* need to come under scrutiny and comprehensive assessment as they are in the USA.
- But this will not be easy. Football is in different cultural locations in different parts of Europe. In some countries sport has political and social dimensions which it does not have in America, such that tycoons are willing to buy and pay players for clubs or put their own fortune into clubs, or sometimes the state will intervene to aid clubs. Real Madrid has huge debts but a convenient planning deal with the city authorities for developing its training centre will soon clear these. A sensitivity to the complexities of the cultural location of the sport, an acknowledgement of the variety of sources of funds, and the way that funding football can serve other aims – political, even profit maximisation in other sectors – all these nuances need to be part of analyses rather than simply seizing on any data sets or financial figures that happen to be around. Partly because of this, what is needed are more studies of the political economy of football, analyses that acknowledge social, political, and cultural specificities. For football in Europe, purely economic analysis will never be enough, even when it actually is trying to address the truly critical issues confronting the sport.

BIBLIOGRAPHY

Agence France Presse (various dates) news releases.
Bell, A. (2000), 'Sport and the Law: the Influence of European Competition Policy on the Traditional League Structures of European Football', in Hamil et al. (2000).
Garland, J. et al. (eds) (2000), *The Future of Football*, London: Frank Cass.
Hamil, S. et al. (eds) (1999), *A Game of Two Halves: The Business of Football*, Edinburgh: Mainstream.

Hamil, S. et al. (eds) (2000), *Football in the Digital Age; Whose Game is it Anyway?*, Edinburgh: Mainstream.

Hoehn, T. and S. Szymanski (1999), 'The Americanization of European Football', *Economic Policy*, **28**, April.

Levin, R. et al. (2000), The Report of the Independent Members of the Commissioner's Blue Ribbon Panel on Baseball Economics, New York: Major League Baseball.

Moorhouse, H.F. (1987), 'Scotland against England: football and popular culture', *International Journal of Sports History*, **4** (2).

Moorhouse, H.F. (1993), 'The Economic Effects of the Transfer System in Professional Football: Evidence from Scotland 1982–1991', research paper no. 6, Training and Employment Research Unit, University of Glasgow.

Moorhouse, H.F. (1995), 'The Consequences for European Football of Ending the Traditional Transfer System and UEFA's "Three Foreigner Rule"', a report for The European Commission (Directorate General 5).

Moorhouse, H.F. (1999a), 'Football Post-Bosman: The Real Issues', in C. Jeanrenaud and S. Kesenne (eds), *Competition Policy in Professional Sports: Europe after the Bosman Case*, Antwerp: Standaard Editions.

Moorhouse, H.F. (1999b), 'The Economic Effects of the Traditional Transfer System in European Professional Football', *Football Studies*, April.

Moorhouse, H.F. (2000), 'The Redistribution of Income in European Professional Football: past, present and future', *Reflets et Perspectives de la Vie Economique*, **309** (2 and 3), June.

Morrow, S. (1999), *The New Business of Football: Accountability and Finance in Football,* London: Macmillan.

Newspapers and magazines (various dates)
Celtic View
Le Monde
L'Equipe
The Financial Times
The Independent
The Guardian
The Herald
The Daily Record
The Scotsman
The Sunday Herald
The Sunday Telegraph
The Sunday Times
The Times

Reuters (various dates) news releases.

UEFA (2000), *Financial Distribution of UEFA Champions League Marketing Revenues 1999/2000*.

UEFA.com (various dates).

www.scotprem.com.

PART 2

Economic Theory and Team Sports

4. Improving the competitive balance and the salary distribution in professional team sports

Stefan Kesenne

1. INTRODUCTION

Sport is competition, and the peculiarity of the economics of professional team sports is the so-called 'inverted joint product', meaning that two firms or clubs are necessary to supply the product which is playing a match, and at least two to organize a league championship. Moreover, the competitive balance between the teams in a league is an important determinant of the spectator interest and the total revenue of the league (see Neale, 1964). Given the unequal drawing potential of clubs for playing talent and supporters in big cities and small towns, the general concern is that a free agency player market will cause a very unequal distribution of playing strength among teams. Because the winner takes all, the stronger financial position of the big city teams will also allow them to hire or buy the best players from the small town teams. This cumulative effect results in a distribution of playing talent that is too unequal to keep the spectators interested, which will result in a decrease of the clubs' revenue.

In the past league authorities have taken different measures to regulate the labour market and control the move of professional players in order to guarantee a reasonable competitive balance. The best known and most controversial of these measures is the retain and transfer system or reservation system. It did not allow end-of-contract players to move from one club to another unless both clubs agreed on the transfer fee that had to be paid. In the US this reservation system disappeared in the 1970s in all major league sports. In Europe the transfer system has been abolished by the so-called Bosman verdict in 1995 (European Court of Justice, 15 December 1995).

Most American major leagues also have some arrangement to share revenue among clubs. Revenue sharing is meant to help the small clubs to keep up with the big guys, for instance the NFL knows a gate sharing arrangement that gives the visiting club a share of no less than 40 per cent.

Moreover the federal broadcast rights are equally distributed among all clubs in the league. Also the European Champions League redistributes television rights among the participating clubs. After the abolition of the reservation system in the US, and the following explosion of player salaries, most leagues started to bargain about salary caps. A salary cap is in fact a payroll cap that limits the total amount a team can spend on player salaries. Recently, for the first time in American history, the NBA also accepted an individual salary cap, which restricts the maximum salary level of star players (see Staudohar, 1999).

In some US major league sports like basketball (NBA) and football (NFL) the rookie player draft is yet another measure that aims at equalizing the playing strength of clubs. It implies that the young and talented players in the minor leagues and the college competitions can be hired by the major league clubs in reverse order of their league standing. Given the history and the structure of professional sports in Europe no rookie draft exists in European sports like soccer, rugby, basketball and volleyball.

The aim of this chapter is to discuss to what extent these measures are effective to improve the distribution of playing talent among clubs in a league and to hold down the star players' salaries. In the literature one can find different studies dealing with this issue and the conclusions turn out to differ depending on the hypotheses of the models that are used. In particular the objective of the club – profit or win maximization – and the arguments of the revenue function – the relative and/or absolute quality of the team – seem to be the most crucial factors. In this contribution we discuss the most important measures that are relevant for the US, Europe and Australia like the retain and transfer system, revenue sharing and salary caps. In Section 2 we specify a model with a general revenue function and an objective function that includes both profits and wins. A third section discusses the impact of the different regulations. Conclusions are given in section 4.

2.   THE MODEL SPECIFICATION

In the literature one can observe a striking difference between the alleged objective of professional sports clubs in the US, Europe and Australia. In the US most economists assume clubs to behave like profit-maximizers, whereas in Europe and Australia some kind of a utility maximization seems to be the clubs' objective. This can include the team's playing success or the winning percentage, the average game attendance, the health of the league and so on (see Sloane, 1971; Dabscheck, 1975). However, it cannot be denied that this gap between the US and Europe is narrowing. Some US economists like Quirk and El-Hodiri (1974) and Noll (1974) admit that besides making profits winning the championship is also important, even if it reduces profits (see also Rascher, 1997). In the world of European soccer, being the most professional and commercial sport, not only winning but also making profits is becoming part of the game. In England's Premier League, Manchester United is a profitable club and already more than 20 other clubs are floating on the market. Also, in other countries like Italy and even Holland, going to the market is considered to be the next thing to do to attract more capital and to raise a club's budget. In order to be successful on the stock exchange a reasonable profit rate, among other things, seems to be inevitable. It follows that in the near future, and even today, the gap between the extreme objectives like pure win or profit-maximazation, is closing. It is more realistic to start from an objective function that is a mix of the two, and this is an important issue because it turns out to affect the effectiveness of several player market regulations (see Rascher, 1997; Kesenne, 2000a).

In our opinion the objective of most sports clubs in all parts of the world is to increase their playing success but not at all costs. Professional sports clubs, also in Europe, are becoming commercial companies, starting to behave like any other firm in a competitive industry and feeling the need to be profitable. Owners, stockholders or investors need a return on their investments, so that a certain profit rate is necessary. This puts a restriction on the management of the club that wants to increase the playing strength of the team by hiring more playing talent.

We therefore start from the hypothesis that it is a club's objective to maximize the winning percentage under the restriction of guaranteeing a reasonable profit rate, which can be high or low, or even zero. In the short run, assuming the capital stock of the club to be constant, a fixed profit rate also means a fixed amount of profits. So the objective function can be written as

$$\max w + \lambda[\pi^0 - (r - c)], \tag{4.1}$$

where w is the season winning percentage of a team, r and c are total season revenue and cost and π^0 is a given level of season profits; λ is the Lagrange multiplier. Based on most empirical research (for a survey see Cairns et al., 1986), a club's total season revenue depends primarily on the size of its home market, the winning percentage of that club and the absolute quality of the teams in the league. The positive impact of the winning percentage, however, shows decreasing marginal returns because a league needs a reasonable degree of uncertainty of outcome to keep spectators interested. It seems obvious that both the relative and the absolute quality of a team depend on the quality of the players. Because it is not the number of players but rather the total number of playing talents of all players together that counts, most models are specified in terms of playing talents. However, such a player labour market model is not capable of telling the whole story. One important shortcoming is due to the fact that each sports team cannot play with more than a fixed number of players fielded at the same time, for instance 11 for a soccer team, 5 for a basketball team and so on. It follows that a soccer team is better off with, say, 15 top players, each of them having 20 talents, than with 60 regular players with 5 talents each. But in this model, both add up to a total of 300 talents. One way to tackle this problem is to start from two types of players, top players and regular players. Under a few reasonable assumptions the model can be reformulated in terms of the number of top players. If we call the top players l_1 and the regular players l_2, we assume that the productivity of a regular player, which is the individual contribution of a player to a club's winning percentage, is only a fraction (a) of the productivity of a star player. So the winning percentage of the home team can be written as the following positive function

$$w = f(l_1 + al_2) \text{ with } 0 < a < 1. \tag{4.2}$$

A team can only have a fixed number of players (l) on the field so a club faces the restriction that

$$l_1 + l_2 = l. \tag{4.3}$$

After the substitution of (4.3) into (4.2), a club's season revenue function can be written as

$$r = r[m, al + (1-a)l_1, l_s], \tag{4.4}$$

where m is the size of the market, and l_s is the total supply of top players as an indication of the absolute quality in the league.

On the cost side we assume that a club's total season cost c consists of labour and capital cost. The capital cost c_0 is constant in the short run and the player labour cost is the only variable cost of a club. If c_1 is the labour cost or the salary of a top player and c_2 is the unit cost of a regular player, we can write the cost function, given constraint (4.3), as

$$c = (c_1 - c_2)l_1 + c_2 l + c_0. \tag{4.5}$$

Because the regular players are in excess supply, their salary c_2 is simply a fixed minimum wage. The salary c_1 of the top players, however, is determined by the demand and supply conditions on the player labour market. We assume the supply of top players l_s to be independent of the salary level.

Given this model, one can easily derive that the demand for top players is given by the net average revenue curve in terms of top players, that is: after subtracting the fixed profit level, the fixed capital cost and the fixed labour cost from total revenue, that is

$$AR^N = \frac{R - \pi^0 - c_2 l - c_0}{l_i} = c_1 - c_2. \tag{4.6}$$

Given the properties of the revenue function, this demand curve is downward sloping in terms of the difference between the salary level of top players and regular players. On a free agency player market, the labour market equilibrium can be found where the sum of the demand for top players of all clubs in the league equals the supply of top players. In a two-club market with a big club and a small club the situation is pictured in Figure 4.1.

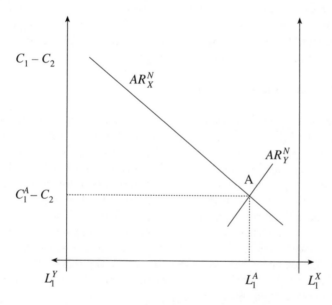

Figure 4.1   Player market equilibrium under free agency

On the horizontal axis the total supply of top players is indicated by the distance between the two origins. The demand for the big club X is higher than for the small club Y because the big club has the largest budget, which is based on the size of the market giving the big club the best opportunities to attract players talent and spectators. This difference in drawing potential is the main determinant of the difference in financial strength of the clubs. One can see that, *ceteris paribus*, the big club has the largest share of the available top players. However, one has to point out that this outcome also depends on the capital cost of the club, as well as on the profits a club wants to make. Both can be different for different clubs. The more profitable a club wants to be, the smaller will be its hiring of top players, *ceteris paribus*. It is obvious that also the slope of the demand function matters. A club with winning elastic revenues will hire more top players than a club with winning inelastic revenues because the demand curve of the last one is steeper. In the following analysis we assume this winning elasticity to be the same for all clubs.

3.   THE IMPACT OF PLAYER MARKET REGULATIONS

If equation (4.6) is the demand curve for top players on the player labour market with a given supply of playing talents, how do league regulations like a retain and transfer system, a revenue sharing arrangement or a salary cap affect the competitive balance in a league?

3.1.   Retain and Transfer System

It has already been shown in the US literature that, if all clubs are profit-maximizers, a player reservation system, or its European variant, a retain and transfer system, does not change the distribution of playing talent among clubs in a league (see Noll, 1974; Quirk and Fort, 1992). This so-called invariance proposition is also supported by much empirical evidence. Indeed, since the abolition of the reserve clause in the US major leagues in the 1970s, the competitive balance has not been changed. There is some evidence that the free agency system might even have improved the competitive balance (see Quirk and Fort, 1992). So far it is not clear to what extent this result has also been caused by the salary caps that have been imposed in the major leagues after the abolition of the reserve clause that has led to a rise in top player salaries.

Because there are some doubts about the relevance of the profit-maximizing hypothesis, even in the US major leagues, the question is whether the same conclusion can been drawn if we start from win maximization under the restriction of a fixed profit rate. The empirical evidence (see Szymanski and Kuypers, 1999) shows that small clubs are net sellers of playing talent on the transfer market. Given the player labour demand equation (4.6), one can easily derive that, if a small club receives a transfer fee from the big club as a financial compensation for the loss of one of its players, the small club's total revenue increases, and so does its net average revenue. It follows that in Figure 4.1 the small club's demand curve for playing talent shifts to the right, the big club's demand curve shifts to the left, so that the new market equilibrium results in a better competitive balance in the league. However, this positive effect of the transfer system will not be very significant. It would be more significant if the initial distribution of top players, that is before clubs start to trade players on the transfer market, were more equal. But this is not the case, certainly not in Europe which does not have a rookie draft system. By definition a small club is a club with a weak drawing potential, not only for spectators, but also for players so that the initial player market equilibrium under free agency is already found far to the right in Figure 4.1. It follows that there is little to trade from small to big clubs so that the market equilibrium under a transfer system will stay in the neighbourhood of the free agency equilibrium point. Anyway, why would a big club engage in transfer arrangements that worsen its competitive position? Only occasionally will a star player be bought by the big club which will allow the small club to attract one or two regular players instead.

One of the implications of this model, compared with the profit-maximizing model, is that the combination of a *rookie draft* and a transfer system can have a favourable impact on the competitive balance, because the initial distribution of playing talent is more equal so that trading players afterwards increases the small clubs' revenue which can be spent on more or better players (see Lavoie, 2000).

Given the powerful monopsony position of club owners under the reservation or transfer system, it is not a surprise that players have been exploited. Scully (1974) showed that under the profit-maximizing assumption MLB baseball players were paid far below their marginal productivity before 1975. Many years later, under the free agency system, this underpayment has stopped (see Scully, 1999). In a win-maximizing league players are on average not exploited. Starting from the monopsony model of the labour market one can show that playing talent will be overpaid. In Figure 4.2, where the number of playing talents are on the horizontal axis and the salary level on the vertical axis, it can be seen that the salary level is above marginal productivity at the break-even point, where the net average revenue and the supply curve intersect.

This view is also supported by the general impression that in many European soccer clubs players are paid above their individual contribution to club revenue. However, one should point out that monopsonists also have the power to discriminate, so that some players can still be exploited, like J.-M. Bosman by The Football Club of Liege, while others are overpaid. The conclusion is that the impact of the transfer system on the

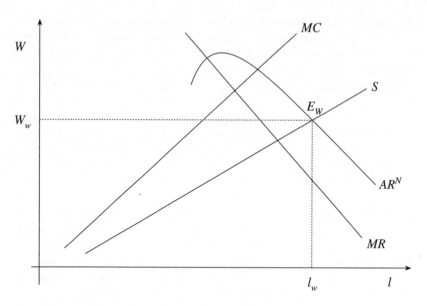

Figure 4.2   Monopsony under win maximization

competitive balance in a league will be marginal, but that it endows too much power to the club owners, putting the players in a weak position. So why should one stick to an illegal and ineffective system, which deprives the fundamental right of a professional worker to choose a new employer at the end of his contract, when other regulations exist that are both legal and more effective.

3.2.   Revenue Sharing

One of the alternative regulations to improve the competitive balance is a system of revenue sharing among clubs. Because small clubs are net sellers of playing talent on the transfer market, the transfer system has somehow functioned as a financial redistribution system. So, after the abolition of the transfer system, league administrators were considering alternative redistribution systems. In the history of the American major leagues like baseball (MLB) and football (NFL) revenue sharing has already become common practice. However, the economic literature is not very consistent in its approach to the impact of revenue sharing on the competitive balance in a league. In his pioneering contribution Rottenberg (1956) argued that under the profit-maximizing assumption revenue sharing among clubs does not affect the distribution of playing talent. Later on, this result was formally proven by El-Hodiri and Quirk (1971). Also Vrooman (1995) and

Rascher (1997) agree that revenue sharing does not affect competitive balance. Atkinson et al. (1988), using a more general model, showed that revenue sharing does have an impact on the distribution of playing talent. Also Marburger (1997), modelling attendances as an increasing function of the absolute quality of both the home and the visiting team, found that: 'the increased sharing of revenues may enhance competitive balance'. However, in a recent paper taking the perspective of Contest Theory, Szymanski (2001) shows that revenue sharing enhances the degree of imbalance because of the imbalance in revenue generating potential of big and small clubs.

How does revenue sharing affect the competition balance if one starts from the model specification in section two? Kesenne (1996, 2000a) has shown that, if all revenue is shared between the home and the visiting team according to a fixed share parameter in a win maximizing scenario, the big clubs will reduce their demand for playing talent and the small clubs will expand their demand so that the distribution of playing talent improves. This results holds regardless of the specification of the revenue function in terms of absolute or relative quality, and regardless of the size of the profit rate. Because the model specification in Section 2 is the same as in Kesenne (2000a), only reformulated in terms of top players and regular players, a similar impact of revenue sharing can also be derived. The situation is pictured in Figure 4.3.

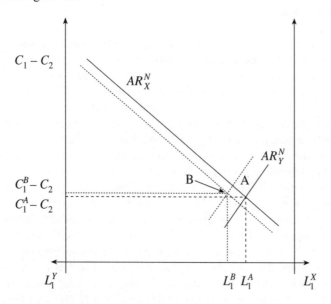

Figure 4.3   The impact of revenue sharing

The big club's demand curve for top players shifts downwardly whereas the small club's demand curve shifts upwardly. It is important to notice that in the upward shift the small club's demand curve is larger than the downward shift of the big club's demand curve. The reason is the demand curves in this model are average revenue curves. If a certain amount of total revenue is shifted from the big to the small club, the downward shift of the big club's average revenue is smaller because the big club has more top players. It follows that initially a limited revenue sharing arrangement increases the top player salaries so that the salary distribution also becomes more unequal. Because the regular players' salaries are fixed at the minimum wage, the average level of player salaries goes up, which is different from the impact of revenue sharing in a profit-maximizing league. However, if the degree of revenue sharing is raised high enough so that a more equal competitive balance than the profit-maximization labour market equilibrium emerges, the top player salary and the average salary level will come down again. The reason is that total league revenue is at its maximum level at the profit-maximizing equilibrium. Because the salary level in the win-maximizing equilibrium is simply the ratio of the net total league revenue (after subtracting the total fixed capital cost) and the total supply of playing talent, it follows that the salary reaches its highest level where total revenue is at its highest level.

3.3 Salary Caps

One of the main conclusions of Fort and Quirk (1995) in their well-known review article in the *Journal of Economic Literature* is: 'The problem of maintaining financial viability for teams located in weak-drawing markets is a major one for sports leagues. The analysis here argues that an enforceable *salary cap* is the only of the cross-subsidization schemes currently in use that can be expected to accomplish this while improving the competitive balance in a league'. Investigating the impact of salary caps is no easy matter, because there are so many different variants. There are hard and soft salary caps, depending on the exceptive clauses that allow clubs to exceed the maximum payroll. There are also salary caps that are combined with a minimum amount that a club is forced to pay on salaries so that some cross-subsidization is necessary. In that case a salary cap is linked to a revenue-sharing arrangement. There is also the system of the so-called luxury tax, that imposes a tax whenever a club's payroll exceeds the salary cap. Recently a collective bargaining agreement after the NBA-lockout has resulted in an individual salary cap on top of the existing salary (that is payroll) cap (see Staudohar, 1999). Quirk and Fort (1992) and Fort and Quirk (1995) show that a salary cap can improve the competitive balance in a league, albeit that this salary cap is a combination of a salary cap and a revenue-sharing arrangement. Vrooman (1995), using a more general model, argues that the impact on the competitive balance of this type of a salary (payroll) cap is only a myth. Marburger (1997) and Rascher (1997) basically agree with the view of Fort and Quirk, although Marburger, concentrating on the impact of the luxury taxes, is concerned about the disincentives these measures might create. Kesenne (2000b) shows that the impact of a pure salary cap, meaning that only a maximum amount is imposed on the payroll of a club, improves the distribution of playing talent among teams. However, all these studies start from a profit-maximizing hypothesis. The question is whether the same conclusion can be drawn if one starts from the model specification in Section 2.

A pure salary cap, without any cross-subsidization, can be written in terms of the number of top players as

$$c_1 - c_2 = \frac{cap - c_2 l}{l_1},$$ (4.7)

where *cap* is the amount of the hard salary cap. This hyperbolic function is at the same time the big club's demand function for top players. They simply have the choice to hire more top players at a lower salary level or fewer top players at a higher salary level. The demand function of the small club Y is the same as before, because it is reasonable to assume that their payroll always stays below the cap so that the imposed salary cap is not effective. This is shown in Figure 4.4.

The intersection of both demand curves, which fixes the new labour market equilibrium, is now found at point B. Because the equilibrium point has shifted from A to B, it follows that the competitive balance in a league can indeed be improved by a salary cap, and the big club X will hire fewer top players than before. Comparing A and B on the vertical axis, it can be seen that the salary difference between top players and regular players will be smaller, so that a more equal salary distribution can be expected. Because the salary of the moderate players is the official minimum wage, it follows also that the average level of player salaries will be lowered by the salary cap. One of the implications of imposing a salary cap in this model is that, *ceteris paribus*, each club is making a higher profit than planned.

The negotiations during the 1998 dispute between NBA club owners and players ended, among other regulations and for the first time ever in sports, in the acceptance by the players of an individual cap (see Staudohar, 1999). Not only the total payroll, but also the individual player salaries now face a maximum amount, based on years of service. The impact of an individual salary cap can also be seen in Figure 4.4 where the horizontal line on the level CAP_i indicates the individual cap. It is

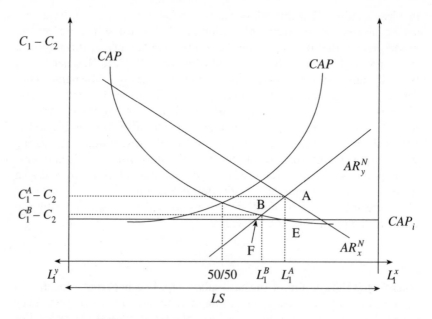

Figure 4.4　The impact of a salary cap

obvious that, in order to be effective, this individual cap has to be lower
than the equilibrium top player salary in point B. One of the consequences of an individual cap on top player salaries is that it creates an
excess demand for top players. This rationing of top players results in any
equilibrium point somewhere between the points E and F, the new profit-
maximizing points for the big and small club respectively. It is more likely
that the outcome will be closer to E, implying that more top players will
play for the big team, and for good reasons. If the top players are free to
choose their club under the free agency system, they will prefer to play for
the better team and the more prestigious club. Moreover, the richer club
can offer the star players more non-wage or fringe benefits on top of their
salary. So, if we compare the market equilibrium with and without the
individual cap, points E and B, the profit-maximizing rich club hires more
top players than they would without the individual cap. The small club is
rationed and has to fill up its roster with more regular players. The result
of an individual cap is that the competitive balance becomes more
unequal than under a payroll cap. The more positive outcome is that an
individual cap further improves the salary distribution between stars and
regulars.

4. CONCLUSION

Based on this partial analysis one can assert that the abolition of the reservation system or the retain and transfer system is the right thing to do. It does not improve the competitive balance compared with free agency and it creates too much monopsonistic exploitation and discrimination of players. If the transfer system compensates the small clubs for their youth formation and strengthens their financial position, the effect is small and the loss can be made up easily by more legal and targeted compensation systems for youth training. This model further shows that revenue sharing and salary caps have more to offer in terms of improving the competitive balance, the salary distribution and the financial survival of small clubs.

REFERENCES

Atkinson S.E., L.R. Stanley, J. Tschirhart (1988), 'Revenue sharing as an incentive in an agency problem: an example from the National Football League', *RAND Journal of Economics*, **19** (1).

Cairns J., N. Jennett and P. Sloane (1986), 'The economics of professional team sports: a survey of theory and evidence', *Journal of Economic Studies*, (13), 1.

Dabscheck, B. (1975), 'Sporting equality: labour market versus product market control', *Journal of Industrial Relations*, **7** (2), 174–90.

El-Hodiri, M. and J. Quirk (1971), 'An economic model of a professional sports league', *Journal of Political Economy*, **79**, 1302–19.

Fort, R. and J. Quirk (1995), 'Cross-subsidization, incentives and outcomes in professional team sports leagues', *Journal of Economic Literature*, **XXXIII**, 1265–99.

Kesenne, S. (1996), 'League management in professional team sports with win maximizing clubs', *European Journal for Sports Management*, **2** (2).

Kesenne, S., (2000a), 'Revenue sharing and competitive balance in professional team sports, *Journal of Sports Economics* **1** (1), 56–65.

Kesenne, S. (2000b), 'The impact of salary caps in professional team sports', *Scottish Journal of Political Economy*, **47** (4).

Lavoie, M. (2000), 'La proposition d'invariance dans un monde où les équipes maximisent la performance sportive', *Reflets Perspectives de la vie économique*, **XXXIX**, (2–3), 85–93.

Marburger D.R. (1997), 'Gate revenue sharing and luxury taxes in professional sports', *Contemporary Economic Policy*, **XV**, April.

Neale, W.C. (1964), 'The peculiar economics of professional sports', *Quarterly Journal of Economics*, **78** (1), 1–14.

Noll, R. (ed.) (1974), *Government and the Sports Business*, Washington, DC: Brookings Institution.

Quirk, J. and M. El-Hodiri (1974), 'The Economic Theory of a Professional Sports League', in R.G. Noll (ed.), *Government and the Sport Business*, Washington, DC: Brookings Institution.

Quirk, J. and R.D. Fort (1992), '*Pay Dirt. the Business of Professional Team Sports*, Princeton, NJ: Princeton University Press.

Rascher, D.A., (1997), 'A Model of a Professional Sports League', in W. Hendricks, (ed.), *Advances in the Economics of Sport*, volume 2, Greenwich, Conn.: JAI-Press Inc.

Rottenberg, Simon (1956), 'The baseball players' labour market', *Journal of Political Economy*, **64**.

Scully, G.W. (1974), 'Pay and performance in major league baseball', *American Economic Review*, **64** (6), 915–30.

Scully, G.W. (1999), 'Free Agency and the Rate of Monopsonistic Exploitation in Baseball', in C. Jeanrenaud and S. Kesenne (eds), *Competition Policy in Professional Sports*, Antwerp: Standaard Editions Ltd, pp. 59–69.

Sloane, P. (1971), 'The economics of professional football: the football club as a utility maximizer', *Scottish Journal of Political Economy*, **17** (2).

Staudohar, P. (1999), 'Labor relations in basketball: the lockout of 1998–99', *Monthly Labour Review*, U.S. Department of Labor, April, pp. 3–9.

Szymanski, S. (2001), 'Competitive Balance and Income Redistribution in Team Sports', Discussion paper, Imperial College Management School, London, 24 pp.

Szymanski, S. and T. Kuypers (1999), *Winners and Losers, the Business Strategy of Football*, London: Viking, 408 pp.

Vrooman, J. (1995), 'A general theory of professional sports leagues', *Southern Economic Journal*, **61** (4).

5. Equality of opportunity and equality of outcome: static and dynamic competitive balance in European and North American sports leagues

Stefan Szymanski and Ron Smith

1. INTRODUCTION

Sports leagues in Europe and North America have developed distinctive institutions over their long histories. From a policymaker's perspective, many of these institutions have evolved to promote a competitive balance among the teams. Moreover, without the justification of competitive balance many of these institutions might be considered to violate the antitrust laws. In North America these include the reserve clause in baseball, draft rules, restrictions on player trades and income sharing. In Europe the chief mechanism for promoting balance, through equality of opportunity, has been the promotion and relegation mechanism. Moreover, the European antitrust authorities have in recent years challenged other agreements between the leagues said to promote competitive balance, most notably in the Bosman case. This chapter evaluates the extent to which the degree of competitive balance found in the more cartelised North American leagues matches that found in the more 'competitive' European leagues.

Competitive balance is widely perceived as an essential feature of successful professional team sports. Closely contested matches, championship races in which many teams can win and whose outcome is uncertain, are widely thought to add to the attractiveness of a league competition. However, there have been relatively few studies that have set out to examine the extent to which sports leagues are in fact competitively balanced. Most studies have tended to seek out a link between fan interest in a match, (demand) and some measure of competitive balance, usually based on individual fixtures in a season, (see for example Noll (1974), Peel and Thomas

(1988), Knowles et al., (1992); Szymanski and Kuypers (1999) provides a brief survey).

Some other papers have examined the relationship between aggregate attendance at league matches and the competitive balance of that league, (for example Schmidt and Berri, 2001). For this purpose some measure of the competitive balance of a league as a whole is required. The most popular approach has been to use some indicator of the variance of outcomes, such as the standard deviation of winning percentages, (for example Scully, 1989; Noll, 1991 and Quirk and Fort, 1992). However, this is an essentially static measure and gives no weight to the identity of winners over time. Thus a league with a standard deviation of winning percentages equal to 0.10 might be considered less balanced than one with a standard deviation of 0.05, even if in the former case the identity of the top five teams changed each year and in the latter case it were always the same.

Generating a measure that might reflect dominance of a league by one or a small number of teams over time is less easy since the appropriate measure is not obvious. One approach, adopted by Buzzachi et al. (2001) is to examine the expected turnover in a perfectly balanced league in the top k ranks of a league and compare this with the actual distribution, providing a type of Gini index of inequality. The approach adopted here, however, follows Balfour and Porter (1991), Vrooman (1996) and Ross and Lucke (1997). These studies considered an autoregressive model of contest success in which winning percentages depend on club characteristics (which can be represented as fixed effects) and past performance. The standard deviation of the fixed effects can then be interpreted as the intrinsic balance of the teams, while the coefficient on the lagged dependent variable measures the speed of adjustment to the long-term trend. Moreover, the R^2 of the regression measures the inherent predictability of league performance over time.

There have been relatively few attempts to compare competitive balance across sports. Quirk and Fort (1992) compare win percent frequencies over many years and compare the distribution to the normal distribution which would be observed if all teams were equally likely to win. The excess tail frequencies are then compared across the US major leagues. However, there has been no attempt to compare competitive balance in the US majors to the European soccer leagues. The comparison is important since the anti-trust treatment of sports differs greatly in each regime, even though the importance of competitive balance is recognised in each. The US leagues operate a closed system in which membership is fixed by agreement among the owners, income is redistributed and labour market restraints are imposed with the stated purpose of promoting competitive balance. Employment terms and conditions are largely fixed by collective bargaining agreements. In Europe the top ranking soccer league in each country operates under a system of promotion and relegation where the worst performing teams at the end of each season are replaced by the best performing teams in the immediately junior league. Income redistribution is negligible, player trading is openly accepted and there is little or no collective bargaining. Such labour market restraints as existed have been successfully challenged by the European competition authority in recent years.

This chapter compares four European soccer leagues – the English Premier League and Football League, Italy's Serie A, Spain's Liga Primera and the Portuguese top division – with Major League Baseball, the National Football League and the National Hockey League in North America. Data was collected on win percentages for the last 30 years. The data shows:

(i)   The standard deviation of win percentages for European Leagues are similar to those of the North American leagues.

(ii)   There are more entrants and exitors in the European leagues than in the North American leagues, but short-term entrants fare significantly worse than the long-run survivors in Europe.

(iii)   Using a simple autoregressive model with fixed effects a greater proportion of the variation in win percent can be explained in the European leagues than in North America.

(iv)   The fixed effects are jointly significant in all leagues (implying that there is no regression to a common mean), and there is greater variation in the estimated fixed effects in Europe.

(v)   The size of the lagged dependent variable (LDV) implies convergence to the fixed effects for all leagues, but the speed of adjustment is faster in Europe, so that shocks tend to persist longer in North America than in Europe.

These results provide a mixed picture on competitive balance. While the static picture measured by the standard deviation of win percent in each year suggests a similar degree of static competitive balance across leagues, the dynamic story highlights important differences. The greater predictability and greater variance of the fixed effects in Europe suggests greater inequalities and less long-term balance in Europe. However, against this must be weighed the greater openness of the European leagues due to the institution of promotion and relegation. Over the last 30 years the North American leagues have expanded to around 30 teams in total, and while there has been entry, there has been almost no exit. However, in the European leagues there have been between 40 and 50 teams which have appeared in the top division (consisting of around 20 teams). The greater speed of adjustment may suggest that the larger pool of eligible teams in

Europe may generate more uneven contests and therefore more rapid adjustment in the face of random shocks.

The picture that seems to emerge is one in which redistribution measures in the closed North American leagues preserve greater equality among incumbents than is found in Europe, while the existence of promotion and relegation in Europe has ensured access for lesser teams and greater risk for bigger teams. In short, North American leagues create equality of outcome for the select incumbents, while European leagues display equality of opportunity without equality of outcomes.

2.   A MODEL OF COMPETITIVE BALANCE

Professional teams compete for success on the field by hiring playing talent. The market for playing talent in the major leagues is highly competitive, with many buyers and sellers and readily observable ability. In the European soccer leagues, where there is only limited interference with the free market in talent allocation and virtually no collective bargaining, this relationship is extremely powerful, as has been documented by, for example, Szymanski and Kuypers (1999). In North American leagues, where there are many mechanisms for interfering with the free market, such as player draft rules, collective bargaining, salary caps, league minimum wages, restrictions on player trades and cash sales, the relationship is much weaker, but nonetheless present. Figures 5.1 and 5.2 illustrate these points for English soccer and Major League Baseball over the period 1985–98. On each chart the horizontal axis measures the wage bill of each team, expressed as a fraction of the average of all other teams in each year, and then averaged over the sample period. The vertical axis measures win percent (in the English case as a percentage of decisive matches only). In England the raw data has an R^2 of 0.79, while for Major League Baseball the R^2 is only 0.38 (see Hall et al. (2002) for a more detailed comparison). A similar pattern emerges for revenue generation – successful teams attract higher income, through ticket sales, merchandising, TV rights and so on, and hence revenue has a strong positive correlation with league performance, and once again the correlation is weaker in North America than in Europe (Szymanski and Smith (1997) examine this relationship for English soccer). One interpretation of these relationships might be as follows:

(1)   Current expenditure on talent determines current success: $w_{it} = a + b\,E_{it}$
(2)   Current expenditure is proportional to current revenues: $E_{it} = \lambda\,R_{it}$
(3)   Current revenues depend on past success: $R_{it} = c + d\,w_{i,t-1}$

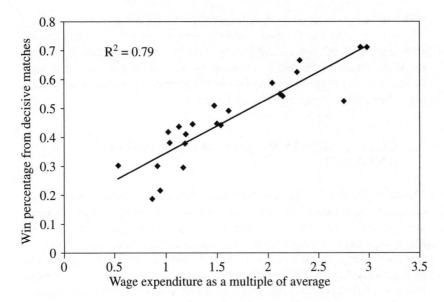

Figure 5.1   Win percentage and wage expenditure for English clubs,
1985–98

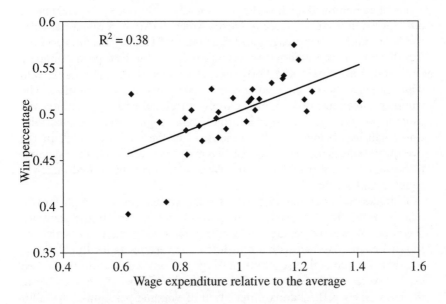

Figure 5.2   Win percentage and wage expenditure for Major League
Baseball, 1985–98

which implies a reduced form autoregressive relationship $w_{it} = \alpha + \beta\, w_{i,t-1}$ where $\alpha = a + b\lambda c$ and $\beta = b\lambda d$. Note that a model of this kind implies that static measures of competitive balance will be affected by factors such as the distribution of financial resources across the league, and that such differences may manifest themselves in the long-run persistence of success (or failure) through the estimate of the parameter β.

3. STATIC MEASURES OF COMPETITIVE BALANCE

The most popular approach to measuring competitive balance has been to compare the standard deviation of winning percentages to an idealised average constructed on the assumption that each team has an equal probability of success in each match.[1] This measure has been used not only to compare competitive balance over different periods within the same league (for example Scully, 1989; Noll, 1991) but also to compare competitive balance across leagues (Quirk and Fort, 1992; Vrooman, 1995). In the latter case these comparisons have concerned only North American leagues. In this chapter we compare North American leagues with some European soccer leagues.[2]

The data compiled for this chapter consists of 30 years of performance data for seven leagues – three in North America (Major League Baseball, the National Football League and the National Hockey League) and the top division of the national soccer leagues of four European countries (England, Italy, Spain and Portugal). The focus of the analysis is team winning percentages, since these can be compared across countries. The winning percentage of a team is closely correlated with league rank, the usual measure of performance in professional league soccer – the correlation coefficient being typically somewhere in the region of 0.95. In the European leagues the percentage of tied matches is very high: they account for around one-third of all results. We assume here that a tied match is equal to half a win.[3]

To make valid comparisons across different leagues it is important to take into account the playing schedule of each league. If the standard deviation of win percentage in a particular season were the same for Major League Baseball with a schedule of 182 games as for the National Football League with a schedule of 16 games one would not say the two leagues were equally balanced. The greater the number of games played, the more likely is the standard deviation of winning percentages to fall if all teams have an equal chance of winning. Thus it makes sense to express the actual standard deviation as a ratio of the idealised standard deviation assuming equal playing strengths. On this assumption the mean winning percentage of a team would be 0.5 and the standard deviation would be $0.5/\sqrt{m}$ where m is the number of matches in the season (see Quirk and Fort, 1992 p. 1267 for a derivation).[4] Table 5.1 was produced by calculating this ratio for each league in each year and then averaging it over the three decades considered.

Table 5.1 *Actual standard deviation of winning percentages divided by the idealised standard deviation assuming equal playing strengths, averaged for each decade*

	1970s	1980s	1990s
Italy	1.42	1.30	1.56
Spain	1.13	1.41	1.45
Portugal	1.82	1.71	1.65
England	1.95	1.96	1.88
NFL	1.57	1.44	1.48
MLB	1.84	1.63	1.65
NHL	2.54	1.94	1.82

Note: for Spain, MLB and NFL decades cover x0–y9, for Portugal and NHL decades cover x1–yO and for England and Italy decades cover x9–y8.

The lowest ratio for any league in the data is for Spain during the 1970s,[5] while the highest was registered by the National Hockey League in the same decade. However, over time the two leagues have converged so that in the 1990s the ratios were almost identical. In recent years there has been much talk in Europe about the growing inequality among teams, but there is no obvious trend in the standard deviations.

A different picture emerges when we look at standard deviations by club. In the European soccer system promotion and relegation permits new teams to enter the market, but these teams may not prove very successful. Table 5.2 divides teams into one of three groups – teams in the league for up to one decade, between one and two decades and between two and three decades. The table shows the number of teams in each category, the win percentage and standard deviation of win percentages.[6] In the North American system new entry may occur through expansion franchises, but there are few cases of exit. Thus for these leagues the table illustrates the speed with which new franchises catch up.

In the European leagues there is a clear gap between the numerous short-term entrants and the relatively small number of long-term survivors. For example, in Italy, Spain and Portugal the average win percentage of the top

Table 5.2   Standard deviations of win percentage by club over three decades

League	Clubs in the league between 2 and 10 years			Clubs in the league between 11 and 20 years			Clubs in the league between 21 and 30 years		
	Average win percent	Standard deviation of win percent	Number of teams	Average win percent	Standard deviation of win percent	Number of teams	Average win percent	Standard deviation of win percent	Number of teams
Italy	0.37	0.10	24	0.42	0.13	7	0.61	0.15	9
Spain	0.39	0.10	16	0.43	0.10	12	0.57	0.11	11
Portugal	0.36	0.08	25	0.40	0.10	10	0.62	0.11	9
England	0.41	0.11	15	0.45	0.12	14	0.55	0.12	14
NFL	0.44	0.14	7	0.51	0.19	5	0.50	0.18	25
MLB	0.46	0.05	7	–	–	0	0.50	0.06	26
NHL	0.42	0.10	5	–	–	0	0.51	0.10	22

Note: periods covered are the same as in Table 5.1.

group is about two standard deviations higher than the mean of the short-term entrants. The difference is less pronounced in England, but even there the gap is much greater than in any of the North American leagues. The gap between the long-term survivors and the rest is most pronounced in Portugal, where only three teams have won the League Championship over the sample period (Benfica, Porto and Sporting), and of these three none has finished lower than fifth.

Dividing teams into groups based on length of time inside the league already introduces a dynamic element into analysis of competitive balance. Table 5.3 takes this one stage further by illustrating the distribution of tenure by teams in the top soccer divisions of four European countries and in three of the North American major leagues. The table shows that although the North American leagues tend to be larger, they have fewer participants over time than the European leagues, reflecting the impact of promotion and relegation in Europe. While there is little exit in the sense of teams folding completely in the North American case, there is some turn-over from the point of view of the fans due to franchise relocation. For the purposes of Table 5.3 teams that relocate are treated as if they were new teams.

Table 5.3   Team participation in selected leagues over the last 30 years

League	Average league size	Number of teams participating	Average team tenure	Standard deviation of team tenure	Observations
Italy	17	43	12	10	500
Spain	19	45	13	10	564
Portugal	17	54	9	9	510
England	22	48	13	10	647
MLB	28	34	22	11	839
NFL	26	33	24	11	784
NHL	20	26	23	9	591

Averaged over 30 years the European leagues admitted more than two teams for every league place available, while in North America there were less than 1.5 teams per available slot. This higher level of team turnover is obviously the product of the promotion and relegation system in Europe. Looking at team tenure, the average European team managed to remain in the top division for just over 10 years (one-third of the period) compared to an average tenure of over 20 years in North America, where there is entry but almost no exit. The standard deviation of tenure was around 10 years in all leagues, implying a coefficient of variation in Europe that is about twice the level observed in North America.

The important policy question that arises is whether this greater variability in tenure translates into a comparable variability in playing performance within the leagues. Given the greater emphasis of the North American leagues on redistributive measures to promote competitive balance, are the effects of this offset by the variability induced by promotion and relegation?

4.   A DYNAMIC MEASURE OF COMPETITIVE BALANCE

The variance of win percentages in a given season gives some idea of the closeness of a Championship race, but it is a far from complete indicator of competitive balance. One obvious factor that reduces variance in the European system of open leagues is that teams performing poorly face relegation to a lower division, which means that teams with low league rankings seldom stop trying. In a closed league the absence of relegation can lead to indifferent end of season performance and with a reverse-order-of-finish draft system teams may even try to lose matches. Thus when comparing soccer leagues in Europe with the North American system, the annual standard deviation of win percentages is not very informative.

We want to develop and analyse the dynamic factors that may influence the evolution and level of variance of performance in a league. The basic structure we use is a simplified version of that used to analyse dispersion of per capita income in Lee et al. (1997), but the approach goes back to Galton's work on regression to the mean and has been used to analyse a variety of issues. In the context of sports leagues Balfour and Porter (1991), Vrooman (1996) and Ross and Lucke (1997) have also looked at dynamic specifications. We begin by developing the econometric theory based on the simple model described in Section 2.

The win proportion of a particular team can be thought of as having two components, one based on the ability of the team w^*_{it} and one based on chance c_{it}. Thus

$$W_{it} = w^*_{it} - c_{it}$$

The size of the chance component will depend on the nature of the game and the number of games in a season. For exposition, we will begin with the case where there are no innate advantages, and ability depends on past performance (for example this year's team contains much the same personnel as last year's) and the extent of the investment made in the team relative to the other teams, e_{it}:

$$w_{it}^* = \beta w_{i,t-1} + e_{it}$$

We assume depreciation is not complete (that is clubs do not hire a completely new team every year), so that the persistence of performance, β, is greater than zero. Thus observed performance evolves according to

$$w_{it}^* = \beta w_{i,t-1} + \varepsilon_{it} \tag{5.1}$$

where we assume that $\varepsilon_{it} = c_{it} + \varepsilon_{it}$ is independently normally distributed with constant variance $\varepsilon_{it} \sim IN(0, \sigma^2)$ and is uncorrelated with $w_{i,t-1}$. In this framework we cannot distinguish chance and investment. In the absence of chance and differential investment the long-run equilibrium is equality of win percentage ($w_{it} = 0.5$). What is crucial is not the level of investment by each club, but relative effort. Thus it is the variance of ε_{it} that is important. One could investigate whether this variance changes over time, for example with changes in the incentives clubs face, but we will assume it is constant. Then squaring (5.1), summing over N, dividing by N and assuming $N^{-1} \sum w_{i,t-1} \varepsilon_{it} = 0$, because the errors and regressors are uncorrelated, we get

$$N^{-1} \sum_{i=1}^{N} w_{it}^2 = \beta^2 \left[N^{-1} \sum_{i=1}^{N} w_{i,t-1}^2 \right] + N^{-1} \sum_{i=1}^{N} \varepsilon_{it}^2$$

Assuming the sample is large enough that we can replace $N^{-1} \sum_{i=1}^{N}$ by expected values, this gives

$$\omega_t^2 = \beta^2 \omega_{t-1}^2 + \sigma^2. \tag{5.2}$$

Since the variance ω_t^2 is bounded, we require $\beta^2 < 1$, which excludes random walks in performance. Noting that the coefficient of determination in a single cross section regression is

$$R^2 = 1 - \frac{\sigma^2}{\omega_t^2}$$

we can also write this relationship as

$$\frac{\omega_t^2}{\omega_{t-1}^2} = \frac{\beta^2}{R^2}$$

thus the evolution of the variance is determined by the balance between persistence and predictability, when there are no innate differences between clubs. The conventional wisdom and broadly the pattern of our data is that ω_t^2 is roughly constant over time. This requires $\beta^2 = R^2$, but this could be achieved in a lot of ways, such as high values of both or low values of both. The equilibrium variance is

$$\omega^2 = \frac{\sigma^2}{1 - \beta^2}$$

thus competition becomes less balanced the larger the dispersion of annual relative investment and of chance, and the greater the persistence of performance. The variance will tend upwards or downwards to this level depending on whether the initial variance was greater or less than equilibrium. Note R^2 changes as ω_t^2 changes.

If we now allow for innate differences in advantage, performance is determined by:

$$W_{it}^* = \alpha_i + \beta w_{i,t-1} + \varepsilon_{it} \tag{5.3}$$

where the α_i sum to zero across clubs. When this is estimated by least squares it decomposes win proportion into three components: a club-specific component, a component that can be predicted by past performance and a residual component that is uncorrelated with past performance. Each of these contributes to the degree of competitive balance in different ways. If we assume that the competition started a long time ago then

$$w_{it} = \frac{\alpha_i}{1 - \beta} + \sum_{j=0}^{\infty} \beta^j \varepsilon_{t-j}$$

the expected long-run win proportion for club i is $\alpha_i/(1 - \beta)$ and the benefits of past investment depreciate over time.[7] Noting that $E(\varepsilon_t^2) = \sigma^2$ and $E(\varepsilon_t \varepsilon_{t-j}) = 0 \ (j \neq 0)$, and taking expectations over time

$$E(w_{it}^2) = \left(\frac{\alpha_i}{1 - \beta}\right)^2 + \frac{\sigma^2}{1 - \beta^2}$$

then taking expectations over clubs assuming that $\alpha_i \sim N(0, \varphi^2)$ the equilibrium variance is

$$\omega^2 = \frac{\varphi^2}{(1 - \beta)^2} + \frac{\sigma^2}{1 - \beta^2}$$

thus we can decompose the factors that determine competitive balance into the contributions of (a) the dispersion of ability (φ^2), (b) the dispersion of investment and luck (σ^2) and (c) the persistence of success (β).

Higher persistence of success multiplies both dispersions and reduces competitive balance, but multiplies innate ability by more than differences in investment.

Our regressions estimates are summarised in Table 5.4. European leagues exhibited considerably higher predictability as measured by the R^2 than either the NFL or MLB. The NHL was similar in this respect to the European leagues apart from Portugal, which exhibited the greatest degree of predictability.

Table 5.4   Regression estimates

League	R^2	Coefficient of lagged dependent variable (β)	Coefficient of variation of fixed effects in the long run
Italy	0.45	0.30	0.48
Spain	0.49	0.08	0.29
Portugal	0.73	0.19	0.40
England	0.43	0.21	0.36
NFL	0.25	0.36	0.23
MLB	0.23	0.39	0.11
NHL	0.44	0.51	0.12

Note: data covers the same 30 year period used in the other tables. The estimating equation was $wpc_{it} = \alpha_i + \beta\ wpc_{it-t} + \varepsilon$. For each league the lagged dependent variable was significant at the 1 per cent level, except for Spain, where it was not significant at either the 1 per cent or 5 per cent level. The fixed effects were jointly significant at the 1 per cent level in every league except the NHL, which was jointly significant at the 5 per cent level. Long-run coefficients are given by $\alpha_i/(1 - \beta)$. For the leagues with promotion and relegation (Italy, Spain, Portugal and England) the data was restricted to teams present in both the current and previous season.

The lagged dependent variable was noticeably larger for the North American leagues, suggesting relatively sluggish adjustment toward the long-run mean. This implies that random shocks will persist longer – perhaps because limited contractual freedom experienced by players in North America makes its harder to turn a losing team into a winning team by buying talent, and that once a winning team is assembled, it only breaks up once the players approach the end of their careers.[8] From the discussion of the previous section, a high value of the lagged dependent variable is consistent with a high degree of persistence in player investment which can in turn enable dynasties to persist over time.[9]

The final measure of competitive balance is presented in column 3 of Table 5.4. The coefficient of variation of the fixed effects indicates a much greater long-term imbalance in the European leagues compared to the US. In particular it appears that Major League Baseball and the National Hockey League display less variability in the fixed effects than the NFL which is often considered one of the most balanced leagues. However, it may be that in the NFL teams have a greater tendency to long-term stability while in baseball and hockey there have been fewer consistently successful teams over 30 years. The estimates for the European leagues are consistent with the observation that over the last 30 years there have been a small number of well-known teams that have dominated competition.

5.   DISCUSSION AND CONCLUSIONS

Measured simply by the standard deviation of win percentage in each league season there appear to be few differences in competitive balance between Europe and North America. By analysing the data differently this chapter has demonstrated that while more teams have access to the highest level of competition through the system of promotion and relegation, there appears to be less dynamic competitive balance in Europe. This is consistent with the observation that there are more of league rules promoting competitive balance in North America.

The chapter has also shown that the lower degree of dynamic competitive balance is generally consistent with an underlying model of playing success in which the impact of player investment persists over time. However, the larger estimated coefficient on the lagged dependent variable of win percentages for the North American leagues works in the opposite direction. It may be that redistributive measures in North American sports promote equality of access to talent, but that once a particular club obtains the services of the most highly talented athletes, restrictions in the labour market enable them to retain their services and therefore the team's performance level over a longer period of time.

The fundamental difference between the two league systems on either side of the Atlantic is best described as the distinction between equality of opportunity and equality of outcomes. In the North American leagues relatively few have access, but those that do have a fair chance of competing at the highest level. In Europe, by contrast, while entry is open to all, access to the ruling elite remains beyond the grasp of all but a small minority.

NOTES

1. Other static measures include the Gini coefficient (Quirk and Fort, 1992), relative entropy (Horowitz, 1997) and the Hirschman–Herfindahl index (Depken, 1999)
2. A similar exercise is to be found in Kipker (2000).
3. The issue is this: if we take only the percentage of matches won, strong teams look less successful than they really are. If we consider only the percentage wins over decisive matches (that is those not drawn) we artificially reduce the length of the season and so we should reduce the idealised standard deviation according to the sum of decisive matches in each season. Treating draws as half a win is thus much simpler and more consistent.
4. Note that if each team had an identical probability of winning its home games higher than 50 per cent and played the same number of home and away matches, then the standard deviation of team average winning percentages would be zero even though the standard deviation of match winning percentages would be positive.
5. In 1975 the Spanish Championship was won by some margin by Real Madrid, while Real Murcia finished some way adrift at the bottom of the table. However, the gap between the remaining teams was so small that the gap between the second placed team and the second-to-last was equal to four wins. Given that each team plays every other team home and away, the gap is no more than a win in each of these games.
6. Teams with only one year in the league are excluded: in Italy there were three teams with an average win percentage of 0.25, six in Spain with an average of 0.28, ten in Portugal with an average of 0.28, five in England with an average of 0.25, two in the NFL with an average of 0.48 and none in MLB or the NHL.
7. Strictly speaking, this equation, and what follows, requires that all teams have been continually present in the league. If we are dealing with leagues based around promotion and relegation we must either take the truncation into account when looking at win percentages in a particular division or use a different measure of performance such as league rank (see for example Szymanski and Smith, 1997) since win percentages across divisions are not comparable.
8. Vrooman (1996) finds that the coefficient of the LDV in baseball has fallen considerably since the introduction of free agency.
9. The data for the European leagues is in fact censored, since teams that are relegated do not disappear, but compete at a lower level of competition where they also achieve some level of performance. To consider the implication of this for the estimates a regression was run for the 99 teams appearing in the four English professional divisions over the 30-year period. In this case the dependent variable was league rank (where the top position in the league immediately below the top division was measured as $n + 1$, where n is the number of teams in the top division, and so on) since win percentages are not comparable across divisions. The estimate on the lagged dependent variable for the truncated sample was 0.22, while the estimate for the full sample was 0.68. This suggests that there is much more sluggishness in the adjustment process when the interlocking hierarchy of leagues is considered as a whole.

REFERENCES

Balfour, A. and P. Porter (1991), 'The Reserve Clause in professional sports: legality and effect on competitive balance', *Labor Law Journal*, **42**, 8–18.

Buzzachi, L., S. Szymanski and T. Valletti (2001), 'Static versus Dynamic Competitive Balance: Do teams win more in Europe or in the US?', Imperial College Management School Discussion paper.

Depken, C. (1999), 'Free-agency and the competitiveness of Major League Baseball', *Review of Industrial Organization*, **14**, 205–17.

Hall, S., S. Szymanski and A. Zimbalist (2002), 'Testing causality between team performance and payroll: the cases of Major League Baseball and English soccer', *Journal of Sports Economics*, **3** (2), 149–68.

Horowitz, I. (1997), 'The increasing competitive balance in Major League Baseball', *Review of Industrial Organization*, **12**, 373–87.

Kipker, I. (2000), 'Determinanten der Zuschauernachfrage im professionellen Teamsport: Wie wichtig ist die sportliche Ausgeglichenheit?' Unpublished chapter of PhD dissertation.

Knowles, G., K. Sherony and M. Haupert (1992), 'The demand for major league baseball: a test of the uncertainty of outcome hypothesis', *The American Economist*, **36**, 72–80.

Lee, K., M. Pesaran and R. Smith (1997), 'Growth and convergence in multi-country empirical stochastic Solow model', *Journal of Applied Econometrics*, **12** (4), 357–92.

Noll, R. (1974), 'Attendance and price setting', in R. Noll (ed.), *Government and the Sports Business*, Washington, DC: Brookings Institute.

Noll, R. (1991), 'Professional Basketball: Economic and business perspectives', in P. Staudohar and J. Mangan (eds), *The Business of Professional Sports*, Urbana: University of Illinois.

Peel, David and Dennis Thomas (1988), 'Outcome uncertainty and the demand for football', *Scottish Journal of Political Economy*, **35**, 242–9.

Quirk, J, and R. Fort (1992), *Pay Dirt: The Business of Professional Team Sports*, Princeton, NJ: Princeton University Press.

Ross, S. and R. Lucke (1997), 'Why highly paid athletes deserve more antitrust protection than unionized factory workers', *Antitrust Bulletin*, **42** (3), 641–79.

Schmidt, M. and D. Berri (2001), 'Competitive Balance and Attendance: the Case of Major League Baseball', *Journal of Sports Economics*, **2** (2), 145–67.

Scully, G. (1989), *The Business of Major League Baseball*, Chicago: University of Chicago Press.

Szymanski, S. and T. Kuypers (1999), *Winners and Losers: The Business Strategy of Football*, Penguin Books.

Szymanski, S. and R. Smith (1997), 'The English football industry: profit, performance and industrial structure', *International Review of Applied Economics*, **11** (1), 135–53.

Vrooman, J. (1995), 'A general theory of professional sports leagues', *Southern Economic Journal*, **61** (4), 971–90.

Vrooman, J. (1996), 'The baseball players market reconsidered', *Southern Economic Journal*, **62** (3), 339–60.

PART 3

Cost–Benefit Analysis and Sports

6. Bidding for the Olympics: fool's gold?

Robert A. Baade and Victor Matheson

INTRODUCTION

Governments have spent billions to accommodate the Olympic Games in recent times. While the motivations for hosting the Games are complex, those who seek public funding for them use the promise of substantial economic returns to justify public subsidies. Do the Olympic Games represent an extraordinary economic opportunity for nations and cities worthy of significant taxpayer support? The purpose of this chapter is to assess the economic impact of the Olympics and the wisdom of the use of public funds to support them. Particular attention is focused on the Summer Olympic Games in Los Angeles in 1984 and Atlanta in 1996. The evidence gleaned from the experiences of these two cities indicates that the economic impact was more modest than that projected by those promoting the event in those cities.

Economic theory casts doubt on a substantial windfall for the host city from the Olympic Games. Cities competing with one another for the Games would theoretically bid until their expected return reached zero. In theory the International Olympic Committee (IOC), the monopolist supplying the Games, would appropriate any economic rents from the Games directly through bribes from the suitors and indirectly through mandating that potential hosts assume all costs incurred relating to the event. Two things could prevent this from happening. First, the monopoly power of the IOC could be countered if there existed only a single suitor for the Games. In fact, Los Angeles was the sole city bidding for the 1984 Summer Olympic Games.[1] Second, the weight of public opinion could be sufficiently strong to convince the IOC to share the event's monopoly rents. Recent criticisms directed at the IOC have resulted in reforms designed to thwart the acceptance of under-the-table payments to IOC members. These illegal payments, however, represent a small portion of the financial demands the IOC imposes on the host communities. IOC Rule 4, which requires the host city to assume financial liability for the Games, constitutes the most significant financial responsibility. Despite the existence of the IOC monopoly, cities continue to compete for the Games. The sheer size and scope of the Olympics may well blind the suitors for the Games to the substantial financial risks.

The Olympic Games epitomize the concept of a 'mega-event' to borrow a phrase from the literature devoted to economic impact. The word mega conjures up images of vast numbers of alien spendthrifts descending on the lucky host city. The impression of a substantial inflow of money created by the crowds and the excitement at Olympic venues is hard to dispute, but does a sober appraisal of the change in economic activity after the event support those first impressions? Few after-the-fact audits are performed because studies of this sort provide little benefit to cities that have hosted such events. Potential host cities, however, may well derive utility from economic post-mortems. In particular, cities contemplating Olympian expenditures would undoubtedly find useful a dispassionate appraisal of economic benefits to assist them in formulating a representative bid.

The first section of this chapter reviews the literature as it relates to an assessment of the impact of mega-events. In the next section, the strengths and shortcomings of the theory and techniques used by those who advocate using public funds to host the Games are examined. In the subsequent section of the chapter, we discuss the after-the-event model that we propose to estimate the impact. Actual estimates are presented in the chapter's next section. Conclusions and policy implications are articulated in the final section of the study.

REVIEW OF THE LITERATURE

The Olympics qualify as a 'mega-event' in contemporary phraseology. To justify on theoretical grounds public subsidies for mega-event infrastructure, such investments must exhibit substantial externalities or be construed as 'public goods'. Boosters offer staggering claims regarding the amount of economic activity a mega-event can generate. For example, in bidding for the Olympic Games in 2012, the chairman of Dallas 2012 conservatively estimated a $4 billion impact and observed:

> How much is $4 billion? It's very close to the 1998 net income for Metroplex giants J.C. Penney Co. Inc., EDS Corp., Kimberly-Clark Corp., Texas Instruments Inc., Halliburton Co. And Texas Utilities Co. – combined.
> That $4 billion will benefit most every business in the Metroplex – from hotels to restaurants, from real estate to transportation, from communications to health care.

Beyond that, Dallas 2012 says landing the Olympic bid would give the city a specific reason to improve local infrastructure: Streets, freeways, the DART rail, even the Cotton Bowl and Fair Park. (Cawley, 1999)

Dallas 2012's optimism runs counter to some mega-event experiences elsewhere in the world. In assessing some of these event experiences Mary-Kate Tews observed:

> Throughout the 1980s, World's Fairs and Olympic organizers turned to the mega-event as a panacea, a solution to the myriad of problems caused by economic hard times. Instead of solving such problems, however, they often found themselves involved in very high-stakes, high-risk enterprises that had devastating after-effects. Such was the case in New Orleans, where researchers posed serious questions about the efficacy of the mega-event as a means of achieving economic development goals after Expo '84 declared bankruptcy. (Tews, 1993, p.3).

Philip Porter offered a similarly negative assessment of the impact that 'Super Bowls', the distinctly American mega-event, have on their host communities. After reviewing short-term data[2] on sales receipts for several American football championship games, Porter concluded:

> Investigator bias, data measurement error, changing production relationships, diminishing returns to both scale and variable inputs, and capacity constraints anywhere along the chain of sales relations lead to lower multipliers. Crowding out and price increases by input suppliers in response to higher levels of demand and the tendency of suppliers to lower prices to stimulate sales when demand is weak lead to overestimates of net new sales due to the event. These characteristics alone would suggest that the estimated impact of the mega-sporting event will be lower than impact analysis predicts. When there are perfect complements to the event, like hotel rooms for visitors, with capacity constraints or whose suppliers raise prices in the face of increased demand, impacts are reduced to zero. (Porter, 1999)

The widespread disagreement on the economic impact of mega-events offered in bidding for the events and appraising their contributions after the fact begs for a resolution. Have the Olympic experiences in Los Angeles in 1984 and Atlanta in 1996 been good investments for those cities, and do they suggest that properly run mega-events in economies with some slack can match the optimistic claims of event boosters? Reconciling the rosy claims offered to secure the public funding necessary to host the event and the dreary assessments of some events after the fact is essential to insuring future reasonable appraisals of mega-event economic impact. Such reconciliation requires first an assessment of the underlying theoretical issues.

THEORETICAL ISSUES

Miscalculations regarding the economic effects of hosting the Olympics are most likely, arguably, to occur in assessing the economic benefits from hosting the games and the opportunity costs involved in doing so. With regard to opportunity cost, even if a sports project does generate positive net benefits, public funds should be invested only if the net benefits exceed those from an alternative use of the funds (Kesenne, 1999). The analysis performed in this study, therefore, has been developed with an eye toward ensuring that the benefits are not exaggerated and the opportunity costs have not been ignored. Consider first the issues relating to benefit hyperbole.

There are standard techniques for estimating economic impact that have evolved over time, but in general represent an application of standard macroeconomic theory. Technically speaking, an expenditure or incomes approach could be used to estimate the economic impact. The expenditure approach requires as a first step estimates of direct expenditures attributable to the event or project. These first-round, or direct expenditure changes are then used to estimate indirect expenditures through the use of a 'multiplier'. Briefly, multipliers are thought to exist because one person's spending becomes income for others who in turn spend a portion of that new income creating income for still others, and so on. The indirect spending converges to some amount because only a fraction of any income increment received as a consequence of someone's spending is spent again. In other words, some of the money leaks from this system through savings, taxation, or money spent outside the host economy (imports). Using this technique, if a mistake is made in estimating direct expenditures, those errors are compounded in estimating indirect expenditures. The secret to generating credible economic impact estimates using the expenditure approach is to estimate precisely direct expenditures.

A precise measure of changes in direct expenditures is fraught with difficulties. The most prominent among them relates to accurately assessing the extent to which spending in conjunction with the event or project would have occurred in the absence of the event. For example, if an estimate was sought on the impact of professional sport on a local economy, consideration would have to be given to the fact that spending on sports may well merely substitute for spending that would occur on something else in the absence of professional sport. Therefore, if the fans are primarily indigenous to the community, sport may not provide much impact because its availability in a community may serve primarily to reallocate leisure spending while leaving spending overall fundamentally intact. This distinction between gross and net spending has been cited by economists as a chief reason why professional sports does not seem to contribute as much to metropolitan economies as boosters claim (Baade, 1996). One of the attributes of a mega-event is that gross and net spending changes induced by the event are more likely to converge. This is so because spending at a mega-event is more likely to be categorized as export spending since most of it is thought to be undertaken by people from outside the community. Skilled researchers will often eliminate the spending undertaken by local residents at a mega-event because it is likely to be inconsequential relative to that consumption which is undertaken by those foreign to the host community (Humphreys and Plummer, 1995).

Eliminating the spending by residents of the community would at first blush appear to eliminate a potentially significant source of bias in estimating direct expenditures. Surveys on expenditures by those attending the event, complete with a question on place of residence, would appear to be a straightforward way of estimating direct expenditures in a manner that is statistically acceptable. However, while surveys may well provide insight on spending behaviour for those patronizing the event, such a technique offers no data on changes in spending by residents not attending the event. It is conceivable that some residents may dramatically change their spending during the event's play given their desire to avoid the congestion at least in the venue(s) environs. In general, a fundamental shortcoming of economic impact studies is not with information on spending for those who are included in a direct expenditure survey, but rather with the lack of information on the spending behaviour for those who are not.

A second potentially significant source of bias in economic impact studies relates to leakages from the circular flow of spending. For example, if the host economy is at or very near full employment, it may be that the labour essential to conducting the event resides in other communities where there is a labour surplus or unemployment.[3] To the extent that this is true, then the indirect spending that constitutes the 'multiplier effect' must be adjusted to reflect this leakage of income and subsequent spending.

Labour is not the only factor of production that may repatriate income. If hotels experience higher than normal occupancy rates during a mega-event, then the question must be raised about the fraction of increased earnings that remain in the community if the hotel is a nationally owned chain.[4] In short, to assess the impact of mega-events, a balance of payments approach should be utilized. That is to say, to what extent does the event give rise to dollar inflows and outflows that would not occur in its absence. Since the input–output models used in the most sophisticated *ex ante* analyses are based on fixed relationships between inputs and outputs, such models do not account for the subtleties of full employment and capital ownership noted here. As a consequence, it is not clear if economic impact estimates based on them are biased up or down.

The potential shortcomings for calculating the multiplier values described above applies to the uncustomized versions of the most recent US Department of Commerce's Regional Input–Output System (RIMS II) which is a popular tool used by forecasters. Even when the models used to forecast are customized, the possibility remains that essential pieces of information are ignored and the forecast may miss the mark as a consequence. The models constructed by Regional Economic Models, Inc. (REMI) to their credit specify an endogenous labour sector which gives more accurate readings on the employment and wage implications of an 'event', but the accuracy of the REMI projection depends on the quality of the model that predicts the future of the regional economy in the absence of an event (control forecast) and the economy's future if the event occurs (alternative forecast). The event's impact is estimated as the difference between the control and alternative forecasts. An *ex post* analysis differs from the REMI approach in that it looks at the economic landscape of a locality or a region before and after an event, and attributes the difference in important economic indicators to the event. The key to the success of this approach is to isolate the event from other changes that may be occurring simultaneously and that may exert a significant impact on the local economy.

As an alternative to estimating the change in expenditures and associated changes in economic activity, those who provide goods and services directly in accommodating the event could be asked how their activity has been altered by the event. In summarizing the efficacy of this technique Davidson opined:

> The biggest problem with this producer approach is that these business managers must be able to estimate how much 'extra' spending was caused by the sport event. This requires that each proprietor have a model of what would have happened during that time period had the sport event not taken place. This is an extreme requirement which severely limits this technique. (Davidson, 1999)

An expenditure approach to projecting the economic impact of mega-events is likely to yield the most accurate estimates. Do the estimates on the economic impact of the Olympic Games hosted by Los Angeles in 1984 and Atlanta in 1996 conform to *ex ante* estimates of the economic impact these mega-events have on their host cities? In the next section of the chapter, the model that is used to develop after-the-fact estimates is detailed.

THE MODEL

As noted above, to provide credible estimates on the economic impact of a mega-event, an *ex post* model must account for the impact of other changes in an economy that occur in concert with the event. Since a mega-event's impact is likely to be small relative to the overall economy, isolating the event's impact is not a trivial task. On the other hand, there is evidence to suggest that estimates of direct and indirect expenditures that are induced by sports and mega-events are exaggerated in prospective studies. This is so in part because estimating net spending changes as a consequence of an event requires information not only on how people attending the event consume, but how residents of the city not attending the event alter their consumption as well. More generally speaking, there are details with respect to dollar inflows and outflows as a consequence of an event that cannot be easily or fully anticipated. Furthermore, *ex ante* studies in general ignore opportunity costs. The model that we have constructed has been inspired by a recognition of the challenges and deficiencies common to both *ex ante* and *ex post* analyses.

In constructing a model to estimate the impact an event has had on a city, several approaches are possible and suggested by past scholarly work. Previous models used to explain metropolitan economic growth have been summarized by Mills (1992). They identified five theories: export base, neo-classical growth, product cycle, cumulative causation, and disequilibrium dynamic adjustment. All these theories seek to explain growth through changes in key economic variables in the short run (export base and neo-classical) or the identification of long-term developments that affect metropolitan economies in hypothetical ways (product cycle, cumulative causation, and disequilibrium dynamic adjustment). Our task is not to replicate explanations of metropolitan economic growth, but to use past work to help identify how much growth in metropolitan employment is attributable to the Summer Olympic Games. To this end we have selected explanatory variables from past models to help establish what employment would have been in the absence of the Olympics. We then compare that estimate to actual employment levels to estimate the contribution of the Games. The success of this approach depends on our ability to identify those variables that explain the majority of observed variation in growth in employment in those cities that have hosted the Summer Olympic Games.

To isolate the mega-event's impact, both external and internal factors need to be considered. External factors might include, for example, a relocation of people and economic activity from the 'rust/frost belt' to the 'sun belt', changes in the disposition of the federal government toward revenue sharing, and changes in the demographic character of urban America. Internal factors might include a change in the attitude of local politicians toward fiscal intervention, a natural disaster, or unusual demographic changes. One technique would be to carefully review the history of cities in general and particular and incorporate each potentially significant change into a model. An alternative is to represent a statistic for a city for a particular year as a deviation from the average value for that statistic for cohort cities for that year. Such a representation over time will in effect 'factor out' general urban trends and developments. For example, if we identify a particular city's growth in employment as 10 per cent over time, but cities in general are growing by 5 per cent, then we would conclude that this city's pattern deviates from the norm by 5 per cent. It is the 5 per cent deviation that requires explanation and not the whole 10 per cent for our purposes in this study.[5]

In modelling those factors that are unique to individual cities, it is helpful to identify some conceptual deficiencies characterizing the demand side of *ex ante* and *ex post* models that exaggerated economic impact estimates. Many prospective economic impact studies, particularly those that are older, fail to make a distinction between gross and net spending changes that occur as a consequence of hosting a mega-event. In *ex post* studies failure to factor out the city's own secular growth path could embellish an estimate of the contribution of the Olympic Games. *Ex ante* studies even in very sophisticated forms are based usually on the premise that important economic relationships remain unchanged. It is, after all, historical experiences that define the statistics upon which prospective impact estimates are based. However, if the event is significant in a statistical sense, will not the event modify historical experience? We cannot claim a significant impact, and at the same time claim that history will be unaltered. Our model, therefore, in various ways 'factors out' the city's historical experience. To continue with our example from above, if history tells us that a city that experiences a growth in employment that is 5 per cent above the national average, before and after a mega-event, then it would be misguided to attribute that additional 5 per cent to the mega-event. If, after the event, the city continued to exhibit employment increases 5 per cent above the national norm, the logical conclusion is that the mega-event simply supplanted other economic developments that contributed to the city's above-average rate of growth. It will be particularly interesting to see if rates of employment growth forecast for Los Angeles and Atlanta approximate what an *ex post* model not adjusted for a city's secular growth path would conclude.

The alternative to the technique outlined to this point, would be to carefully review the history of cities in general and particular, and explicitly incorporate each potentially significant change into the model. This technique has practical limitations to which past studies attest. Economists who have sought to explain growth using this technique have followed traditional prescriptions, and have developed demand- or supply-centred models through which to explain growth.[6] Some scholars have combined both demand and supply arguments.[7] Both supply and demand models have strong theoretical underpinnings. Those who utilize a demand approach with some version of employment as the independent variable base their theory on the notion that the demand for labour is ultimately derived from the demand for goods and services. Those who favour a supply approach would argue that cost factors are the most critical in explaining employment in a metropolitan statistical area (MSA) or region.

Given the number and variety of variables found in regional growth models and the inconsistency of findings with regard to coefficient size and significance, criticisms of any single model could logically focus on the problems posed by omitted variables. Any critic, of course, can claim that a particular regression suffers from omitted-variable bias, it is far more challenging to address the problems posed by not including key variables in the analysis. In explaining regional or metropolitan growth patterns, at least some of the omitted variable problem can be addressed through a careful specification of the dependent variable. As noted above, representing relevant variables as deviations from city norms leaves the scholar a more manageable task, namely that of identifying those factors that explain city growth after accounting for the impact of those forces that generally have affected regional or MSA growth. For example, a variable is not needed to represent the implications of federal revenue sharing, if such a change affected cities in ways proportionate to changes in demographic characteristics, for example population, used to calibrate the size of the revenue change for any particular city. Of course instead of representing the MSA dependent variable as a deviation from a national mean and its own secular growth path, a national mean and the MSA's growth path can be represented as independent variables. In fact, we chose to represent the mean rate of employment growth for MSAs and the city's growth path for employment for the previous three years as independent variables.

Following the same logic, independent variables should also be normalized, that is represented as a deviation from an average value for MSAs or as a fraction of the MSA average. It is important, for example, to model the fact that relocating a business could occur as a consequence of wages increasing in the MSA under study or a slower rate of wage growth in other MSAs. What matters is not the absolute level of wages in city I, but city I's wage relative to that of its competitors. What we propose, therefore, is an equation for explaining metropolitan employment growth which incorporates those variables that the literature identifies as important, but specified in such a way that those factors common to MSAs are implicitly included.

The purpose of *ex ante* studies is to provide a measure of the net benefits a project or event is likely to yield. To our knowledge there is no prospective model that has the capacity for measuring the net benefits of a project relative to the next best alternative use of those funds. If we assume that the best use of funds has always occurred prior to a mega-event, then the growth path observed for a city can be construed as optimal. If this 'optimal growth path', identified by the city's secular growth trend, decreases after the mega-event occurs, then the evidence does not support the hypothesis that a publicly subsidized mega-event put those public monies to the best use. A negative or even insignificant coefficient for the Olympics variable is *prima facie* evidence that the mega-event is less than optimal.

Our particular focus in this study is to assess changes in employment in Los Angeles and Atlanta that were attributable to their hosting of the Summer Olympic Games in 1984 and 1996, respectively. Equation (6.1) represents the model used to predict changes in employment.

$$\partial N_t^i = \beta_0 + \beta_1 \sum_{i=1}^{n} \frac{\partial N_t^i}{n_t} + \beta_2 \, \partial N_{t-1}^i + \beta_3 \, \partial N_{t-2}^i + \beta_4 \, \partial N_{t-3}^i + \beta_5 \, Pop_t^i + \beta_6 y_t^i +$$

$$\beta_7 W_t^i + \beta_8 T_t^i + \beta_5 OB_t^i + \beta_5 REG_t^i + \beta_5 SOG_t^i + \beta_5 MSA_t^i + \beta_5 TR_t^i + \varepsilon$$

Where for each time period t,

∂N_t^i	=	% change in employment in the ith metropolitan statistical area (MSA),
n_t	=	number of cities in the sample,
Pop_t^i	=	log of the population of the ith MSA,
y_t^i	=	real per capita personal income in the ith MSA as a percentage of the average for all cities in the sample,
W_t^i	=	nominal wages in the ith MSA as a percentage of the average for all cities in the sample,
T_t^i	=	state and local taxes in the ith MSA as a percentage of the average for all cities in the sample,
OB_t^i	=	a dummy variable for oil boom and bust cycles for selected cities and years,
REG_t^i	=	dummy variables for eight geographical regions within the United States,
SOG_t^i	=	dummy variable for the Summer Olympic Games,
MSA_t^i	=	dummy variable for ith MSA,
TR_t^i	=	annual trend,
–	=	stochastic error.

For the purposes of our analysis the variables are specified as percentage changes unless otherwise indicated, and the functional form is linear in all the variables included in equation (6.1). As mentioned previously, rather than specifying all the variables that may explain metropolitan growth, we attempted to simplify the task by including independent variables that are common to cities in general and the ith MSA in particular. In effect we have devised a structure that attempts to identify the extent to which the deviations from the growth path of cities in general ($\_\partial N_t^i/n_t$) and city I's secular growth path ($\partial N_{t-1}^i, \partial N_{t-2}^i$, and ∂N_{t-3}^i)[8] are attributable to deviations in certain costs of production (wages and taxes), demand-related factors (population, real per capita personal income), dummy variables for the oil boom/bust cycle and the region in which the MSA is located, and the presence of the Summer Olympic Games. If the Olympic Games dummy variable emerges as significant, then we intended to use the value of the coefficient to estimate the employment effect of the Games directly. Since the coefficient did not emerge as significant,[9] equation (6.1) was used to predict the growth path for employment, and this predicted value was compared to the actual growth in employment to formulate a conclusion with regard to the effect the Games had on employment in Los Angeles in 1984 and Atlanta in 1996. Of course, the credibility of this procedure depends on a robust equation for predicting employment growth.

Relative values of population, real per capita personal income, wages, and tax burdens are all expected to help explain a city's growth rate in employment as it deviates from the national norm and its own secular growth path. As mentioned above, past research has not produced consistency with respect to the signs and significance of these independent variables. Some of the inconsistency can be attributable to an inability to separate cause and effect. For example, we would expect higher relative wages over time to reduce the rate at which employment is growing in an MSA relative to other cities. That would be true, *ceteris paribus*, if wages determined employment. If, however, high rates of employment increased an MSA's wage relative to that of other cities, it may be that the opposite sign emerges. We do not have as a consequence *a priori* expectations with regard to the signs of the coefficients. That should not be construed as an absence of theory about key economic relationships. As noted earlier, we included those variables that previous scholarly work found important.

Fifty-seven cities constituted our sample, representing all MSAs that were among the 50 largest by population in the United States in either 1969 or 1997. The cities and years for which we had data are identified in the appendix to this report. A bibliography of data sources appears in the general bibliography which follows the conclusions and policy implications.

Cost–benefit analysis and sports

RESULTS

The results from the regressions run for equation (6.1) with Atlanta and Los Angeles included are recorded in Tables 6.1 and 6.2, respectively. The t-statistics are represented in the parentheses following the coefficient estimates.

Table 6.1   Regression results for pooled MSA data with Atlanta included

Statistic/Value[a]	Coefficient values and (t-statistics)
b_0 (constant)	$-0.436\ (-3.91)^c$
$b_1\ (\partial N_t^{ij}\_\partial N_t^{ij}/n_t)$	$0.883\ (32.78)^c$
$b_2\ (\partial N_t^{ij}/\partial N_{t-1}^i)$	$0.379\ (17.64)^c$
$b_3\ (\partial N_t^{ij}/\partial N_{t-2}^i)$	$-0.113\ (-4.84)^c$
$b_4\ (\partial N_t^{ij}/\partial N_{t-3}^i)$	$0.127\ (6.77)^c$
$b_5\ (\partial N_t^{ij}/Pop_t^i)$	$-0.0089\ (-5.27)^c$
$b_6\ (\partial N_t^{ij}/y_t^i)$	$0.000736\ (0.21)$
$b_7\ (\partial N_t^{ij}/W_t^i)$	$-0.0084\ (-2.17)^d$
$b_8\ (\partial N_t^{ij}/T_t^i)$	$0.0054\ (1.58)$
$b_9\ (\partial N_t^{ij}/OB_t^i)$	$0.0183\ (8.27)^c$
$b_{10}\ (\partial N_t^{ij}/REG_t^i)^a$	$-0.006\ (-3.69)^c$
$b_{11}\ (\partial N_t^{ij}/SOG_t^i)$	n.a.
$b_{12}\ (\partial N_t^{ij}/Atlanta)$	$0.0075\ (2.38)^c$
$b_{13}\ (\partial N_t^{ij}/TR_t^i)$	$0.00025\ (4.417)^c$
R^2	0.707
Adjusted R^2	0.703
F-statistic	184.92^c
Durbin-Watson	$1\ .83^b$

Notes:
[a] $k-1$ of the regions identified for the United States by the Department of Commerce were represented by a dummy variable. Those regions include: New England, Mideast, Great Lakes, Plains, Southeast, Southwest, and Rocky Mountain. The West region served as the residual. Therefore, each of the regional coefficients identifies the extent to which the particular regional growth in employment differs from the West region. Values for other regional coefficients were calculated and used to estimate employment growth. Atlanta is located in the Southeast region, and only the value for that coefficient for that regional dummy was recorded in this table. Since our sample included eight other MSAs in the Southeast region, the coefficient recorded for the dummy variable for Atlanta identifies how it is that Atlanta's growth in employment varies from that of other MSAs in the Southeast region. Given the presence of other cities in the Southeast region in the sample, the dummy variables for the Southeast region and Atlanta are not identical.
[b] Inconclusive region.
[c] Result was significant at the 99 per cent level.
[d] Result was significant at the 95 per cent level.

Table 6.2   Regression results for pooled MSA data with Los Angeles included

Statistic/Value[a]	Coefficient values and (t-statistics)
b_0 (constant)	-0.422 (-3.78)*
b_1 $(\partial N_t^{ij}\_\partial N_t^{ij}/n_t)$	0.88 (32.79)*
b_2 $(\partial N_t^{ij}/\partial N_{t-1}^i)$	0.379 (17.63)*
b_3 $(\partial N_t^{ij}/\partial N_{t-2}^i)$	-0.112 (-4.84)*
b_4 $(\partial N_t^{ij}/\partial N_{t-3}^i)$	0.127 (6.74)*
b_5 $(\partial N_t^{ij}/Pop_t^i)$	-0.0065 (-3.62)*
b_6 $(\partial N_t^{ij}/y_t^i)$	-0.0006 (-0.18)
b_7 $(\partial N_t^{ij}/W_t^i)$	-0.009 (-2.3)**
b_8 $(\partial N_t^{ij}/T_t^i)$	0.0048 (1.41)
b_9 $(\partial N_t^{ij}/OB_t^i)$	0.0184 (8.29)*
b_{10} $(\partial N_t^{ij}/REG_t^i)^a$	-0.003 (-1.34)*
b_{11} $(\partial N_t^{ij}/SOG_t^i)$	n.a.
b_{12} $(\partial N_t^{ij}/\text{Los Angeles})$	-0.00879 (-2.62)*
b_{13} $(\partial N_t^{ij}/TR_t^i)$	0.00025 (4.417)*
R^2	0.707
Adjusted R^2	0.703
F-statistic	185.13*
Durbin-Watson	1.809^b

Notes:
[a] See the corresponding note for Table 6.1. The regional coeffcient recorded in this table is for the Rocky Mountain region, and it estimates the extent to which growth in the Rocky Mountain region differs from that in the West region. Once again the West region was used as the numeraire.
[b] Inconclusive region.

The F-statistic indicates that the equation for both Atlanta and Los Angeles was significant at the 1 per cent level, indicating that the model is robust. The adjusted correlation coefficients indicate that equation (6.1) 'explains' approximately 70 per cent of the variation in employment growth rates. The population and wage variables were significant at the 95 per cent level or better while the real per capita income and tax variables were not statistically significant. The signs of the population and wage variables are reasonable. That is, it is not unreasonable to expect that large cities would exhibit slower rates of employment growth than smaller cities, and cities for which money wages are high could be expected to exhibit slower rates of employment growth.

The estimated coefficients for the Summer Olympic Games variable did not emerge as statistically significant in either Los Angeles or Atlanta, and as a result the impact of the Summer Olympic Games could not be directly estimated using the value of the coefficient for the dummy variable representing the Games. The technique used to estimate employment gains attributable to the Summer Olympic Games involved estimating the employment growth path using equation (6.1) and comparing the predicted values in employment growth to the actual gains in employment. The difference between the predicted and actual employment figures represented an estimate of the employment gains induced by the Summer Olympic Games in Atlanta and Los Angeles. In the case of Atlanta, this estimate is likely to be generous since not all the employment gains can be attributed to the Olympics in a city that grew faster on average than cities in the region and the country. Using this technique, the estimates on employment gains for Atlanta and Los Angeles are represented in Tables 6.3 and 6.4, respectively.

Table 6.3   Employment gains for Atlanta attributable to the 1996 Summer Olympic Games

Model[a]	Employment Gains (Losses)
Model 1	3 467
Model 2	21 767
Model 3	42 448

Note:
[a] The models are distinguished according to the manner in which the growth path for employment was specified. In particular the growth path for employment could be calculated to include 1994 and 1995 observed growth in employment. Since it is likely that employment growth in 1994 and 1995 did reflect elevated expenditure levels as a consequence of investments in infrastructure by the Atlanta Committee for the Olympic Games (ACOG), the 1996 estimate for employment growth was less likely to show a substantial increase in job growth above the high levels that characterized 1994 and 1995. Since it is unclear when the infrastructure investments and other direct expenditures in conjunction with the Olympics occurred and exerted an impact on the Atlanta economy, we have specified three models. Model 1 assumes that most of the direct, indirect, and induced expenditures occurred in 1996. Model 2 estimates job growth using a growth path for employment that includes 1994, and, therefore, measures the impact of the Olympics on job growth for 1995 and 1996 beyond that expected based on equation (6.1) estimated through 1994. Model 3 differs from model 2 in that the contribution of the Olympics to employment growth is measured using an estimate for equation (6.1) that includes the sample period through 1993. The evidence suggests that the bulk of expenditures for the Olympic Games for Atlanta occurred between 1994 through 1996. This assertion is based on the breakdown of expenditures into direct, indirect and induced categories identified in the study commissioned by the AOCG by Humphreys and Plummer (1995). Humphreys and Plummer define indirect economic expenditures as 'that portion of spending by out-of-state visitors that purchases goods and services produced by Georgia's industries to satisfy the additional demand'. Since Humphreys and Plummer estimate that more than 50 per cent of total spending is indirect, then the majority of job growth is attributable to spending that occurred for the most part in 1996. Nonetheless, there is an argument that can be made for using any of the three models that we have specified here even though the Humphreys and Plummer estimates on economic impact are based on Olympic expenditures from 1991 to 1997.

Table 6.4   Employment gains for Los Angeles attributable to the 1984 Summer Olympic Games

Model[a]	Employment gains (losses)
Model 1	5 043

Note:
[a] The only model specified for Los Angeles theoretically corresponds to model 1 in Table 6.3. Since the infrastructure for the 1984 games in Los Angeles was largely in place and substantial government expenditures by the State of California or the City of Los Angeles were not undertaken in support of the Olympic Games, the expenditure boost provided by the Games was felt primarily, if not exclusively, in the year in which the games were conducted.

As the evidence recorded in Tables 6.3 and 6.4 makes clear, the job implications for the Los Angeles and Atlanta Summer Olympic Games were fundamentally different. We attribute the difference to the fact that The City of Atlanta and the State of Georgia spent enormous sums of money on infrastructure for the 1996 Games while the City of Los Angeles and the State of California were miserly by comparison. The infrastructure expenditures for Atlanta as far as we can determine were substantial in 1994 and 1995 although there was some spending in conjunction with the Olympics beginning in 1991. Los Angeles, by contrast, did not spend a substantial amount prior to their Games, and the expenditure boost was largely confined to 1984. The employment impact, therefore, appears to have been felt only in 1984.

In the case of Atlanta, it is not entirely clear when the infrastructure and other preliminary Olympic expenditures occurred and influenced the economy. As a consequence we calculated job growth estimates for three possibilities or models (see the note following Table 6.3) which took into account accelerated employment growth attributable to pre-Olympic spending. Specifically if the employment growth was recalculated to account for an accelerated rate of job growth beginning in 1994 induced by substantial preparatory expenditures beginning in that year, that is, model 3, we estimated the Summer Olympic Games in 1996 generated cumulative job growth in 1994–96 of 42 448 full- and part-time jobs. On the other hand if preparatory expenditures were not substantial enough to accelerate job growth until 1995, that is, model 2, we estimate that the Atlanta Olympics created 21 767 full- and part-time jobs. Finally, if expenditures were not substantial until 1996, then the Atlanta Olympics accounted for only 3 467 jobs. Models 1 and 3, therefore, represent upper- and lower-bound estimates on job growth induced by the 1996 Summer Olympic Games hosted by Atlanta, Georgia.

The model 3 estimate conforms in order of magnitude to job growth estimates provided by Humphreys and Plummer (1995) who projected that the Olympics would create approximately 77 000 new jobs in the State of Georgia with 37 000 of those materializing in Atlanta.[10] It must be kept in mind, however, that the 42 448 estimate tacitly assumes that all job growth that falls outside the pattern established before 1994 is attributable to the Olympics. Technically speaking, in estimating the cumulative employment impact of all the spending that occurred in conjunction with Olympics, we have factored out all the job growth from other sources in 1994 and 1995. It would appear, as a consequence,that the 42 448 is an estimate that casts the Olympics in the most favourable light by attributing all incremental job growth to the 1996 Summer Games. It is arguable that Atlanta's job growth accelerated more rapidly in 1994 in concert with the business cycle. Employment figures for 1991–93 suggest that Atlanta's recovery from the nation's recession that ended in the spring of 1991 did not seem to gather much momentum until 1993. The Olympics is, therefore, credited with job creation that should be attributed to other developments and events.[11]

Those who championed public subsidies for the Atlanta Olympics contend that the impact of the Games endures. Our evidence, however, indicates that the Olympic legacy is likely to be small. In other words, the evidence suggests that the economic impact of the Olympics is transitory, one-time changes rather than a 'steady state' change. This outcome is likely to be true unless great care is taken to insure that the Olympic infrastructure is compatible with the resident economy. If the infrastructure for the Games lacks synergy, or worse, if it displaces or competes with resident or established capital and labour, then the job gains are likely to be short-lived. Job growth estimates for 1997 derived through adjusting the model to reflect the higher rates of job growth induced by the Olympics indicate that between 17 706 and 32 768 jobs were 'given back'. In other words, at least 40 per cent (and perhaps more) of the jobs were transitory. The City of Atlanta and the State of Georgia spent approximately $1.58 billion (see Humphreys and Plummer, 1995, p.41) to create 24 742 permanent full- or part-time jobs in the best case scenario (model 3) which averages out to $63 860 per job created.[12] It is conceivable that once opportunity costs are considered with the possibility that Olympic venues could compete for limited leisure dollars, the Olympics could actually generate a cumulative long-term job loss. Indeed models 1 and 2 indicate a loss of jobs long-term of 29 301 and 4 540, respectively. These estimates would be credible if for some reason the growth in jobs in 1994 or 1995 was not the result of spending undertaken in conjunction with the Olympics games. This should sound a warning to potential host cities particularly since Atlanta did appear to recognize the need to utilize Olympic infrastructure in meaningful ways after the Games. Recognizing the need for synergy is no guarantee that the plan which it inspires will be free of misconceptions and successful. For example a significant amount of the Olympic infrastructure expense, 71 per cent of the new construction budget and 12 per cent of total ACOG expenditures, was devoted to the Olympic stadium which became Turner Field, the home of the Atlanta Braves, a Major League Baseball (MLB) team. Turner Field changed the baseball venue, but did it add anything that generates net new spending and permanent jobs? There is ample evidence to indicate that new stadiums add little if anything to a metropolitan economy.[13]

Other evidence on the nature of ACOG expenditures invites scepticism about a substantial Olympic economic legacy. Only 31 per cent of the ACOG expenditures were in areas that could reasonably be expected to provide a measurable economic legacy. To be more precise, $485 million was spent on 'new construction', 'electric and electronic', 'transportation', and 'communication'. By contrast wage and salary disbursements ('Households') and 'business services' accounted for $740.5 million or 47 per cent of the ACOG expenditures (Humphreys and Plummer, 1995).

Furthermore, recent studies on metropolitan growth have emphasized the importance of sectoral clustering. Mills observed:

> At one level, the issue (metropolitan growth) can be stated simply. Many studies have found that similar sectors tend to cluster together in metropolitan areas . . . find that localization economies are more important than urbanization economies. That means that growth of employment within a sector tends to depend more on the size of the sector than on the size of the metropolitan area. I interpret the strong findings about localization to be findings about the importance of clustering among related but not identical sectors. (Mills, 1992)

The Olympics arguably do not generate the sort of clustering that is characteristic of high growth areas. To a significant degree the Olympics represents an alien industry, one that does not connect or mesh well with established businesses. In addition to the Olympic Stadium (Turner Field), the ACOG created an International Horse Park of 1400 acres, spent $17 million on the Wolf Creek Shooting Complex, and another $10 million on the Lake Lanier Rowing Center. These facilities may be unique, but explanations are required for how these rather esoteric developments fit with other industries and contribute to the economies of scale arguments that underlie, at least in part, the sectoral clustering, cumulative causation and disequilibrium dynamic adjustment models that represent contemporary explanations for the rapid growth we observe in some MSAs to include Atlanta. Indeed, to the extent that the Olympics are quite alien and divert the MSA from a higher growth path, the Summer Olympic Games could contribute negatively to job growth. This, in all likelihood explains the negative job growth outcomes of models 1 and 2 for Atlanta for 1997.

We estimate that the Summer Olympic Games contributed 5043 jobs to the Los Angeles economy in 1984. The empirical evidence indicates that the jobs were clearly transitory. Our model fails to reveal any net job gains in 1985 and beyond as a consequence of the Olympic Games. This outcome is probably attributable to the fact there was no significant investment in infrastructure in conjunction with the Games.

CONCLUSIONS AND POLICY IMPLICATIONS

The purpose of this chapter was to assess the economic impact of the Summer Olympic Games on Los Angeles in 1984 and Atlanta in 1996. In so doing, it was our hope that we could provide some useful information to cities bidding for the Games. It is conceivable that an after-the-fact sober appraisal of the economic contribution of the Games could help temper some of the excesses that have been brought to light by the well-publicized 'overzealous' behaviour of those who succeeded in bringing the Olympics to Salt Lake City and Atlanta.

Los Angeles and Atlanta represent an interesting contrast in terms of their approaches to the bidding process. This difference reflects to a substantial extent past financial experiences. In the wake of the financially troubled Montreal and Moscow Olympic Games in 1976 and 1980, only Los Angeles bid for the 1984 Games. This fact explains the absence of significant public sector financial support in Los Angeles, and, perhaps, the private financial success the 1984 Games are thought to have enjoyed. The increase in economic activity attributable to the 1984 Games, as represented by job growth, an estimated 5043 full-time and part-time jobs using our model, appears to have been entirely transitory, however. There is no economic residue that can be identified once the Games left town. Los Angeles was not visibly affected by the experience; certainly it was not transformed by it.

Atlanta represented a return to the extraordinary levels of public spending associated with the Olympic Games in 1976 and 1980, a phenomenon not coincidentally associated with several cities bidding for the right to host the Games. In an environment where bidding is intense among a number of cities, economic theory would suggest that the winning bid would be consonant with a zero economic return on the investment if opportunity costs are included in the bidding calculus. The Summer Olympic Games, however, are not ordinary investments, given their substantial political content, and we could expect negative returns on the economic investment as a consequence. In other words government is willing to pay something for perceived political gains. In light of this, it is not surprising that the best case scenario for the Atlanta Games of 1996 is consistent with what we could reasonably expect to find for public investments in general. More specifically, if beginning in 1994 all the economic growth beyond Atlanta's normal experience could be attributable to public expenditures in conjunction with the Olympics, Atlanta spent approximately $63000 to create a permanent full- or part-time job. To create a permanent full-time job equivalent, past public works programmes have spent approximately the same amount of money. It needs to be remembered, however, that the $63000 job creation figure for Atlanta applies to part-time as well as full-time employment. The statistics on job growth for Atlanta, therefore, do not permit the development of a statistic that is comparable to the cost of what amounts to full-time job creation through the implementation of the Local Public Works Capital Development and Investment Act of 1976 (LPW I) and the Local Public Works Capital Employment Act of 1977 (LPW II).

The best-case scenario does not necessarily equate with that which is most likely to occur. There are compelling reasons to expect that Atlanta's experience deviated from that which we identified as the best case. One reason has to do with the fact that the business cycle for Atlanta and the United States in general are not in perfect harmony. Atlanta's recovery from the national recession that ended in the spring of 1991 was tardy. Employment statistics for Atlanta indicate that 1994, the year in which our model began to account for the impact of substantial ACOG spending, was still relatively early in the recovery phase of Atlanta's business cycle. Of course one could argue that that is suggestive of the potency of ACOG spending, but there are theoretical reasons to suspect otherwise.

Contemporary theory that attempts to explain metropolitan economic development emphasizes the economies of scale imparted by sectoral clustering or specialization of particular industries within an urban economy. The Olympics industry is by its very nature exceptional in terms of its infrequency and the particular and immediate demands it makes on a host economy. Rather than fitting in, the host economy has to make changes to accommodate the event. This hurricane of economy activity can have a permanent impact only to the extent that its infrastructure demands translate into permanent uses that build on resident capital and labour rather than substituting for them. Atlanta worked hard to create the necessary synergy, but the Olympics may well represent an industry that emphasizes infrastructure that is infrequently or incompletely utilized. There are limited uses for shooting ranges and sports stadiums. Diverting scarce capital and other resources from more productive uses to the Olympics very likely translates into slower rates of economic growth than that which could be realized in the absence of hosting the Olympic Games. Our other scenarios for Atlanta indicate job gains during the Olympics, but long-term job losses. The outcomes of the scenarios that we have identified as models 1 and 2 for Atlanta seem more likely.

In considering the policy implications of our research, consider first the collective interests of cities. If cities are intent on hosting the Olympic Games they must do the obvious, that is they must take steps to counteract the monopoly power of the IOC. It is in the collective interest of potential host cities to devise means to change the nature of the bidding process. The Los Angeles experience is instructive because in the absence of cities competing with one another, Los Angeles and the IOC were on roughly equal footing in negotiating the financial terms of the Games. As a consequence Los Angeles experienced short-term job gains without jeopardizing their economic future. Los Angeles got from the Olympics what they were capable of providing. Stated somewhat differently, they got that for which they paid. The revamping of rules regarding gifts to IOC members is an obvious way in which cities have recognized their shared interests and prevented the IOC from exercising their monopoly prerogatives. One obvious suggestion is to do away with the current arrangement where IOC officials visit suitor cities. Replace the raucous, open bidding process that currently exists with a single 'sealed bid' complete with details on the city's capability of effectively hosting an event of this size.

Where individual cities are concerned, they must be realistic about what the Olympics offer economically. Thorough investigations of past experiences will not only provide a filter through which the promises of boosters can be run, but it might well indicate the most effective methods for integrating Olympic infrastructure needs with the present economy and a vision of its future. In the absence of careful and directed planning, cities that succeed in hosting the Olympics may well only find fools' gold for their efforts.

NOTES

1. This could explain why the 1984 Olympics may have been profitable for Los Angeles. Indeed, the City refused to sign a contract with the IOC on IOC terms. That is LA Mayor Tom Bradley insisted that his City be exempted from the infamous IOC Rule 4 (Shaikin, 1988).
2. Porter's use of monthly sales receipts is important. If the researcher can compress the time period, then it is less likely that the impact of the event will be obscured by the large, diverse economy within which it took place. The use of annual data surely has the potential to mask an event's impact through the sheer weight of activity that occurs in large economies over the course of a year unless steps are taken to isolate the event.
3. The stadium construction accident at Miller Park in Milwaukee on 14 July, 1999 illus-

trates this point. A crane collapsed killing three ironworkers and seriously injuring the crane operator. Of these four people, only two of them resided in the Milwaukee MSA. The third steelworker was from Kimberly, Wisconsin, and the crane operator was from Houston, Texas.

4. It is not altogether clear whether occupancy rates increase during mega-events. It may be that the most popular convention cities, those most likely to host the Olympic Games, would experience high occupancy even if they are not successful in hosting them. Evidence, however, suggests that room rates increase substantially during the Olympics and the Super Bowl, but questions regarding the final destination of those additional earnings remain.

5. It should be remembered that our intent here is not to focus on what accounts for all growth in cities. Rather our task is to determine how much a mega-event contributes to a city's economy. It is true that trend-adjusting does not provide any economic insight about those factors responsible for metropolitan growth, but adjusting for trends enables us to focus attention on a smaller component of growth for a city which a mega-event may help explain.

6. To assess the relationships between costs and growth see: Mills and Lubuele (1995), Terkla and Doeringer (1991), and Goss and Phillips (1994).

7. See, for example, Duffy (1994) and Wasylenko and McQuire (1985).

8. Growth rates for employment in the three previous years were used to account for estimation problems created by a single aberrant year that could occur for a variety of reasons to include a natural disaster or a change in political parties with accompanying changes in fiscal strategies. Technically speaking the model was more robust with this specification, and the values for the cross correlation coefficients did not suggest a multicolinearity problem.

9. We estimated that the Summer Olympic Games would have to induce an increase of approximately 70000 jobs in Atlanta to surface as statistically significant.

10. Humphreys and Plummer estimate that the increase in jobs throughout the State of Georgia as a consequence of the Olympics is proportionate to the fraction of the state's population in any particular locale. Since approximately 48 per cent of the State's population resides in Atlanta, then 48 per cent of the estimated increase of 77000 jobs in the State will be based in Atlanta. This manner of allocating job gains across the State seems inappropriate in light of the fact that arguably more then 48 per cent of the Olympic expenditures occurred in Atlanta and environs. A more reasonable estimate of Atlanta's job growth should be based on the fraction of expenditures occurring in the metropolitan area. This would surely yield an estimate of more than 37000 jobs in Atlanta even after taking into account the multiplier effect which, of course, expands with the area of analysis.

11. There is some evidence to support the fact that Atlanta's accelerating growth in employment was attributable to factors other than the Olympics. This possibility is supported ironically by Humphreys. He was part of a three-person team that performed an analysis on the impact of the 1994 Super Bowl hosted by Atlanta, and they estimated that the Super Bowl was responsible for 1974 and 2736 jobs in the City of Atlanta and the State of Georgia, respectively (Humphreys et al, 1993 and Humphreys, 1994).

12. It is important to note that these are not figures per person-year or full-time employment. To estimate that would require a breakdown of part-time and full-time jobs. To our knowledge no such breakdown exists. To provide some context, it has been estimated that the Local Public Works Capital Development and Investment Act of 1976 (LPW I) and the Local Public Works Capital Employment Act of 1977 (LPW II) created direct and indirect jobs at an average cost of $37000 for a person-year (Hall, 1980). If the cost of creating those jobs doubled between 1980 and 1996, the average cost per person-year would be $74000 or roughly the same magnitude as the cost of creating a combination of part-time and full-time jobs through Atlanta's hosting of the Summer Olympic Games.

13. See for example Baade (1996) and several articles in Noll and Zimbalist (1997).

REFERENCES

Baade, Robert A. (1996), 'Professional sports as a catalyst for metropolitan economic development', *Journal of Urban Affairs*, **18** (1), 1–17.

Cawley, Rusty (1999), 'The Olympic race: the Metroplex Bid for the 2012 Games has a parallel in Atlanta, where the '96 Games generated less gold than expected', Dallas Business Journal, April 5.

Davidson, Larry (1999), 'Choice of a Proper Methodology to Measure Quantitative and Qualitative Effects, of the Impact of Sport', in Claude Jeanrenaud (ed.), *The Economic Impact of Sports Events*, Neuchatel, Switzerland: Centre International d'Etude du Sport, pp. 9–28.

Duffy, N. (1994), 'The determinants of state manufacturing growth rates: a two-digit-level analysis', *Journal of Regional Science*, **34**, 137–62.

Goss, E. and J. Phillips (1994), 'State employment growth: the impact of taxes and economic development agency spending', *Growth and Change*, **25**, 287–300.

Hall, Robert L. (1980), 'Public Works as a Countercyclical Tool', *Hearings Before the Joint Economic Committee, 96 Congress, 1 sess.*, Washington, DC: Government Printing Office, June 17, p. 9.

Humphreys, Jeffrey M. (1994), 'The economic impact of hosting SuperBowl XXVIII on Georgia', *Georgia Business and Economic Conditions* May–June.

Humphreys, Jeffrey M., et al. (1993), 'The economic impact of hosting the 1994 Super Bowl in Atlanta', *Georgia Business and Economic Conditions*, November–December.

Humphreys, Jeffrey M. and Michael K. Plummer (1995), 'The Economic Impact on the State of Georgia of Hosting the 1996 Summer Olympic Games', Mimeograph, Athens, Georgia: Selig Center for Economic Growth, The University of Georgia.

Kesenne, Stefan (1999), 'Miscalculations and Misinterpretations in Economic Impact Analysis', in Claude Jeanrenaud (ed.), *The Economic Impact of Sports Events*, Neuchatel, Switzerland: Centre International d'Etude du Sport, pp. 29–39.

Mills, Edwin (1992), 'Sectoral Clustering and Metropolitan Development', in E. Mills and John McDonald (eds), *Sources of Economic Growth*, Brunswick, New Jersey: Centre for Urban Policy Research, pp. 3–18.

Mills, E. and L. Lubuele (1995), 'Projecting growth of metropolitan areas', *Journal of Urban Economics*, **37**, 344–60.

Noll, Roger and Andrew Zimbalist (1997), 'The Economic Impact of Sports Teams and Facilities', in R. Noll and A. Zimbalist (eds), *Sports, Jobs and Taxes: The Economic Impact of Sports Teams and Stadiums*, Washington, DC: Brookings Institution Press, pp. 494–508.

Porter, Philip (1999), 'Mega-Sports Events as Municipal Investments: A Critique of Impact Analysis', in J. Fizel, E. Gustafson and L. Hadley, (eds), *Sports Economics: Current Research*, New York: Praeger Press.

Shaikin, Bill (1988), *Sport and Politics: The Olympics and the Los Angeles Games*, New York: Praeger Press.

Terkla, D. and P. Doeringer (1991), 'Explaining variations in employment growth: structural and cyclical change among states and local areas', *Journal of Urban Economics*, **29**, 329–40.

Tews, Mary-Kate (1993), 'The Mega-event as an Urban Redevelopment Strategy:

Atlanta Prepares for 1996 and Beyond', Mimeograph, New Orleans: College of Urban and Public Affairs, October.
Wasylenko, M. and T. McQuire (1985), 'Jobs and taxes: the effect of business climate on states' employment growth rates', *National Tax Journal*, **38**, 955–74.

APPENDIX

Table 6A.1   Cities and years used to estimate model in Tables 6.1 and 6.2

City Name	1969 Population	1969 Rank	1997 Population	1997 Rank	Wage Data availability	Region
Albany, NY	797010	50	873856	57	1969–97	Mideast
Atlanta, GA	1742220	16	3634245	9	1972–97	Southeast
Baltimore, MD	2072804	12	2475952	18	1972–97	Mideast
Bergen, NJ	1354671	26	1335665	43	1969–97 (State data 1969–97)	Mideast
Boston, MA	5182413	4	5826816	4	1972–97	New England
Buffalo, NY	1344024	27	1163149	47	1969–97 (Average of cities)	Mideast
Charlotte, NC	819691	49	1351675	42	1972–97	Southeast
Chicago, IL	7041834	2	7883452	3	1972–97	Great Lakes
Cincinnati, OH	1431316	21	1607001	32	1969–97	Great Lakes
Cleveland, OH	2402527	11	2227495	22	1969–97	Great Lakes
Columbus, OH	1104257	33	1456440	41	1972–97	Great Lakes
Dallas, TX	1576589	18	3123013	10	1972–97	Southwest
Dayton, OH	963574	42	952060	55	1969–97	Great Lakes
Denver, CO	1089416	34	1901927	26	1977–97	Rocky Mountains
Detroit, MI	4476558	6	4468503	7	1976–97	Great Lakes
Fort Lauderdale, FL	595651	55	1472927	38	1969–97 (State data 1988–97)	Southeast
Fort Worth, TX	766903	51	1554768	33	1976–97 (State data 1976–83)	Southwest
Greensboro, NC	829797	48	1153447	48	1972–97	Southeast
Hartford, CT	1021033	39	1106695	50	1969–97	New England
Houston, TX	1872148	15	3846996	8	1972–97	Southwest
Indianapolis, IN	1229904	30	1504451	36	1989–97	Great Lakes
Kansas City, MO	1365715	25	1716818	28	1972–97	Plains
Las Vegas, NV	297628	57	1262427	45	1972–97	Far West
Los Angeles, CA	6989910	3	9116506	1	1969–97 (State data 1982–87)	Far West
Louisville, KY	893311	43	994537	54	1972–97	Southeast
Memphis, TN	848113	45	1082526	53	1972–97	Southeast
Miami, FL	1249884	29	2128987	24	1969–97 (State data 1988–97)	Southeast

Table 6A.1 continued

City Name	1969 Population	1969 Rank	1997 Population	1997 Rank	Wage Data availability	Region
Middlesex, NJ	836616	47	1105804	51	1969–97 (State data 1969–97)	Mideast
Milwaukee, WI	1395326	23	1459760	40	1969–97	Great Lakes
Minneapolis, MN	1991610	13	2794939	13	1972–97	Plains
Nashville, TN	689753	53	1136607	49	1972–97	Southeast
Nassau, NY	2516514	9	2660623	16	1969–97	Mideast
New Haven, CT	1527930	19	1626327	3C	1969–97 (Average of cities)	New England
New Orleans, LA	1134406	31	1308127	44	1972–97	Southeast
New York, NY	9024022	1	8650425	2	1969–97	Mideast
Newark, NJ	1988239	14	1943455	25	1969–97 (State data 1969–97)	Mideast
Norfolk, VA	1076672	36	1544781	34	1972–97 (State data 1973–96)	Southeast
Oakland, CA	1606461	17	2273911	21	1969–97 (State data 1969–87)	Far West
Orange County, CA	1376796	24	2663561	15	1969–97 (State data 1982–87)	Far West
Orlando, FL	510189	56	1462958	39	1972–97 (State data 1988–97)	Southeast
Philadelphia, PA	4829078	5	4939783	5	1972–97	Mideast
Phoenix, AZ	1013400	40	2842030	12	1972–97 (State data 1972–87)	Southwest
Pittsburgh, PA	2683385	8	2359824	19	1972–97	Mideast
Portland, OR	1064099	37	1789790	27	1972–97	Far West
Providence, R1	839909	46	904301	56	1969–97	New England
Riverside CA	1122165	32	3047741	11	1969–97 (State data 1982–87)	Far West
Rochester, NY	1005722	41	1084215	52	1969–97	Mideast
Sacramento, CA	737534	52	1503900	37	1969–97 (State data 1982–87)	Far West
St. Louis, MO	2412381	10	2559065	17	1972–97	Plains
Salt Lake City, UT	677500	54	1250854	46	1972–97	Rocky Mountains
San Antonio, TX	892602	44	1506573	35	1972–97	Southwest
San Diego, CA	1340989	28	2723711	14	1969–97 (State data 1982–87)	Far West
San Francisco, CA	1482030	20	1669697	29	1969–97 (State data 1982–87)	Far West
San Jose, CA	1033442	38	1620453	31	1972–97 (State data 1982–87)	Far West

Table 6A.1 continued

City Name	1969 Population	1969 Rank	1997 Population	1997 Rank	Wage Data availability	Region
Seattle, WA	1430592	22	2279236	20	1972–97 (State data 1982–97)	Far West
Tampa, FL	1082821	35	2224973	23	1972–97 (State data 1988–97)	Southeast
Washington, DC	3150087	7	4609414	6	1972–97	Southeast

Complete data on population and employment was available for all cities from 1969 to 1997. This implies that data on employment growth and employment growth lagged from 1 to 3 years was available from 1973 to 1997. Tax data was available for all cities from 1970 to 1997, and was obtained from the Tax Foundation in Washington, DC. Wage data from the Bureau of Labor Statistics was available for cities as described above. When city data was not available, state wage data was used in its place. When possible, the state wage data was adjusted to reflect differences between existing state wage data and existing city wage data. For MSAs that included several primary cities, the wages of the cities were averaged together to create an MSA wage as noted in Table 6A.1.

The 'Oil Bust' dummy variable was included for cities highly dependent on oil revenues including Dallas, Denver, Fort Worth, Houston and New Orleans. The variable was set at a value of 1 for boom years, 1974–1976 and 1979–81, and at −1 for the bust years, 1985–88. While this formulation does imply that each boom and bust is of an equal magnitude, the variable does have significant explanatory value nonetheless.

Each city was placed in one of eight geographical regions as defined by the Department of Commerce. The region to which each city was assigned is shown in Table 6A.1. Employment, income and population data were obtained from the Regional Economic Information System at the University of Virginia which derives its data from the Department of Commerce statistics.

7. Economic impact of sporting events: what has to be measured?

J.J. Gouguet

The measurement of the economic impact of the biggest sporting events is a source of controversy between economists (Barget and Gouguet, 2000). Overall, two main questions have to be asked:

- how to carry out such a measure ?
- which function has to be given to these results ?

The first question gives rise to important problems of methodology which the authors of impact studies do not always completely master. The result is often a substantial over-evaluation of the real repercussions of sporting events. The second, which is more fundamental, has been abundantly treated mainly in English literature: are governmental subsidies or public aid for the construction of big stadiums justified compared to the extent of economic impact that these sporting events would create? (Lavoie, 1997). It is then often demonstrated by academic economists that organizers ask for these subsidies in the name of an economic impact which would not, in fact, exist (Baade and Matheson, 2000). Nonetheless, it appears to us that this answer is not totally satisfactory, as the justification of the subsidy should not be only considered in relation to the amount of the economic impact of the event.

So, we are going to try in this chapter to show on which analytical bases it is possible to talk about all these controversial questions which reflect the increasing financial stakes linked to the biggest sporting events: does the construction of sport infrastructure have to be subsidized? Is public aid to professional clubs justified? To answer such questions correctly, it seems that there is often confusion between the economic impact and the economic efficiency of sporting events and it has to be avoided.

The legitimacy of a project (a big stadium, for example) has to be measured against the social utility it gives rise to and not against the scope of its economic impact, for fear that it could end up with absurdity (Stringer, 1980). We will show in this way that, in the view of decisional help, only a complete calculation of the economic performance based on the global economic value of this project (and not a calculation of the economic impact) is valid.

1. THE TOTAL ECONOMIC VALUE OF SPORTING EVENTS

There are many categories of sporting events which should be first defined. These sporting events do not all present the same difficulties of measurement. In particular, the total economic value of these goods consists partly of specific external effects which cannot be easily integrated.

1.1 Difficulties of Definition

1.1.1 Typology of sporting events

As far as the economic analysis is concerned, the nature of the sporting events considered as economic goods has to be determined, as well as the specificities of its market. For this purpose, the main forms of sporting events have to be counted beforehand so as to draw up a typology. Many criteria can be used in an economic sense to define the sporting events. The three most significant ones have been pointed out here:

- the frequency (see Table 7.1): traditionally, occasional sporting events (a world cup, a grand prix, a trophy, and so on) and regular sporting events (a national championship spreading over one sporting season) have been opposed;
- the economic weight of the event which can be evaluated in many ways: turnover, spectator numbers, television audience (see Tables 7.2–7.5). Until now, economic analysis has especially been interested by mega-events. For instance, Barget (2001) adopts as the minimum threshold one billion television viewers in a cumulative audience and/or 30 countries broadcasting the event;
- the event property: some events belong to and are organized by official sport authorities (international federations, IOC, and so on); other events, on the contrary, belong to big private groups (Amaury with the Tour de France or the Paris Dakar).

Beyond these first criteria to differentiate sporting events, it is most important to understand that all these events do not have the same nature and the same characteristics with regard to economic impact and created social utility. For example, in the case of occasional events, it may be that two

Table 7.1   Typology of sporting events

Frequency	Weight	Property	Examples
Sporadic events	ordinary events	official authority	French Football Cup
		private sector	Cyclist race
	mega events	official authority	Olympic Games
		private sector	Tour de France
Regular events	ordinary events	official authority	French Basketball Championship
	mega events	official authority	National Football Championships
		private sector	Football Super League Project

categories can be distinguished: on the one hand, spectacular events for the general public and on the other hand, official events attracting a well-experienced public. The nature and scope of the economic impact will not be the same according to the type of events:

- in the first case which gets closer to a pure spectacle, the analysis will be the same as any other economic activity which wants to yield a profit. The main difficulty to overcome will be the mobilization of the information which is necessary to test the theory (approach by the economic base, for example);
- in the second case which is closer to an operation of general interest, it has to be asked what is the value of the social utility thus created, which can justify the payment of public subsidies. Here again, the main difficulty is the mobilization of information (concerning the external effects linked to occasional sporting events).

A new typology of occasional sporting events could then appear: some will have an important economic impact but a relatively low social utility; others will present a high degree of social utility in spite of insignificant economic impact. The problem is that a number of consistent elements of this social utility belong to the category of external effects, which inevitably complicates the measurement.

Table 7.2   TV sports rights in USA and in Europe (1999/2000)

Sport, championship	TV rights (in millions of French francs)
American Football	
National Football League (EU)	12 500
Basketball	
National Collegiate Athletic Association (EU)	3 640
Football	
Italian Championship	3 300
French Championship	2 200
English Championship	1 800
Spanish Championship	1 700
German Championship	1 530
Baseball	
Major League Baseball (EU)	1 700
Ice Hockey	
National Hockey League (EU)	700

Source: Bourg and Gouguet (2001).

Table 7.3   World audience for major sporting events (billions of TV spectators–number of countries broadcast)

Events (date)	Cumulative global audience	Number of countries broadcast
Formula One Grand Prix (1999)	57	206
Football World Cup (1998)	41	200
Summer Olympics (1996)	19.6	200
Winter Olympics (1998)	10.7	160
European Football Championship (1996)	6.9	150
World Athletics Championship (1999)	4.2	200
Rugby World Cup (1999)	3	180
Roland Garros Open Tennis (1999)	2.7	160
Tour de France – Cycling (1998)	1	167
Superbowl – Baseball (1999)	1	150
British Open Golf (1995)	1	42

Source: Bourg and Gouguet (2001).

Table 7.4   Number of international major sporting events

Dates	Events
1896	3
1912	20
1977	315
1987	660
1999	800

Source: Bourg and Gouguet (2001).

Table 7.5   Specific sporting examples

Clubs or events (sport, date)	Turnover millions of French francs	Results millions of French francs	%
Roland-Garros (tennis, 1998)	456	+ 216	47.4
Manchester United (football, 1998/1999)	1 100	+ 320	29.1
World Football Cup (1998)	2 400	+ 550	22.9
French Football Championship 1st League (1997/1998)	3 300	+ 474	14.4
Bayern Munich (football, 1998/1999)	825	+ 80	9.8
Summer Olympics (Sydney, 2000)[a]	10 000	− 830	8.3

Note: [a] Forecastings February 2000.

Source: Bourg (2000).

1.1.2   Taking into account external effects

(a) Presentation of externalities.   In general, the analysts take three types of external economies into account:

– the improvement of social cohesion of the host territory which can take many forms: improvement of the social climate, strengthening of local identity around a common project, creation of social links, improvement of social integration, decrease of some discriminations, and so on. These externalities are partially linked to positive social consequences coming from the economic impact of the sporting event (decrease of tensions linked to unemployment for example, to delinquency, to drugs and so on). The example of the last Football World Cup in France is sufficiently explicit and has abundantly been commented on, in particular in relation to the acceptance by public opinion that French society is fundamentally multiracial, as was its team which won the world championship. Furthermore, beyond this global repercussion, it is known that the media broadcasting of the sporting events makes possible the progress of the social recognition of some underprivileged citizen categories: youth from risky areas, women and so on. In relation to this last category, the example of Iranian women who saw the match is an interesting case of external- ity that it could be useful to explore more deeply.

– the improvement of the public image of the territory. This improve- ment can be concretized by a gain in attracting tourists, activities, enterprises, markets and so on. Many studies have thus been run to try to understand the part of sporting events in the promotion of a territory. They all have met problems in gathering information and, beyond the doubtful results because of externalities, they were not able to answer the question of what would have happened without the sporting event.

– the improvement of basic infrastructure of the territory which, here again, can have long-term developing effects: lodging, transport, culture, sport, quality of life, and so on. One of the most convincing examples on the European scale is surely the organization of the Olympic Games at Barcelona in 1992. New major transport infra- structure, new neighbourhoods, and rehabilitation of ancient dis- tricts and so on have contributed to decrease the generalized saturation of the town and to restore its public image. In the long- term, these induced effects may be much more important than only the short-term effects, as they can be measured by a multiplier (Gouguet and Nys, 1993).

So, the impact of a sporting event is not limited to direct market effects but has to integrate all these positive externalities which increase the real value of the event. Nonetheless, beyond these benefits, negative external effects should be taken into account, which is rarely done in most of the studies. In the same way as previously, three types of externalities are gen- erally taken into account:

– a loss of social cohesion through the consequences of the preparation of the sporting event or its progress: hooliganism and spatial segrega- tion (eviction of underprivileged social classes and gentrification of renovated districts). In the first case, instead of being the expression of the identification of a community with a team, the sporting event becomes on the contrary the pretext to violently emphasize one's difference or one's life sickness in relation to the dominant society or to other supporters. Sporting events then reveal the rejection of others. In the second case, the example of the Olympic Games at Barcelona is still a good one with the disappearance of a popular neighbourhood to build the Olympic village, with the relocating of the people involved to outer suburbs, and with the arrival of the well-off in the renovated district.

– damage to the public image of the territory in case of failure of the event or the disfunctioning of the organization and progress. It is first the eviction effects due to the fear of saturation of the territory during a big sporting event. For example, tourists who should have come are going to cancel or postpone their coming. So, to be accurate, the economic impact measure of the event must take into account such eviction effects. There are then all the difficulties met by the territories which get into debt to welcome the sporting event, without their investments generating a real economic development afterwards. The reimbursement of the debt is then made to the detriment of new investments. There are finally the doping or cheating: the gravity and scope of the different scandals relayed by the media may put in danger the public image of some disciplines, of the sport as a whole and so of the host territory.

– damage to the quality of life and environment because of the setting of a huge infrastructure.

All these elements have to be integrated into a cost/advantages calculation of the sporting event, which must not limit itself to the costs and market benefits. Methods of evaluation of such externalities have been originally designed in the field of environmental economy. The problem is to know whether these instruments could be carried to the sports field.

b) Out-market values.   The damage done to the environment has brought back the debate about value. The awareness of the scarcity of resources will lead to the proposal of a new definition of the value, to take into account in the economic calculation not only the market value of goods but their total economic value (See Figure 7.1).

– intrinsic value or value in itself of the goods: how much do some or other goods cost, even if they are useless (a tree, an animal and so on)?
– optional value: even if individuals do not exploit a resource, they can wish to keep it as an option for the future. So, some goods which do

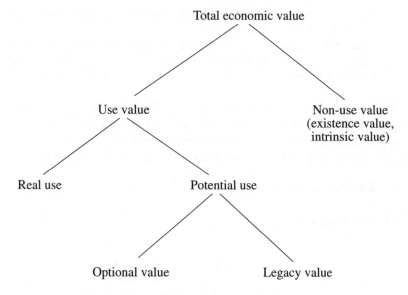

Figure 7.1 Total economic value

not have much use value today can be of a great option value tomorrow, bearing in mind science and technical progress.
– patrimonial value or value of legacy: which value do I give to the fact of renunciation to the immediate use of goods to make the future generations take advantage of it?

The total economic value is the sum of all these values and it is the one which has to be used in economic calculations.

On the grounds that these definitions belong to the environmental economy, it can be said that the total economic value of the sporting event is the measure of the total utility that people from the host territory can take of it. So, one has to know whether the previous diagram can be used to qualify the sporting event. Barget (2001) in his doctoral thesis analyses the following propositions:

– use value: it is the utility effectively felt by the sporting event consumer.
– optional value: it is the amount of the utility felt by the people for the possibility of gaining from the sporting event in the future. The importance is to maintain the option of the organization of such an event, to avoid its disappearance.
– value of legacy: it is the satisfaction felt by the fact of handing a sporting event down to future generations. It is essentially the

measure of all the value that can be given to sporting culture as an inheritance for humanity.
–   value of existence: it is the utility felt by an individual and coming from the fact of knowing that this event exists with all its economic, social, symbolical, cultural repercussions, even if this individual is not present.

The sum of all theses values gives the total economic value of the sporting event. As many of these values are not valuable, economists have tried for 30 years roughly to experiment with many methods to reveal the willingness to pay of agents, which has not been achieved without many difficulties.

1.2   Difficulties in Measuring the Value

1.2.1   Choosing a method

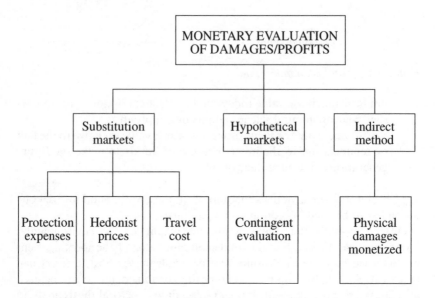

Figure 7.2   Monetary evaluation of damages/profits

(a) General presentation (see Figure 7.2)
(1)   Substitution markets: as far as the environment is concerned, individual preferences are evaluated by examining their behaviour on three markets linked to environment: travel, protection and housing.

   ●   travel costs: time and money necessary to go to the place are evaluated. This gives the value assigned to such places by consumers. This method has been used in the US as early as the 1950s to determine the value of national parks, nature reserves and so on, through the evaluation of the benefits linked to the recreational use of natural assets (fishing, hunting, swimming, walking and so on).

• protection costs: facing damage to their environment, individuals are going to try to protect themselves from these disagreements. The amount of these costs can be used to determine the value granted to the environmental quality.

• hedonist costs: it is generally the real estate market which is used for such an analysis. It is assumed here that the land price or the housing price reflects as well the environmental quality of these goods. If this quality lowers itself, the market will take it into account through a price decrease.

(2)   Direct method: also called method of contingent evaluation, it is increasingly used to estimate the intrinsic value or potential value of environmental goods. The expression 'direct method' is used as individuals' preferences and their willingness to pay is directly examined by questionnaire and interview. The aim is to reveal, through the individual's willingness to pay, the variation of utility that they can anticipate from a modification of their environment. According to Bonnieux and Desaigues (1998), more than 1500 studies produced in 40 countries for 30 years have allowed economists to ameliorate the robustness of this method.

(3)   Indirect method: it is the monetary evaluation of physical effect. First, the physical effect of environmental modification on a given activity (of how much does the ground erosion reduce the agricultural production) is evaluated. Secondly, the monetary value of this change in the production or the costs is estimated.

In spite of much bias, some of these methods coming from environmental economy have been used in the sporting field.

(b) Possibility of transposition to the sporting field.   Among the three methods of the markets of substitution, it may be that only the technique of travel costs could fit for the evaluation of the sporting event. The methods of protection cost or hedonist prices have a more limited interest for the evaluation of more occasional externalities linked to the event (noise and overcrowding, for example).

On the contrary, the sporting event may fit the use of the method of travel costs, as it will be relatively easy to reconstruct the demand curve of the event and to calculate from this curve the consumer surplus. The transposition of the method of natural spaces may not be a problem as the moving of spectators creates the information necessary to the revelation of their willingness to pay.

According to Barget (2001) who has experimented with it, this method is relatively easy to implement with some relatively low costs. It has simply to be remembered that this method consists of three stages (Bonnieux and Desaigues, 1998):

- assessment of the curve of participation, that is the relationship between the price (travel cost) and the quantity asked (participation rate)
- assessment of the function of aggregated demand by adding to the travel cost a right of way to the event
- calculation of the consumer surplus.

This method of the travel cost seems to be efficient for evaluating the use value of sporting events. For the value of no-use or potential use (legacy or option), it is the method of contingent evaluation that has to be resorted to. This method presents many problems of bias but, well-conducted, it can give robust evaluation of the willingness to pay of the agents for the sporting event.

Example

Barget has tested the two methods previously described (travel cost and contingent evaluation) to try to determine the economic value of the Quarter Final of the Davis Cup which took place at Limoges in April 1997. Here are the main problems and the results (see Figure 7.3)

(a) Use value.   Use value can be measured by the willingness to pay of the agents, that is the amount they are going effectively to pay through the entry price enlarged by the maximum amount that they would be ready to pay not to be deprived of the event (consumer surplus). The method of the travel cost used by Barget obeys the main stages previously described:

1. geographical cutting up: five areas have been noted for Limoges;
2. travel cost calculated by taking into account the following items: passed time, fuel, wear of vehicle, housing costs. This cost has been modulated as well according to the travel motivations;
3. rate of assistance by geographical areas calculated from the sample;
4. function of assistance estimated by the least squares method, and so on;
5. function of demand.

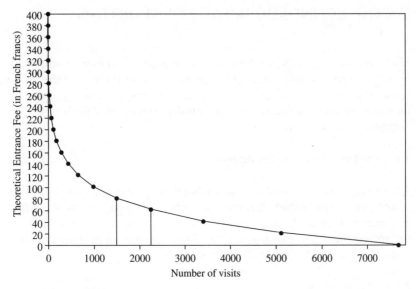

Source: Barget (2001)

Figure 7.3 Demand curve

From this, the consumer surplus could be estimated by the trapezium method to more than 384 120 francs.

(b) Contingent evaluation method. The questionnaire used has been structured so that it is consistent with the studies already written:

- a first part is intended to determine the importance of the sporting events in general for the interviewed person, how much supplementary tax he is ready to pay for their organization in Limousin.
- a second part is intended to determine the willingness to pay specifically for the Davis Cup, as well as the reasons given for such a payment.

The willingness to pay has been estimated to be more than double the organization cost of the event; the reasons given by the consumer are mainly: the improvement of the public image of Limousin, youth education, the impact for the regional economy, and social cohesion. In contrast, the handing down of the event to future generations (legacy) or the possibility to organize the sporting event again in the future (option) have obtained a relatively low score.

So, all in all, the Davis Cup in Limoges has been found broadly in excess (benefits less the costs felt by the population).

2.   THE ECONOMIC IMPACT OF SPORTING EVENTS

Many attempts to evaluate the economic impact of sporting events have been conducted by different institutions and exist now. They are the object of debates amongst the professional economist society which is opposed for two main reasons: the scope of the results obtained and the use of these results for political aims.

2.1   The Uncertainty of the Results

All the regional economists acknowledge that the economic impact of an activity on a given area varies necessarily according to the characteristics of this area. One of the dimensions which can synthesize the whole of the variables is the size of the chosen area. This is why it is usual to oppose large and small areas in the economic impact study.

2.1.1   Large areas

The statement is clear, as is shown in Table 7.6: the results obtained concerning the impact of a sporting event vary a lot according to the events. One has to know as well that the same event evaluated by different authors and methods gives rise to very contrasting results.

Many reasons could be given intuitively to explain such gaps and in particular the specificity of the events or areas at stake. But as the same events have been the subject of very different evaluations, it seems to us that the problem is about the type of method used and the condition of use. Let us recall that the economic impact studies of sporting events generally lie in three types of approach:

- some demand models coming from Keynes which consist in evaluating a macroeconomics multiplier of expenses. The essential difficulty here is the accurate evaluation of some propensities, in particular the propensity to import of the host area.
- some supply models coming from Leontief which measure the effects of intersectorial dragging which spread in the region through the whole relationships of inputs/outputs from the sales/purchases in intermediate consumption around the sporting event. It is acknowledged that in theory this multiplier is the more reliable method, but the lack of data at the regional level considerably limits its implementation. It is to be noted, however, that it has been used in the sporting field to measure the impact of the strike of the professional footballers in Chicago (Miller and Jackson, 1988).

Table 7.6 *Sporting events – economic impact assessment (in millions of French francs 1995)*

Source	Event	Territory	Net injection	Induced effects	Total impact
Economics research associates	Summer Olympics (Los Angeles, 1984)	South California	3615.28	5664.44	9279.72
Victorian tourism commission	Australian Games (Victoria, 1985)	Victoria Metropolitan Area	85.17	28.20	113.37
T.E.T.R.A./Délégation interministérielle...	Winter Olympics (Albertville, 1992)	South-East France			2231.91
J.P.A. Burns, J.H. Hatch, T.J. Mules	Formula One Grand Prix (Adelaide, 1985)	Adelaide Metropolitan Area	113.90	24.83	138.70
			119.46	26.18	145.64
B. Faulkner	World Athletics Cup (Canberra, 1986)	Canberra Metropolitan Area	96.86	364.54	461.40
Centre for applied and business research	Americas' Cup (Fremantle, 1987)	West Australian State	764.00	1140.00	1904.00
P. Frechette, P. Villeneuve, M. Boisvert, G. Leblanc	Winter Olympics (Quebec, 2002)	Great Quebec Quebec Province	2157.19	588.02	2316.80 2745.21
F. Brunet	Summer Olympics (Barcelona, 1992)	Undefined	53514.15	89168.28	142682.43
V. Papin	Americas' Cup (Sète, 1999)	Languedoc-Roussillon Region	590.24 713.54 836.65	277.42 335.37 393.32	867.66 1048.91 1230.17
O. Benezis	World Football Cup (Montpellier, 1998)	Languedoc-Roussillon Region	124.29 152.57	58.42 71.71	182.71 224.28

- some econometric models which test the relationship between the hosting of a sporting event on the one hand and the level of the GNP on the other hand (Baade, 1996; Baade and Dye, 1988, 1990). Here again, the validity of the test depends on the quality of the statistical series that can be collected.

If it is always very difficult to compare the results obtained with different methods it has to be underlined that, whatever are the methods used, many glaring mistakes question the validity of the calculations. Let us quote the more usual:

- inclusion of expenses of local spectators;
- moving in time of expenses coming from spectators who would have come to the area, anyway;
- ignorance of eviction effects. Tourists who do not enjoy sport are going to cancel their planned visit because of the sporting event;
- ignorance of leaks from the territory;
- arbitrary choice of a multiplier;
- non-justified choice of the perimeter of the study.

These reasons often explain the overvaluation of the impact.

2.1.2 Small areas

(a) Choice of a theory.   The case of small areas is radically different from the complexity of the previous cases, but there are still difficulties in the calculation of the impact. The first difficulty is about the choice of a theoretical base and, in this respect, it may be the base theory which could fit for small areas as an explanation of their economic development. The big sporting events, considered as basic activities, can then be considered as a propulsive power of economic growth in these areas. The main problem lies in the identification of the base linked to the sporting event, assuming that there are mixed activities (both basic and non-basic) and linked activities (that some regroup under the name of indirect effects). In particular, at the level of methods of identification, in light of the insufficiency of indirect techniques stemming from the coefficients of localization, it is often more advisable to use direct methods by questionnaire. The cost of such identification in large areas often makes it impossible, as opposed to the case of small areas which can thus be the object of a relatively reliable investigation.

(b) Conditions of implementation.   The spatialized circuit of a sporting event has to be reconstructed by noting all the monetary movements which come into and out of the area (Figure 7.4).

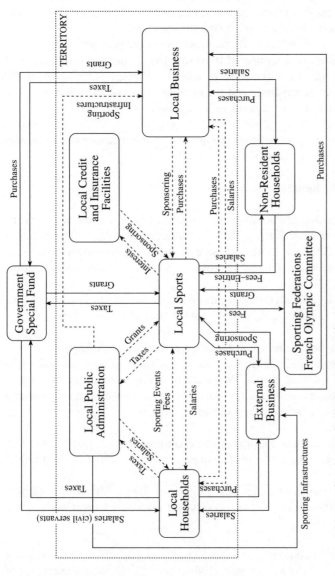

Source: Bourg and Gouguet (1998).

Figure 7.4   Monetary flows associated with sporting events.

167

Many types of difficulties emerge here in being able to report accurately on the real impact:

- estimation of the net injection (gross injections less the leaks). Very often, important sporting events in small areas are profitable in other areas, as the leaks out of the circuit are great.
- estimation of induced effects, which poses the problem of the choice of a multiplier. It appeared to us that the disintegrated multiplier of Wilson, which combines the specificities of responsible agents in the first waves of expenses and the characteristics of the micro regional productive structure, is the more adapted.

As always, it is apparent that the quality of the measure of the impact will depend on the quality of the information collected.

2.2   Use of the Results

Once the economic impact of a sporting event is evaluated, what can be done with the results? It has to be acknowledged that very often there is a real diversity in the use of the measure of the economic impact: demands for State aid, demand to build a stadium, and so on, to the public institutions.

We would like to underline once more that these demands are not legitimate but have to be integrated into another type of justification.

2.2.1   Illegitimacy of the use of the scope of the economic impact

We will not speak again about the meaning of the results of the studies on the impact of sporting events. We would like only to mention that, whatever the party (opponent or partisan), using the economic impact argument to justify or refuse public aids is not acceptable:

- for the partisans, the important economic impact justifies the fact that the government subsidizes a professional team or the building of a stadium.
- for the opponents, the lack of impact means that the taxpayers finance the enrichment of players and owners, which is not the aim of a subsidy.

Vis-à-vis these two points, one should follow the debate which took place in Canada around the Mills report (1998) about the economic incidence of the sport. Nonetheless, in this field, it is Stringer (1980) who has most vigorously condemned the use of the scope of economic impact for political aims. Let us take again the following example, adapted from Stringer: a community has the choice between the building of a large stadium or a hospital. For reasons concerning the economic structure of the territory, the large stadium can be mainly built with local resources (work, capital, and so on), whereas the hospital has to use specialized external enterprises, imported material, and so on. From this fact, the economic impact of the first project is very important, in contrast to the impact of the second one. For all that, must the stadium be built?

One can see very well that this reasoning is not relevant. The choice between the two projects depends on the scope of non-satisfied needs in the sporting or medical fields. If the hospital belongs to a deficient infrastructure, the health of all the population will weigh more in the calculation of cost/profits than the mere entertainment of a small number of inhabitants. One could multiply these typical examples.

This means that even when the calculation of economic impact is accurate, one must not assimilate this impact into the social profitability of the project. This profitability is the difference between the advantages that a population derives from the project and the costs it has to support. The conclusion is clear: it is not sufficient to calculate the economic impact of a project without calculating the utility for the population of such a project. In other words, a calculation of the economic impact cannot, by definition, demonstrate the profitability of a project. It only tells us that the project in question generates a given volume of economic activity, of employment. And that is all. It does not teach us whether this project really deserves to be conducted or not.

2.2.2   An item of the total economic value

If the scope of the economic impact of a project cannot be, by itself, a criterion of decision, one can nonetheless include this item in the calculation of the total economic value of the sporting event. We have shown in the first part of this chapter that a typology of sporting events puts in opposition events with great utility and weak impact and events with weak utility and great impact. The difficulty for comparison stems from the measure of the social utility of projects with, in particular, the evaluation of externalities. It is in this context that one can put the economic impact. It is synonymous with social cohesion, creation of jobs, decrease of delinquency, and so on, and so in this capacity counts among the positive externalities. All in all, the scope of economic impact of a sporting event would thus be an item amongst others of the total economic value of these events.

In conclusion, we will merely say that we wish we could see a little less study of the economic impact of sporting events (more or less serious) and a little more study of the costs/advantages of trying to integrate at best the externalities produced by sporting events. We have tried to suggest that, even if it is not easy, such an exercise is not impossible. In any case, we cannot go on using the calculation of economic impact for aims that are not economically correct.

REFERENCES

Baade, R. (1996), 'Professional sports as catalysts for metropolitan economic development', *Journal of Urban Affairs*, 1.
Baade, R. and R. Dye (1988), 'An analysis of the economic rationale for public subsidization of sports stadiums', *The Annals of Regional Science*, July.
Baade, R and R. Dyer (1990), 'The impact of stadiums and professional sports on metropolitan area development', *Growth and Change: a Journal of Urban and Regional Policy*, Spring.
Baade, R. and V. Matheson (2000), 'An assessment of the economic impact of the American football championship, the Superbowl, on host communities', special edition, *Reflets et Perspectives de la Vie Economique, Sport et mondialisation: quel enjeu pour le XXIe siècle*, Brussels: De Boeck.
Barget, E. (2001), 'Le spectacle sportif ponctuel: essai d'évaluation' (2 vols), PhD, University of Limoges, under the direction of JJ. Gouguet.
Barget, E. and J.J. Gouguet (2000), 'Impact économique du spectacle sportif: revue critique de la littérature', special edition, *Reflets et Perpectives de la Vie Economique, Sport et mondialisation: quel enjeu pour le XXIe siècle*, Brussels: De Boeck.
Bonnieux, F. and B. Desaigues (1998), *Economie et Politiques de l'Environnement*, Paris: Précis Dalloz.
Bourg, J.F. (2000), 'L'Economie du Sport', in P. Arnaud (ed.) *Le Sport en France. Une approche politique, économique et sociale*, Paris: Les études de la Documentation Française.
Bourg, J.F. and J.J. Gouguet (1998), *Analyse Économique du Sport*, Paris: PUF.
Bourg, J.F. and J.J. Gouguet (2001), *Economie du Sport*, Paris: La Découverte, Coll. Repères, (forthcoming).
Gouguet, JJ. and J.F. Nys (1993), *Sport et Développement Économique Régional*, Paris: Dalloz.
Lavoie, M. (1997), *Avantage numérique, l'argent et la ligue nationale de hockey. Vents d'ouest*, Québec: Hull.
Miller H. and R. Jackson (1988), 'The impact of the professional football strike in the Chicago land area', *Illinois Business Review*, 45.
Mills, D. (1998), 'Le sport au Canada: leadership, partenariat et imputabilité', Chambre des Communes, Canada, November.
Stringer, Y. (1980), 'Le faux miracle des retombées économiques', *La Presse*, 18 December 1980, Montreal.

8. The Soccer World Cup 2006 in Germany: choosing match locations by applying a modified cost–benefit model

Bernd Rahmann and Markus Kurscheidt

1. INTRODUCTION

On 6 July 2000, the Fédération Internationale de Football Association (FIFA) awarded the right to host the Soccer World Cup 2006 to Germany. This brought a bidding campaign of the German soccer association (DFB) of over seven years and a (costly) neck-and-neck struggle between five ambitious candidates to an end.[1] Likewise, from an economic perspective, FIFA's voting finished the first level of a *two-stage decision problem* that faces a national soccer association willing to host a World Cup. On the first level, it has to be decided whether it can be rationally justified by socio-economic criteria to bid for the event. On the second level, the soccer association and FIFA must determine, relative to strategic goals, the venues where the World Cup matches are to be held. In practice, besides the usual uncertainty and measurement difficulties, a number of analytical problems as to this two-stage decision comes forth, among others: which evaluation approach and decision rules to choose and how to keep the first-level evaluation consistent with the second-level analysis.

For the case of the Soccer World Cup 2006 in Germany, Rahmann et al. (1998) carried out an *ex ante* study by the use of cost–benefit analysis (CBA) mainly intended to underpin the decision on the first-level problem (see also Kurscheidt and Rahmann, 1999; Rahmann, 1997). They clearly identified three main driving forces of the (socio-)economic impact: (1) the level of stadium investments in the pre-event phase, (2) foreign tourist spending in the present phase, and (3) the net result of operating the stadiums in the post-event phase. The investments play a crucial role since they induce both additional income by multiplier effects, that is benefits, and current capital charges accruing from debt-financed (sports) infrastructure expenditures during the post-event phase. Moreover, they are indirectly positively correlated with the tourist spending as a result of the impact of stadium capacity and regional attractiveness for World Cup tourists. Therefore the effects of venue investments are 'ambivalent' whereas the spending of foreigners will of course be responsible for a considerable economic impulse in the year 2006 which is also reinforced by multipliers. Running the arenas, finally, brings about continuous deficits because the majority of German stadiums are not able to cover operating costs, not to mention capital charges (compare, for example, Vornholz, 2000). Thus, the choice of venues indeed is a crucial strategic task for World Cup organizers which largely determines the overall net impact of the event (Section 2 in this chapter).

Due to diverse uncertainties, nine years prior to the event, Rahmann et al. (1998) were forced to yield their results on the basis of *anonymous* scenarios derived from a portfolio approach which model different spatial constellations of potential match locations (Section 3.1). Now that Germany has been awarded the World Cup 2006, it becomes clearer which German cities are available and likely to be considered as hosting locations. To evaluate the second-level decision problem, the cost–benefit model of the 1998 study can and should be modified in the light of the actual stadium construction plans of the respective cities (Section 3.2). Hence, the *aim of this chapter is to adjust the initial CBA to the simulation of the consequences of alternative sets of locations as decision support for the choice of venues.* Having this in view, the following section examines the two-stage decision problem in further detail. Section 3 describes the modified cost–benefit model of the Soccer World Cup 2006 in Germany. Then, the computed results are presented in the fourth section. Section 5 concludes with some political economy and decision implications of the choice of match locations that may be derived from the previous findings.

2.   THE TWO-STAGE DECISION PROBLEM OF BIDS FOR SOCCER WORLD CUPS

The first level of the two-stage decision problem whether or not to hold a so-called sport mega-event like the Olympics (see Baade and Matheson, Chapter 6 in this volume and Preuss, 2000a) or a Soccer World Cup is no more an exclusive matter of sporting considerations or national sports policies, be it represented by sports federations or governmental bodies. In times of tight public budgets and considerable tax burdens, more and more, such major public projects in the field of sports have to be economically justified as well (Preuss, 2000b; Rahmann et al., 1998; Maennig, 1991). A broad support of the bid can best be guaranteed by demonstrating that there will potentially be a positive overall economic outcome. Consequently, a good deal of the studies commissioned by organizers for this purpose, more or less explicitly and intentionally, have the tendency to overestimate the economic benefits of the event and to underestimate or neglect costs. This problem, as well as their often inappropriate methodology and/or their poor use of measurement techniques, has been analysed and criticized in depth by independent researchers (see among others Baade and Matheson, 2000, as well as in this volume; Davidson, 1999; Dietl and Pauli, 1999; Kesenne, 1999a and b; Preuss, 2000a; Thöni, 1999; Andreff and Nys, 1997; Gouguet and Nys, 1993). But a weak analysis result would indeed suggest the withdrawal of the candidature, unless it is widely accepted that the event generates such high *intangible* benefits for all that the expected economic costs are thought to be warrantable, so to speak, as a 'price' for qualitative returns (Rahmann et al., 1998, pp. 103–6).[2] However, the *first decision level* consists of approximately *assessing the 'value' of the event in terms of money*, relative to a meaningful economic (welfare) criterion.[3] A positive evaluation in that sense would support serious bidding efforts.[4]

Despite its well-known theoretical and analytical deficiencies,[5] it is increasingly agreed among economists that CBA is the most suitable approach to *back-up decisions* on the evaluation problem of sporting events (see, for example, Preuss, 2000b; Jeanrenaud, 1999, pp. 1–3; Kesenne, 1999a and b; Maennig, 1998; Burgan and Mules, 1992; Thöni, 1984, and the comparative analysis of approaches in Kurscheidt, 2000a and 2001). Other approaches frequently used in so-called *economic impact studies* in the field of sports, such as in particular the (pure) expenditure approach in conjunction with (simple) multiplier analysis or input–output analysis, (1) fail to clearly distinguish between positive and negative repercussions of the examined event,[6] (2) often focus just on short-term impacts and, even if a longer period is considered, they are not able to intertemporally evaluate long-term effects, (3) neglect 'intangibles', that is impacts which are difficult or impossible to monetize, (4) do not provide a theoretically underpinned evaluation criterion. In contrast to those approaches, CBA is *explicitly* designed to respond to the analysis requirements of a proper project evaluation: first, it differentiates event-induced effects in clear-cut cost and benefit categories including indirect and intangible impacts; then, they are valuated as far as possible, reckoned up and discounted for time over the whole (long-term) planning horizon; finally, the often complex positive and negative repercussions and interdependencies can be reduced to one aggregated figure, the *net present value* (NPV). As to the evaluation, the first decision rule is straightforward. The project that exhibits the highest NPV, that is the highest aggregated net contribution to GNP, relative to alternative uses of resources should be chosen. Theoretically, the costs of the selected project are represented by the foregone utility of the second-best alternative (opportunity cost principle). Strictly speaking, *all* conceivable alternatives must be known to properly determine the two best projects. But with respect to sporting mega-events, the difficulty is that literally no meaningful alternative can be identified. Their characteristics are so unique, their induced multiple socio-economic effects so far-reaching, and the opportunity to host them so singular in time that there is really nothing comparable, that is any substitute project which serves similar public and social functions (Kurscheidt and Rahmann, 1999; Maennig, 1998; Steiner and Thöni, 1995). Thus, it is a 'do it or leave it' decision which refers to an NPV exceeding at least zero under consideration of the Kaldor–Hicks welfare criterion, that is a *potential* Pareto optimality.[7]

Whereas the first level of the decision problem also arises when planning a bid for other sporting mega-events like the Olympic Games (see Preuss, 2000a and Maennig, 1991) the *second decision level* is specific to Soccer World Cups. They are held by *one* nation or national federation but the respective matches actually take place in *several* cities across the country, in contrast to the Olympics that are hosted by one city in a well-defined local area (Kurscheidt, 2000b; Kurscheidt and Rahmann, 1999).[8] Thus, once the World Cup has been awarded to a certain country, technically speaking, a *strategic decision problem under prior set objectives and institutional constraints* emerges with regard to the choice of match locations. Benefit maximization of course remains the prevailing economic objective, but, because of the vast variety of socio-economic event-induced effects, it has to be weighted by risk and socio-political considerations. Hence, two major strategies of selecting venues may be of particular interest for organizers: (1) *risk-minimizing*, that is stressing economic criteria, (2) pursuing *development goals* including related qualitative sub- or side goals (among others geographical dispersion of venues, distributional equity, urban and regional planning, international competitiveness of sports infrastructure, socio-cultural considerations), that is emphasizing (sports) policy criteria.

However, strategically composed sets of locations that may potentially maximize the achievement of those goals have to meet certain *institutional constraints*. First, only those cities can be considered that have officially submitted a bid for hosting World Cup matches which includes, even up to nine years prior to the event, the binding promise to provide an appropriate venue (OK-Deutschland 2006, 2001a and DFB 1997).[9] Second, there is a number of FIFA regulations governing or at least influencing the choice of locations, in particular the official regulations for the FIFA World Cup

(FIFA, 1999). So the current number of teams and matches at World Cups amounts to 32 and 64, respectively (ibid., Art. 7, paras. 1 and 3).[10] The hosting national soccer association is obliged to establish a Local Organizing Committee (LOC) that is responsible for the preparation and organization of the event (ibid., Preamble, par. 4) under 'the supervision and control of FIFA, which has the last word on all matters' (ibid. par. 5). FIFA is represented by the Organizing Committee for the FIFA World Cup (OCF) (FIFA 1999, Art. 11) which actually is the body that determines the venues and stadiums 'after consultation' (ibid., par. 5B,c) with the LOC and whose decisions are 'final and binding' (ibid., par. 6). Consequently, on the one hand, the freedom of the LOC to set its proper objectives and to choose the corresponding venues is fairly limited. On the other hand, the regulations do not prescribe any criteria for the choice of locations, either with respect to the composition of venues or to their total number. Thus, there is a considerable scope for various options. Finally, FIFA imposes some demanding technical requirements on potential World Cup arenas. The matches are only to be played either in all-seater stadiums or, in the case of venues with standing areas available, the latter must be closed or temporarily converted into seating areas (FIFA 1999, Art. 18, par. 3). For the 48 group matches of the first round, a seating capacity of 40000 and upwards is required, the 16 play-offs need a capacity of about 50000 and the final of 60000 plus. Of course, even bigger arenas of 80,000 seats or more are welcome (FIFA, n.d.). Moreover, a number of features are recommended and, therewith, somehow tacitly demanded at least for some 'exemplary' venues: fully roofed spectator areas or, at best, a retractable roof covering the whole arena, pure soccer stadiums without running tracks, video screens, shops, restaurants, meeting rooms, VIP lounges, business seats and so on (Dietl and Pauli, 2000b; FIFA, n.d.). The investment costs of a new construction of such venues vary with the quality of the equipment and range from about 200 million DM for a 'basic' stadium to 500 million DM or even more for a so-called Superdome with, among other features, a big capacity, high degree of spectators' comfort, retractable roof and removable playing field to maintain the natural turf.

As to the evaluation problem on the second decision level, one faces *several strategic options* of the choice of locations whose net consequences can be revealed by CBA. Thus, in contrast to the first level, the decision rule is now compatible with the opportunity cost principle. The alternative with the highest NPV is to be chosen. But the NPV should still exceed zero since otherwise the conditions for the evaluation of the first decision level may be violated. Here the analytical challenge arises that a first *ex ante* evaluation study prior to a decision on bidding for the event has to be carried out without knowing the exact locations involved in the tournament. After the allocation of the event to a certain country the first analysis has to be modified in a *consistent* way to properly depict possible changes of the initial evaluation and the repercussions of different sets of 'real' venues with data of cities that are actually bidding for hosting World Cup matches. A solution to this problem will be discussed in the next section for the case of the Soccer World Cup 2006 in Germany.

3. MODIFICATIONS OF THE COST–BENEFIT MODEL

3.1   General Structure of the Model

Rahmann et al. (1998) used a portfolio technique to construct significant constellations of the spatial economic structure at potential match locations, that is building *anonymous* scenarios. The approach is straightforward. The main determinant on the *supply side* is the need of investment in facilities which consists of (1) non-sport (yield) interests, especially of private sector investors, (2) the politically desired improvement of infrastructure, and (3) the (existing) (*sport*) *infrastructure endowment* relative to FIFA requirements. Since, *ex ante* on the first evaluation level, the first two components are hardly observable, the latter is sufficient as a proxy for expected investment expenditure. Later, on the second level, the political will of course also becomes public or at least implicitly visible by the stadium investment planned at the respective match location. On the *demand side*, one can only consider the *potential of demand* which is responsible for the future capacity utilization of the new or renovated sports stadiums, that is their profitability. Obviously, there is no appropriate proxy for the local demand because it has a number of elements, such as, for example, population density, purchasing power, propensity to consume, competitive environment in the leisure sector. Considering also financing costs, the local net benefit results from the effects of these determinants.

  The remaining two determinants of the spatial economic structure at the locations, potential of demand and (sport) infrastructure endowment, can be combined with each other in a portfolio matrix. In order to derive meaningful standardized locations, it is sufficient to ascribe three levels to each of the two determinants: (1) low, (2) medium and (3) high. This yields the nine-field portfolio shown in Figure 8.1. For each of these fields, the expected net benefit effect can be assessed both in the short and the long run according to the level of investment and utilization, respectively. Those fields that are not plausible in a meaningful set of locations should be sorted out. Field IX can be omitted since the combination of high infra-

	I	II	III
high	*short term*: B < C, high investment *long term*: B > C, high utilization	*short term*: B ≈ C, medium investment *long term*: B > C, high utilization	*short term*: B > C, low investment *long term*: B > C, high utilization
	IV	**V**	**VI**
medium	*short term*: B < C, high investment *long term*: B ≈ C, medium utilization	*short term*: B ≈ C, medium investment *long term*: B ≈ C, medium utilization	*short term*: B > C, low investment *long term*: B ≈ C, medium utilization
	VII	**VIII**	**IX**
low	*short term*: B < C, high investment *long term*: B < C, low utilization	*short term*: B ≈ C, medium investment *long term*: B < C, low utilization	*short term*: B > C, low investment *long term*: B < C, low utilization
	low	medium	high

Potential of demand

(Sport) Infrastructure endowment

Notes: B = benefits, C = costs.

Figure 8.1 Matrix of potential World Cup locations

structure and low demand is not realistic. Field VII should be dropped because it is (rationally) not desirable to consider locations that clearly lead to a negative local outcome. Grouping the remaining seven fields according to their net effect of short-term and long-term impacts yields four distinct *scenarios*: Scenario 1 (field III) leads to the best result with certain net benefits, scenario 2 (fields II and VI) generates a good result with probable net benefits, whereas the outcome of scenario 3 (fields I and V) is uncertain and, finally, scenario 4 (fields IV and VIII) yields a poor result with probable net costs. It should be kept in mind that political and private preferences could cause a shift of the position of their location in this scheme. If, for instance, a location with a high or medium level of infrastructure decides for any reason to build a new stadium instead of adjusting the old one to basic FIFA requirements by renovation works, it places itself more to the left of the portfolio than it would have been initially categorized, for example a shift from field II to I.[11]

Concerning the composition of at least ten necessary venues, assumptions have to be made on the distribution of these scenarios in hypothetical sets of potential locations. This had been done in the 1998 study in a somewhat technical way by building three hypotheses around a mean assessment, called hypothesis II, based on a stylized normal distribution, that is 2-3-3-2 beginning with scenario 1 up to scenario 4 (see Appendix, Table 8A.1). Money values have now to be ascribed to each scenario in order to compute the aggregated outcome of the hypotheses, that is the model parameters are estimated in currency units. For uncertainty reasons and the well-known measurement difficulties mentioned above, an appropriate spread of the true value around the estimate has to be systematically implemented in the estimation design. This is best done by *worst-* and *best-case analysis* (compare, for example, Boardman et al., 1996; Hanusch, 1994; Mishan, 1988). This method consists of building upper and lower bounds for each estimate. When computing the model, the proper combination of these upper and lower values yields two aggregated results, one for best-case assumptions, and one for worst-case assumptions. All outcomes in between these extremes represent the realistic, or (most) probable range of net benefits (see Appendix, Table 8A.2). The probability that the true result falls within this range actually rises with the number of variables considered in the model. But the interval between the worst and best case, of course, gets larger, too.

A planning horizon of 15 periods is considered, starting in the year 2000 with the FIFA decision on the hosting nation. Furthermore, the general economic setting is held constant (that is absence of inflation, of any politico-economic influences or shocks, of exchange rate or business cycle effects and so on) and all money values (given in Deutschmarks, DM) are based on 1996 prices.[12] The following variables can currently be estimated with sufficient precision and are considered in the model according to their occurrence over time in brackets (for the data see Table 8.1 and Appendix, Table 8A.5): (1) investment costs (at one third of the total amount in $t = 3$ to 5), (2) capital charges, including interests and amortization as an annual percentage of investment costs, and operating costs (both from $t = 6$ to 15), (3) benefits from the utilization of the sport infrastructure, that is especially revenue from rents of soccer clubs, sponsoring, catering, and special events (from $t = 6$ to 15), (4) benefits from foreign tourist spending (in $t = 6$), (5) benefits from additional income induced by multiplier effects of investment (from $t = 4$ to 6) and consumption expenditures (in $t = 7$), (6) benefits from the budget surplus of the LOC, that is revenues minus expenses (in $t = 6$).

3.2   Building Hypotheses on Sets of Locations

Most of the German venues for professional soccer exhibit a considerable need of modernization or have to be replaced by new arenas to reestablish (inter-)national competitiveness (compare Dietl and Pauli, 1999, 2000a and b; Roland Berger & Partner GmbH, 1998). The total amount of required investments for the two professional leagues, *Bundesliga* (1st division) and *2. Liga* (2nd division), could be assessed at about 4 billion DM (Vornholz, 2000). Depending on the composition of venues, the investment needed for the World Cup 2006 ranges between about 1.4 and 2.8 billion DM (based on 1996 prices) in the present analysis (see Appendix, Table 8A.4). There are currently 16 German cities left which have submitted a binding declaration to provide a suitable venue in 2006. As listed in Table 8.1, the degree to which those cities are suitable and prepared to participate in the World Cup can be economically evaluated according to relevant criteria on the local supply and demand side.

The *supply features* are in particular: (1) the current quality and capacity of the soccer stadium, (2) traffic and hotel infrastructure, that is the regional logistics competence, and (3) general touristic attractiveness. Although the evaluation of the latter remains rather subjective, it may be supposed that all those features are significantly positively correlated with the degree of agglomeration. Anyway, the first feature is the most important and can be well observed by hard facts like the need of investment for the World Cup and the planned capacity in 2006 as well as further qualitative considerations with respect to modern stadium construction 'standards' mentioned in Section 2. Therefore, apart from building new hypotheses on the scenario distribution, those data (columns two and three in Table 8.1) make the essential difference to the modified cost–benefit model compared to the 1998 study. It has to be kept in mind that the investment expenditure also

Table 8.1 Evaluation of bidding hosting cities and hypotheses

City	Stadium (supply)			Demand		Evaluation				Hypotheses[a]				
	World Cup compatibility[b]	planned investment[c]	capacity in 2006[d]	population (in 1000)	division of soccer club	supply side[e]	demand side[f]	scenario[g]	selection category[h]	OH	HA	HB	A12	B12
1 Berlin*	low	473	76000	3400	1st	low	high	3	backw.		X	X	X	X
2 Bremen	high	55	43000	550	1st	high	high	1	well	X	X		X	
3 Dortmund*	full	0	52000	595	1st	high	high	1	well	X	X	X	X	X
4 Dusseldorf	low	360	50000	570	3rd	low	medium	4	backw.		X		X	
5 Frankfurt/M	low	246	50000	650	2nd	low	high	3	interm.	X	X	X	X	X
6 Gelsenkirchen*	low	375	52000	285	1st	low	high	3	interm.	X	X	X	X	X
7 Hamburg*	full	0	50000	1700	1st	high	high	1	well	X	X	X	X	X
8 Hannover[i]	low	160	45000	525	2nd	medium	medium	3	interm.	X	X		X	X
9 Kaiserslautern	high	94.5	48000	100	1st	medium	high	2	well	X	X		X	X
10 Cologne	low	215	45000	1000	1st	low	high	3	interm.	X	X		X	X
11 Leipzig*	low	177.1	44000	530	4th	medium	low	4	backw.	X	X	X	X	X
12 Leverkusen[j]	full	5.5	22500	160	1st	high	high	1	well	X				
13 M'gladbach	low	155	43000	270	1st	medium	medium	3	interm.		X	X		X
14 Munich[k]*	low	400	66000	1300	1st	low	high	3	interm.	X	X	X	X	X
15 Nuremberg	low	123	44000	490	1st	medium	medium	3	interm.				X	X
16 Stuttgart	high	102	60000	550	1st	medium	high	2	well	X	X		X	X

Notes:

OH = economically optimal hypothesis of available venues with 10 arenas, HA = risk-minimizing hypothesis with 10 venues, HB = development goal hypothesis with 10 venues, A12 = risk-minimizing hypothesis with 12 venues, B12 = development goal hypothesis with 12 venues.

* Venues considered to be pre-set for (sports) policy reasons in the realistic hypotheses HA, HB, A12, and B12.

[a] Venues chosen for the respective hypothesis are marked by an X.

b World Cup compatibility according to technical requirements of FIFA and international 'standards' of modern venues (compare FIFA n.d.).

c Figures are given in million DM, latest data of 24 October 2001. In the CBA, those values are deflated to basis 1996 using the latest official price index for 2000 to keep the data consistent with the 1998 study. For this reason, the currency DM is kept constant. To find €/Euro values, the figures have to be multiplied by 0.511291 and rounded down.

d Seating capacity planned for the year 2006, latest data of 24 October 2001.

e Evaluation criteria: current quality and capacity of soccer stadium, traffic and hotel infrastructure, touristic attractiveness.

f Evaluation criteria: population and hinterland, local purchasing power, attraction potential (especially league division at the end of 2001 and supporters' enthusiasm) and supposed future performance of the soccer club, competition in the soccer and leisure market (all relative to the planned stadium capacity in 2006).

g Scenario according to the evaluated position in Figure 8.1.

h Selection categories: well prepared (scenarios 1–2), intermediate (2–3), backward (3–4).

i Hannover is not being considered in any hypothesis because of its quite low evaluation (intermediate, scenario 3) and expected financing burdens of the EXPO 2000. Moreover, it is not determined yet whether the venue will be renovated (100 million DM) or newly built (160 million DM, this value is assumed in the table).

j The capacity of the stadium in Leverkusen does not meet the FIFA requirements by far (40000 upwards) but it is very well constructed and equipped. Therefore it is considered at least in hypothesis OH but not in any other although it is likely to be chosen for political reasons by settling a special arrangement, for example as an additional 11th or 13th venue with only 2 instead of 5 or 6 matches (compare Bielicki and Käppner, 2001). Such a contingency cannot yet be consistently introduced in the model.

k The Olympic Stadium in Munich is the only one in Germany which is regularly used by two first division soccer clubs, FC Bayern and TSV 1860 Munich. Thus, it has by far the highest capacity utilization and is likely to be (the most) profitable (venue). Since this is a special case and exact data are not yet available, for consistency reasons, the venue is classified in Figure 8.1 and treated according to the same criteria like all other stadiums, that is the local outcome of Munich in the model is much worse than can be expected in reality. Furthermore, a new stadium project has just lately been approved by a local referendum on 21 October 2001. Hence, there are still a number of uncertainties.

Sources: OK–Deutschland 2006 (2001b), DFB (1999), own judgements.

determines the capital charges after the event and the investment multiplier effects whereas the stadium capacity, weighted by the distribution of matches among venues, is the variable that drives the tourist spending in the model. The *demand side* finally is responsible for the assessment of future benefits of the new sports facilities in the post-event phase (see Appendix, Table 8A.5). The relevant evaluation criteria are, above all: (1) population and hinterland, (2) local purchasing power, (3) attraction potential (especially current league division and supporters' enthusiasm) and supposed future performance of the local soccer club, (4) competition in the soccer and leisure market (all relative to the planned stadium capacity in 2006). The two latter criteria are considered to be decisive in cases of doubts with regard to the exact evaluation because the amount and risk of annual revenues yielded by big arenas in Germany largely depend on high-level soccer, that is at best a long-term successful 1st division club or a traditional club with very loyal fans[13] (compare Dietl and Pauli, 2000b; Vornholz, 2000; Rahmann et al., 1998, pp. 188–94).

According to the judgement on those criteria, the position of the 16 bidding cities in Figure 8.1, and thereby the respective scenario, can be assessed (see Table 8.1). Meaningful hypotheses on their composition in potential sets of match locations have then to be built. For this purpose, it is helpful to introduce a further classification to ascertain the current level of preparation: (1) well prepared, that is scenarios 1 to 2, (2) intermediate, that is scenarios 2 to 3, (3) backward venue, that is scenarios 3 to 4. Now, as discussed in the second section, two major strategies of composing match locations may be assumed. Moreover, for each of them, one set of venues is chosen with ten arenas and one with twelve because this is the range of venues that is thought to be necessary by experienced World Cup organizers.[14] This yields *four realistic hypotheses*: (1) a risk-minimizing hypothesis *HA* with ten venues, (2) a development goals-pursuing hypothesis *HB* with ten venues, (3) a risk-minimizing hypothesis *A12* with twelve venues, and (4) a development goals-pursuing hypothesis *B12* with twelve venues. For all of them, six match locations are considered as being pre-set, three of them for political and three for economic reasons. The LOC already declared that the opening match may take place in Munich and the final in Berlin. Furthermore, to underpin the objective to hold an 'all-German World Cup', at least two venues in the eastern part of Germany have to be involved. Besides Berlin, the DFB designated Leipzig where it was founded in the year 1900. By now, the German federal government has already assured the public financing of both venues. Finally, Dortmund and Hamburg are very likely to be and should be chosen because both of them are important agglomeration areas with well prepared venues and successful soccer clubs (both scenario 1). Gelsenkirchen and its club FC

Schalke 04 have just finished the construction of the first Superdome in Germany and will thus also be considered for its modern and impressive arena. The remaining four to six positions in the hypotheses are selected according to the above strategies and the evaluation of the cities as listed in Table 8.1. For the risk-minimizing strategy, low-cost venues are favoured and, for the development strategy, new stadium constructions and smaller or peripheral cities are preferred. As to the number of the 64 matches played in the stadiums, for consistency reasons, an equal distribution of 60 games is assumed for all hypotheses, that is 6 matches in the ten venues case and 5 in the twelve arenas case, respectively. The remaining 4 encounters (for example opening, final, semi-finals) are allocated to the biggest pre-set venues of Berlin, Munich, Dortmund and Gelsenkirchen.

Bearing in mind the opportunity principle of comparing meaningful alternatives, those hypotheses should be evaluated relative to an *economically 'optimal' set of available venues* that largely neglects any socio-political qualitative considerations. This selection of match locations includes ten venues and follows decision rules that are strictly economic criteria oriented. First, the best-prepared venues are chosen, that is the four scenario 1's and two scenario 2's available. Then, the next-best four scenario 3's which exhibit at least one 'high' evaluation, that is intermediate locations fitting in field I of Figure 8.1, with the lowest investment values are picked out. By this procedure some scenario 3's with quite high investment levels (especially Gelsenkirchen and Munich) are preferred to others with relatively low investment costs (especially M'gladbach and Nuremberg). At first glance, this might seem economically dubious. But it is reasonable to place a higher weight upon the general potential of demand in the case of scenario 3 since the already chosen scenarios 1 and 2 are the strongest venues on the supply side. Six matches are assumed to be played in each arena whereas the remaining four games are allocated to the biggest venues of this selection.[15] The resulting hypothesis OH would be the 'optimal' set of available venues for a rational, risk-averse decision-maker who disregards socio-political aspects. In other words, the inflow of foreign purchasing power of World Cup tourists is 'bought' by the hosting nation at the lowest economic 'price' possible. Furthermore, the result of hypothesis OH (see next section) is close to the outcome of hypothesis I which had been the best and thus recommended in the 1998 study (see also Appendix, Tables 8A.8 and 8A.9). But it has to be stressed that this hypothesis is neither realistic nor suitable to serve even crucial socio-political goals, such as particularly the objective of an 'all-German World Cup' since Berlin and Leipzig would not be involved. Hence, *hypothesis OH is a purely economic reference* that is not claimed to be the best alternative under real world conditions.[16]

4. RESULTS OF THE MODIFIED COST–BENEFIT ANALYSIS

Figures 8.2 and 8.3 show the aggregated result computed by the modified cost–benefit model. The discounted net benefits per period (in million DM, basis 1996) and NPVs, respectively, of the five hypotheses are depicted over time by two graphs for each hypothesis: one for upper bound assumptions and one for lower bound assumptions of the estimated parameters. The heavy line represents the outcome of hypothesis OH as the reference for the evaluation of the alternative sets of match locations. First of all, the pattern shown in both figures is consistent with the findings of the 1998 study. The pre-event phase is dominated by the cost effect of the investment in sports infrastructure, then a considerable upswing occurs in the present phase due to multiplier effects and tourism expenditures whereas constant deficits of operating the sports facilities prevail in the post-event phase (see Appendix, Tables 8A.6 and 8A.7). An essential difference to the 1998 results make the higher peaks of values in Figure 8.2 especially at the upper bound. This is due to the, on average, significantly higher investments, in particular at the lower bound as a result of the more precise data of real stadium construction plans which allows the reduction of the estimation interval (see Appendix, Tables 8A.3 and 8A.4). In contrast, the mean tourist spending is slightly lower than in 1998 (see ibid.) which, except for hypothesis OH in particular at the upper bound,[17] obviously does not have a major influence compared to the former results.

The crucial phase of the planning horizon that clearly differentiates the present results from those of 1998 is actually after the event when the business loss of the venues risks devouring the benefits of the present phase. This can be best seen by the NPVs in Figure 8.3 (for the exact figures see Appendix, Table 8A.9). At the upper bound and for the most probable mean outcome, this is not vital. There, the World Cup 2006 indeed is responsible for a 'hysteresis-like', sustainable shift in economic wealth of about 5 (hypothesis OH) up to 6 billion DM (hypothesis B 12). That means a slightly higher gain than in the 1998 study (see Appendix, Table 8A.8). The average result under base assumptions also remains quite stable on a still considerable level of approximately 2.5 billion DM which is not significantly higher than the 1998 outcome. But, in case of difficult general circumstances, the future financing burdens might generate an overall loss as soon as four (hypothesis B12), five (hypotheses HB) or six years (hypothesis A12) after the event if either the 'twelve venues' solution is preferred or if a development strategy is pursued. This finding is more critical than in the 1998 study. The risk-minimizing hypothesis HA with ten stadiums is the only realistic set of match locations that yields only a slight loss of roughly

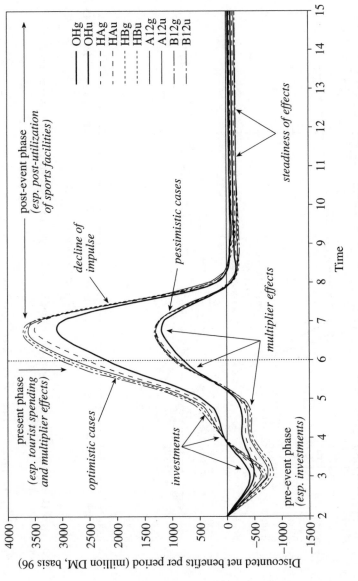

Note: The German language subscripts g (= *günstig*) and u (= *ungünstig*) of the hypotheses indicate the upper and lower bound assumptions, respectively.

Figure 8.2   Discounted net benefits per period of modified hypotheses

185

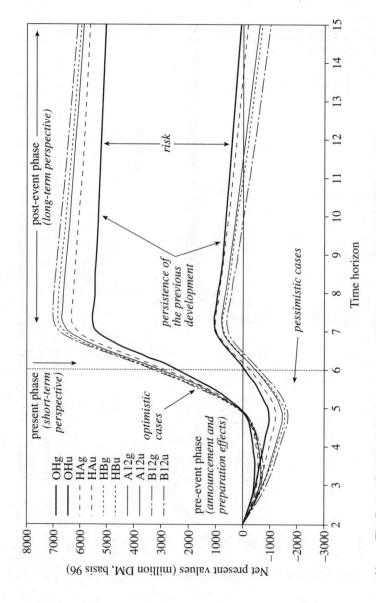

Note: The German language subscripts g (= *günstig*) and u (= *ungünstig*) of the hypotheses indicate the upper and lower bound assumptions, respectively.

Figure 8.3 Net present values of modified hypotheses

57 million DM, and not until eight years after the event. Finally, the economic reference selection of venues, hypothesis OH, is the only one that remains in the gain zone over the whole planning horizon with an NPV of about 48 million DM in 2015. Thus, at the lower bound of the results, it is pretty clear that the host nation might have to pay an 'economic price' in the form of foregone utility for any socio-political concession made, whether for development reasons or to settle a compromise solution of twelve venues if the choice of venues becomes politically delicate. Likewise, even if the general economic forecasts are favourable, it would be gambling rather than rational decision-making to, *ex ante*, trust on and aim at the better upper bound results by choosing a selection of venues equivalent to the hypotheses B12, HB or A12.

5. CONCLUSION: POLITICAL ECONOMY AND DECISION IMPLICATIONS OF CHOOSING MATCH LOCATIONS

The results presented in the previous section confirm that the decision on the second level is indeed crucial since it determines the most important variable, the investments in durable facilities, and thereby the expected range of the overall outcome. Not before two or three years after the event, will it be possible to approximately assess whether the true result may, as expected, be situated in the middle or rather at the upper or lower bound. If the latter is the case a negative aggregated outcome in the medium or long run cannot be excluded any more for any realistic composition of potential match locations. This risk rises with the weight given to socio-political considerations with regard to the venues chosen. Hence, from an economic welfare perspective, risk-minimizing is the dominant strategy in the model. Furthermore, in this sense, the ten venues solution yields a significantly better result than sets of locations with twelve venues. Therefore, the hypothesis HA appears to be the best choice relative to the economically 'optimal' selection of stadiums that strictly favours the best prepared cities.

But some problems of political economy arise in view of defending this set of venues against particular political and lobbying interests since, for this purpose, it will be indispensable to exclude some (prominent) candidates from the participation in the World Cup. Here, clear-cut strategic goals and decision criteria with respect to a consistent choice of locations become most important. The clearer the LOC and OCF shape and reliably communicate their selection strategy and criteria, the less will be the risk of policy- or lobby-driven deviations from the original conception. Otherwise, interest groups may (mis)use the scope of interpretation to exercise political pressures.[18] Even the LOC and OCF can not, of course, be supposed to pursue national welfare goals as, to a certain degree, implicitly assumed here. Enhancing the average quality of German stadiums may be, for instance, a more important concern for both of them. Therefore, making their criteria more transparent would facilitate a public control. But, however, it cannot really be the interest of the LOC and OCF to economically harm the host country, especially if they have to fear that this may be revealed. Moreover, it is desirable for management efficiency reasons to have a precise orientation for the LOC set by strategic objectives. Those define a reference relative to which the efficiency of the organization could be evaluated in terms of goal achievement. Both the LOC and the host country would benefit from an 'exemplary' organization of the event.

An institutional problem may, however, emerge from the bidding procedure that the potential match locations have to face. The final decision on the 16 German candidate cities is not supposed to be taken until mid-2002 or even the end of 2002 and, at least, four venues will have to be sorted out.[19] Therefore, meanwhile, there will be an incentive, in particular for intermediate locations, to upgrade their stadium construction plans to provide a higher quality of sports infrastructure which may enhance their chances of being chosen (relative to other intermediate locations). The same effect could occur, at least on average, due to expectations on additional benefits from hosting the World Cup. Decision-makers in locations which are very likely to be picked out might think that they could (or should) afford a more impressive arena than initially planned in the light of income inflows induced by the event. Hence, the total investment may well tend to rise, whether the respective bidding venues are finally chosen or not. This could even be the case if the LOC and OCF were willing to introduce measures or criteria to dampen this conduct that causes an increase of investment costs. There are, of course, incentives to underestimate costs and overestimate benefits. Finally, this tendency will render it ever more difficult for public investors in sports facilities to attract private partners for a considerable co-financing (see Dietl and Pauli, 2000b).

Both theoretically plausible effects seem actually to be confirmed by the latest developments of the bidding procedure. The total investment sum planned by all 16 German cities rose during the last year from 2.7 billion DM up to 2.94 billion. Any candidate city is anxious to show that it is really determined to construct the promised new arena. Most of them have started already or are about to start the construction works. The result will be that more World Cup compatible venues will be built than needed. Not only will this tendency foster the future competition between stadiums for special events like rock concerts to generate additional income which is necessary to cover capital charges, but also the rise in average quality of sports arenas might cause even non-bidding cities to think about a (costly) modernization of their venues. Either the local soccer club will exercise such pressures because it is the biggest beneficiary or local politicians may feel as if they are missing an important development. Consequently, there could well be a vicious circle of public investment activity in sports infrastructure which in the end will further compete away the revenue per arena to recoup the financing costs. Under such circumstances, potential private investors in the stadium market will prefer to wait or to allocate their resources elsewhere. This has recently seemed to be true. Several cities were seeking private partners in vain or lost partners during the negotiation process. All in all, those patterns of behaviour put the problematic post-event phase even more at risk.

These implications, moreover, lead to the problem of the decomposition of the aggregated outcome of the Soccer World Cup 2006 and the possible necessity of a certain amount of compensation on allocative grounds. In order to potentially meet Pareto-efficiency conditions, care must be taken for future burdens that will be especially vital in some intermediate and backward match locations. Those local jurisdictions might be negatively affected, in particular in case of disadvantageous circumstances and sets of venues close to the hypotheses HB, A12 and B12. Thus, the weaker the overall result, the likelier will be the existence of 'loser locations' and, thereby, the higher could be the need of compensation, but, at the same time, the lower would be the benefits left for compensating. These problems and risks arising at the lower bound of possible results have to be carefully considered and all necessary (strategic) precautions should be taken to avoid such an outcome. The proper choice of match locations is of course one of those, probably the most important (see Kurscheidt, 2000b). The best would be an agreement or alliance between all involved parties, that is FIFA, the LOC, the national government, and the bidding cities. Such a cooperation should aim at securing a reasonable investment planning and fair competition at the decentralized level. FIFA and the LOC should place a high weight upon financial criteria in their choice of venues and the national government ought to support them in pursuing that end or push them to do so. Furthermore, a quick final decision of FIFA which has to approve the LOC's selection would be desirable to finish the bidding competition as early as possible to prevent cities from upgrading their construction plans or building stadiums that ultimately are not picked out for the World Cup. Generally speaking, some national or supranational control of FIFA's conduct in exploiting their monopoly right on the Soccer World Cup might be worth thinking of as well, since FIFA sets off and further fuels the bidding spiral by its high and ever rising requirements to bidders, first between candidate countries and then, in the second round, between cities of the country that won the event.

As independent *ex post* analyses of mega-events like the one of Baade and Matheson in this volume confirm, institutional decisions and thorough planning in the run-up to the event are crucial for the economic success. Every country or city willing to hold such an event should take those tasks very seriously. As for the present chapter, it has been shown for the case of the 2006 tournament in Germany that an analytical approach based on CBA is suitable to deduce appropriate responses to the World Cup-specific, two-stage decision problem (for some theoretical and methodological extensions see Kurscheidt, 2001). What still remains to be done for the future, among other things, is a continuous adjustment of the CBA to new developments, maybe a regionalization of the present CBA to model decentral outcomes of particular locations, as well as a sound (sensitivity) analysis of further strategic variables.

NOTES

1. South Africa, Morocco, England, Brazil and Germany had submitted a bid for the Soccer World Cup 2006. Because of the expected low chances of success, Brazil drew back its candidature shortly before the ballot. Thus, actually, there were only four bids left in the voting on 6 July 2000. The 24 members of FIFA's Executive Committee took the historical decision at the most narrow ballot result possible with 12 votes to 11 and one abstention against the last remaining competitor, South Africa, in the third and final round of voting (Radford, 2000). For Germany, the bidding campaign had begun already on 2 June 1993 with the first submission of the DFB's candidature at the FIFA's seat in Zurich (OK-Deutschland, 2006, 2001a).
2. The assessment that political and reputational benefits justify a potential cost overhang seems to be the case for the Soccer World Cup 2002 which is co-hosted by South-Korea and Japan. Both local organizing committees, KOWOC for Korea and JAWOC for Japan, supply ten cities each as match locations of which a good deal are completely newly built venues (see JAWOC, 1999 and 2000). According to our results in this chapter, the investment and subsequent costs of a set of 20 high quality locations are very likely to lead to a negative overall outcome already in the short run, not to mention the transaction costs of the coordination between both countries. But, apparently, intangible benefits with regard to development and political goals are higher weighted by organizers as statements of the KOWOC Chairman, Park Seh-Jik, confirm: 'I hope there will be progress in Japan–Korea friendship thanks to the World Cup. I would like to strive towards that. . . . we wish each local area to attain well-balanced progress exhibiting both economic improvement and cultural harmony. We hope that each area will benefit from holding the FIFA World Cup' (JAWOC, 1999). Whereas economic net benefits in each hosting region may be wishful thinking, the improvement of the relations between the two countries and the pride of staging, at the same time, both the first World Cup in Asia and the first co-hosted World Cup in FIFA's history, could actually have a very high value that is not monetizable. South Africa followed most probably an analogous reasoning for the quite emotionally led campaign for the World Cup 2006. In both cases, a cost-effectiveness analysis (CEA) would be more appropriate to evaluate alternative institutional designs of hosting the event since the decision to bid is (purely) policy driven (as to the CEA see for example Boardman et al., 1996, pp. 395–410).

3. It is important to distinguish the *economic impact* in the sense of income and employment generated, on the one hand, from the *socio-economic value*, on the other hand. An actual evaluation of the event and the political decision should be based on both, at best, with regard to decision rules derived from suitable economic welfare criteria (see note 7). To that end, Rahmann et al. (1998, pp. 103–5) as well as Barget and Gouguet (2000, p. 32) propose equivalent analysis categories for sporting events.

4. The budget for the bidding campaign ought to be, of course, limited to a reasonable amount with regard to the expected 'value' of the event since those expenses represent *sunk costs* in case of failure of the candidature (Kurscheidt, 2000b). In particular, past campaigns for the Olympics exhibited some excesses in bidding expenses. The DFB, for instance, stresses the fact that the 2006 campaign has been entirely financed by corporate sponsors, well-known big German companies. At the beginning of the campaign, DFB officials had promised to do without public funding (see DFB, 1999, pp. 34–5, and 2000). However, once the candidature has been successful the costs of the campaign have to be considered as event-induced, direct costs and must be incorporated in a cost–benefit calculation.

5. A general critique of the approach used to be that, theoretically and above all in practice, CBA failed to meet the initial pretension to install the rationality and efficiency of the price system on perfect private good markets in the public sector resource allocation. Nowadays, the objectives of CBA are less ambitious and it is widely accepted as a standard tool for public project and policy evaluation. Nevertheless, in practice, the analyst faces a couple of difficult problems like: which prices to use, which discount rate to choose, how to keep the analysis (nearly) objective, that is a clear separation and independence between analyst and decision-maker and so on. For further details see the relevant literature (for example Gramlich, 1997; Boardman et al., 1996; Hanusch, 1994; Mühlenkamp, 1994; Mishan, 1988; for a concise survey as to sporting events see Preuss, 2000b; Rahmann et al., 1998, pp. 94–110, and Thöni, 1984).

6. Negative economic impacts, such as financing costs, can only be modelled as *contractive effects* for instance in an input–output system. This has been done for example by Meyer and Ahlert (2000, pp. 222–38) (see also Ahlert, 2001 and Lager, 1995 who both simulate different scenarios of event financing). Nevertheless, those effects are not equivalent to the costs definition in CBA, nor are they explicitly exposed, that is they, so to speak, 'hide' in the aggregated outcome.

7. The Kaldor–Hicks criterion states the decision rule that the analysed project should be performed if it generates overall benefits which allow the beneficiaries of the project to *potentially* compensate possible losers and to be still better off (Pareto optimality). But, *ex ante*, this compensation is not required for a positive decision. Furthermore, the criterion does not prescribe or recommend any institutional arrangement for the compensation problem. Hence, this is a challenge that remains to be mastered (for a concise survey of welfare criteria and the corresponding CBA decision rules see especially Gramlich, 1997; for an application to Olympic Games see Preuss, 2000a, and see Kurscheidt and Rahmann, 1999, as well as Rahmann, 1997, with respect to Soccer World Cups).

8. The only exception to this 'city principle' that is permitted by the International Olympic Committee (IOC) are the sailing competitions. They are often held in another town (of the same country!) which is situated at the coast if the Olympic city is not (see Preuss, 2000a). Nevertheless, the second-level decision is not so problematic for an Olympic city and often rather a question of urban planning.

9. The binding promise up to nine years prior to the event is no requirement of FIFA. But the bidding national associations have to intensify the preparation of their candidature quite early. The DFB sent a circular letter to all potential hosting cities with a first deadline for their bids for the World Cup 2006 as early as April 1997 (DFB, 1997). Twenty-four of them participated in a first coordinating workshop in October 1997. After four withdrawals, 20 were incorporated in the official enrolment for 2006 handed over by DFB Vice-President and Chairman of the German bid, Franz Beckenbauer, on 27 November 1998. The final and binding deadline for candidatures of cities had been end

of 1998. These venues eventually were part of the comprehensive bidding dossier of 1212 pages (!) submitted on 10 August 1999 (OK-Deutschland 2006, 2001a).

10. The Soccer World Cup 1998 in France was the first to be held with 32 teams (Rahmann et al., 1998, p. 123). This regulation is still valid for the 2002 championship in Korea and Japan (FIFA, 1999, Art. 7, paras 1 and 3) and will certainly hold for 2006 as well. Before that, beginning with the 1982 tournament in Spain, the event was staged with 24 participating teams, that is 52 matches (Rahmann et al., 1998, p. 135).

11. A usual practice of some cities is, for instance, to upgrade their initial construction or modernization plans that are believed to be necessary for maintaining the stadium in the light of expected local benefits from hosting the soccer World Cup. This effect may occur more or less explicitly or intentionally and it is often a result of pressures exercised by local soccer clubs since they are keen on arena features like VIP lounges, meeting rooms, business seats and so on that can be profitably marketed by themselves (see Dietl and Pauli, 2000b; Vornholz, 2000; Rahmann et al., 1998, pp. 190–94). Politicians, in turn, might benefit from the image of the club among voters. However, a World Cup compatible stadium could be realized at construction costs of up to 200 million DM, nevertheless, this amount is significantly exceeded in some cases (see Table 8.1). This may be explained to a certain degree by the above 'upgrading effect' (see also Kurscheidt, 2000b).

12. The study of Rahmann et al. (1998) had been worked out in the course of 1997. Therefore, the appropriate basis of the money values was the preceding year. To maintain the comparability between that study and the present chapter this statistical basis and the currency (DM instead of €) is maintained.

13. It has to be noted that the professional soccer leagues in Europe do apply the relegation principle and, thus, there are no relocations of teams as in the franchise system of US major leagues. In the German 'soccer culture', the local identification with the team plays a crucial role.

14. At the World Cup 1998 in France, the number of venues had been ten. DFB officials repeatedly stated that they would consider a set of match locations of ten up to twelve stadiums. But they did not pronounce a clear preference with respect to this issue. In view of the fact that ten venues are actually sufficient, the twelve stadium solution may be interpreted as a 'compromise' solution if the decision on the venues to be sorted out appears politically delicate in practice. However, the latest statements of LOC officials seem to suggest this compromise choice (see for example Bielicki and Käppner, 2001).

15. Those venues are Dortmund, Stuttgart, Gelsenkirchen and Munich with seven matches each.

16. It may even be said that hypothesis OH is 'technically economic'. Considering also interdependencies between quantitative and qualitative effects induced by the event, it is actually even not economically desirable since it would put at risk a good deal of intangible benefits, that is integration of the eastern and western part of Germany, the overall image of the event and so on, and therewith also the economic success of the World Cup. This could be due to negative reactions or rejections of consumers and soccer fans.

17 In the case of hypothesis OH both the involvement of the low capacity of Leverkusen (22 500) and doing without the high capacity of Berlin (76000) seem to be the reason for the significantly lower tourist expenditure than in all other hypotheses, the 1998 results included.

18. It is most likely that the corporate sponsors of the DFB and the LOC would appreciate that the city of their headquarters be chosen (for example Bayer Group in Leverkusen, Daimler-Chrysler in Stuttgart, Lufthansa in Frankfurt). Likewise, state governments (*Landesregierungen*) might favour their state capital and so forth (among others the quite weakly rated cities Dusseldorf, Frankfurt and Hannover).

19. The complete and official bid of the cities has to be submitted by 15 December 2001. The LOC will hand their suggestion for the number and composition of venues as well as the location of the media centre over to the OCF by 31 March 2002. The latter will then alter or approve this suggestion of the LOC. So the final decision will most probably be taken by mid-2002 or at the end of 2002 (for current information on this issue see http://www.ok-deutschland2006.de).

REFERENCES

Ahlert, G. (2001), 'The Economic Effects of the Soccer World Cup 2006 in Germany with Regard to Different Financing', *Economic Systems Research*, **13** (1), 109–27.

Andreff, W. and J.-F. Nys (1997), *Economie du sport*, 3rd edn., Paris: Presses Universitaires de France.

Baade, R. and V. Matheson (2000), 'An Assessment of the Economic Impact of the American Football Championship, the Super Bowl, on host communities', *Reflets et Perspectives de la Vie Économique*, **39** (2–3), 35–46.

Barget, E. and J.-J. Gouguet (2000), 'Impact économique du spectacle sportif: analyse critique de la littérature', *Reflets et Perspectives de la Vie Économique*, **39** (2–3), 17–33.

Bielicki, J. and J. Käppner (2001), 'Neue Arenen der Erlebniswelt', *Süddeutsche Zeitung*, 23 October 2001.

Boardman, A.E., D.H. Greenberg, A.R. Vining, and D.L. Weimer (1996), *Cost–Benefit Analysis: Concepts and Practice*, Upper Saddle River: Prentice Hall.

Burgan, B. and T. Mules (1992), 'Economic Impact of Sporting Events', *Annals of Tourism Research*, **19**, 700–710.

Davidson, L. (1999), 'Choice of a Proper Methodology to Measure Quantitative and Qualitative Effects of the Impact of Sport', in C. Jeanrenaud (ed.), *The Economic Impact of Sport Events*, Neuchâtel: Editions CIES, pp. 9–28.

DFB (1997), Circular letter of the Vice-President and General Secretary of the DFB to the proprietors of potential hosting venues, Frankfurt/M, 12 February 1997.

DFB (1999), *Willkommen im Fussball-Land – Bewerbung des Deutschen Fußball-Bundes um den FIFA-Weltpokal 2006*, candidature brochure, Frankfurt/M, March 1999.

Dietl, H. and M. Pauli (1999), *Wirtschaftliche Auswirkungen öffentlich finanzierter Stadionprojekte*, Arbeitspapiere des Fachbereichs Wirtschaftswissenschaften N.F. 61, University of Paderborn.

Dietl, H. and M. Pauli (2000a), *Private Funding of Sports Stadiums in the U.S. and Germany: How to Solve the Hold Up Problem*, Business and Public Policy Working Paper, BPP-77, Institute of Management, Innovation & Organization, University of California, Berkley, June 2000.

Dietl, H. and M. Pauli (2000b), *Möglichkeiten privater Stadionfinanzierung im deutschen Profifußball vor dem Hintergrund der WM 2006*, mimeo, University of Paderborn, August 2000.

FIFA (n.d.), *Technical Recommendations and Requirements for the Construction or Modernisation of Football Stadia*, 3rd edn., Zurich, available on FIFA online, http://www.fifa2.com.

FIFA (1999), *Regulations 2002 FIFA World Cup Korea/Japan*, Zurich, July 1999, available on FIFA online, http://www.fifa2.com.

Gouguet, J.-J. and J.-F. Nys (1993), *Sport et développement économique Régional: analyse théorique – cas pratiques*, Paris: Dalloz.

Gramlich, E.M. (1997), *A Guide to Benefit–Cost Analysis*, 2nd edn., Prospect Heights: Waveland Press.

Hanusch, H. (1994), *Nutzen-Kosten-Analyse*, 2nd edn., Munich: Vahlen.

JAWOC (1999), 'Our Job is to build "bridges" between Japan and Korea: Interview KOWOC Chairman Park Seh-Jik', *JAWOC News,* **22**, http://www.jawoc.or.jp/news_e/vol22/interviewtoPaku.htm.

JAWOC (2000), 'Venues in Japan', http://www.jawoc.or.jp/siryo_e/venues/venues-map.htm., seen and printed on 1 September 2000.

Jeanrenaud, C. (ed.) (1999), *The Economic Impact of Sport Events*, Neuchâtel: Editions CIES.

Kesenne, S. (1999a), 'Miscalculations and Misinterpretations in Economic Impact Analysis', in C. Jeanrenaud (ed.), *The Economic Impact of Sport Events*, Neuchâtel: Editions CIES, pp. 29–39.

Kesenne, S. (1999b), 'Kosten-Nutzen-Analysen von Sport Events', in H.-D. Horch, J. Heydel and A. Sierau (eds), *Professionalisierung im Sportmanagement*, Aachen: Meyer und Meyer, pp. 337–42.

Kurscheidt, M. (2000a), 'Le poids macro-économique du sport et le spectacle sportif: Méthodologie, résultats empiriques et perspectives économiques pour le cas de l'Allemagne', *Reflets et Perspectives de la Vie Économique*, **39** (2–3), 47–60.

Kurscheidt, M. (2000b), *Strategic Management and Cost–Benefit Analysis of Major Sport Events: The Use of Sensitivity Analyses Shown for the Case of the Soccer World Cup 2006 in Germany*, Arbeitspapiere des Fachbereichs Wirtschaftswissenschaften N.F. no. 69, University of Paderborn.

Kurscheidt, M. (2001), 'Evaluating, Bidding for, and Managing Sports Mega Events: Theoretical and Methodological Issues of an Integrated Approach to the Economic Analysis of Sporting Events, *The Economic Impact of Sports*, Athens: Panhellenic Association of Sports Economists and Managers (PASEM), pp. 95–104.

Kurscheidt, M. and B. Rahmann (1999), 'Local Investment and National Impact: The Case of the Football World Cup 2006 in Germany', in C. Jeanrenaud (ed.), *The Economic Impact of Sport Events*, Neuchâtel: Editions CIES, pp. 79–108.

Lager, C. (1995), 'Volkswirtschaftliche Wirkungen "OWS Graz 2002" – Simulationen mittels eines multisektoralen dynamischen Modells', in M. Steiner and E. Thöni, *Sport und Ökonomie: Eine Untersuchung am Beispiel der Bewerbung 'Olympische Winterspiele Graz 2002'*, Graz: Leykam, pp. 23–70.

Maennig, W. (1991), 'Kosten-Nutzen-Analysen Olympischer Spiele in Deutschland', *List Forum für Wirtschafts- und Finanzpolitik*, **17**, 336–62.

Maennig, W. (1998), 'Moglichkeiten und Grenzen von Kosten-Nutzen-Analysen im Sport', *Sportwissenschaft*, **28** (3–4), 311–27.

Meyer, B. and G. Ahlert (with collaboration of C. Schnieder) (2000), *Die ökonomischen Perspektiven des Sports: Eine empirische Analyse für die Bundesrepublik Deutschland*, Schorndorf: Hofmann.

Mishan, E.J. (1988), *Cost–Benefit Analysis*, 4th edn., London and New York: Routledge.

Mühlenkamp, H. (1994), *Kosten-Nutzen-Analyse*, Munich: Oldenbourg.

OK-Deutschland 2006 (2001a), 'Von der Bewerbung zur WM', http://www.ok-deutschland2006.de/archiv index.html, seen and printed on 2 October 2001.

OK-Deutschland 2006 (2001b), Homepage of the LOC for Germany 2006, http://www.ok-deutschland2006.de/stadien/, 24 October 2001.

Preuss, H. (2000a), *Economics of the Olympic Games: Hosting the Games 1972–2000*, Sydney: Walla Walla Press.

Preuss, H. (2000b), *Kosten-Nutzen-Analysen von sportlichen Großveranstaltungen*, mimeo, University of Mainz, August 2000.

Radford, P. (2000), 'Germany pip South Africa in 2006 World Cup bid', Reuters press release, in FIFA online, http://www.fifa2.com, Zurich, 6 July 2000.

Rahmann, B. (1997), *Cost–Benefit Analysis of the Football World Cup 2006 in*

Germany: Selected Conceptional and Theoretical Aspects, paper presented at the 1st Kölner Sportökonomie-Kongress, Institut für Sportökonomie und Sportmanagement, Sporthochschule Köln, Cologne, Germany, 13–15 November, 1997; published in German language as 'Kosten-Nutzen-Analyse der Fußball-Weltmeisterschaft 2006 in Deutschland – Ausgewählte konzeptionelle Aspekte und Ergebnisse', in H.-D. Horch, J. Heydel and A. Sierau (eds), *Professionalisierung im Sportmanagement*, Aachen: Meyer und Meyer, 1999, pp. 355–73.

Rahmann, B., W. Weber, Y. Groening, M. Kurscheidt, H.-G. Napp and M. Pauli (1998), *Sozio-ökonomische Analyse der Fußball-Weltmeisterschaft 2006 in Deutschland: Gesellschaftliche Wirkungen, Kosten-Nutzen-Analyse und Finanzierungsmodelle einer Sportgroßveranstaltung*, Cologne: Sport und Buch Strauss.

Roland Berger & Partner GmbH (1998), *Fußballstadien in Deutschland: Situation, Trends, Herausforderungen*, presentation slides, Munich, June 1998.

Steiner, M. and E. Thöni (1995), S*port und Ökonomie: Eine Untersuchung am Beispiel der Bewerbung 'Olympische Winterspiele Graz 2002'*, Graz: Leykam.

Thöni, E. (1984), 'Sport und Ökonomie: Kosten-Nutzen-Analyse als Entscheidungshilfe für Sport (Groß-) Veranstaltungen', *Schimmelpfeng-Review*, **33**, 89–92.

Thöni, E. (1999), 'Zur Evaluierung der sozio-ökonomischen Effekte von Sportgroßereignissen (Olympische Spiele, Weltmeisterschaften)', in H.-D. Horch, J. Heydel and A. Sierau (eds), *Professionalisierung im Sportmanagement*, Aachen: Meyer und Meyer, 343–54.

Vornholz, G. (2000), 'Die Arena – Veranstaltungshalle ohne ausreichende ökonomische Perspektive', *Der langfristige Kredit*, **14**, 13–19.

APPENDIX

Table 8A.1   Distribution of scenarios for 10 locations in 1998 hypotheses

Scenarios (fields in Figure 8.1)	Hypothesis I maximum	Hypothesis II mean	Hypothesis III minimum
scenario 1 (III)	3	2	1
scenario 2 (II, VI)	4	3	2
scenario 3 (I, V)	2	3	4
scenario 4 (IV, VIII)	1	2	3
expected NET BENEFIT	$NB_I > NB_{II}$	$NB_I > NB_{II} > NB_{III}$	$NB_{III} \leq 0$ or $NB_{III} \geq 0$ (?)

Table 8A.2   Hypotheses of the 1998 CBA and estimation intervals

Valuation	estimation interval H_I		estimation interval H_{II}		estimation interval H_{III}	
	upper bound H_{Iu}	lower bound H_{II}	upper bound H_{IIu}	lower bound H_{III}	upper bound H_{IIIu}	lower bound H_{IIII}
Net present value	NPV (H_{Iu})	NPV(H_{II})	NPV (H_{IIu})	NPV (H_{III})	NPV (H_{IIIu})	NPV (H_{IIII})
Cases	best-case		realistic or (most) probable range			worst-case

Table 8A.3   Total investment costs and tourist spending of 1998 hypotheses

	Hypothesis I		Hypothesis II		Hypothesis III	
	upper bound	lower bound	upper bound	lower bound	upper bound	lower bound
total investment (in million DM 96)	1620	560	2020	690	2420	820
total tourist spending (in million DM 96)	*(for all hypotheses)*		1463.57 (upper bound)		813.09 (lower bound)	

Note: The slightly higher values of the tourist spending relative to the modified hypotheses are due to the bad quality of data on the seating capacity in 1997 (see Rahmann et al., 1998, p. 136, especially footnote 232). This information is now much more precise and the 1998 assessments appear to be slightly overestimated.

Table 8A.4   Total investment costs and tourist spending of modified hypotheses

	OH		HA		HB		A12		B12	
	upper bound	lower bound	upper bound	lower bound	upper bound	lower bound	upper bound	lower bound	upper bound	lower bound
total investment* (in million DM 96)	1628.6	1416.2	2063.4	1794.3	2619.2	2277.6	2465.9	2144.3	2856.5	2483.9
total tourist spending (in million DM 96)	1325.7	736.5	1451.9	806.6	1431.8	795.4	1424.2	791.2	1403.3	779.6

Note: *The lower bound of the investment estimation for each venue is represented by the official assessment of the stadium owners made in 2001 deflated to the basis 1996 in the model (see Table 8.1 in the text). Since the true construction costs in most of the cases significantly exceed the initial assessment, the upper bound is estimated at 115 per cent of the lower bound.

Table 8A.5 Data inputs to the modified CBA model and their occurrence over time

Variables (Time t)		Estimation intervals	
		Upper bound	Lower bound
investment costs*† (according to plans of bidding cities) (at 1/3 in t = 3 to 5)	scenario 1	55 million DM (Bremen)	0 million DM (e.g. Dortmund)
	scenario 2	102 million DM (Stuttgart)	94.5 million DM (Kaiserslautern)
	scenario 3	473 million DM (Berlin)	123 million DM (Nuremberg)
	scenario 4	360 million DM (Dusseldorf)	177 million DM (Leipzig)
benefits on investment in sport facilities (from t = 6 to t = 15)	scenario 1	9.6 million DM	6.4 million DM
	scenario 2	9.6 million DM	5.0 million DM
	scenario 3	9.6 million DM	5.0 million DM
	scenario 4	6.4 million DM	1.5 million DM

scenario distribution* (from t = 0 to t = 15):

		Upper bound		Lower bound		
	hypotheses	OH	HA	HB	A12	B12
	scenario 1	4	3	2	3	2
	scenario 2	2	2	0	2	1
	scenario 3	4	4	6	6	7
	scenario 4	0	1	2	1	2

Variables (Time t)	Upper bound	Lower bound
operating costs (from t = 6 to t = 15)	(for all scenarios) 9.6 million DM	(for all scenarios) 6.4 million DM
capital charges (from t = 0 to t = 15)	(for all scenarios) 9.5 per cent of investment as annuity (interest + repayment)	
capacity utilization	90 per cent	75 per cent
proportion 'foreign tickets'	(for all scenarios) 32 per cent of total tickets	
proportion 'journalists' tickets'	(for all scenarios) 0.36 per cent of total tickets	

expenditure per 'foreign ticket'		*in t = 6*: 1440 DM		*in t = 6*: 960 DM	
surplus of LOC	(*in t = 6*)	150 million DM		0 DM	
multipliers‡ for investment expenditures	*time:*	*in t = 4:* 1.1§	*in t = 6:* 0.8	*in t = 4:* 0.4§	*in t = 5:* 0.2 *in t = 6:* 0.2
for tourist expenditure		*in t = 5:* 1 *in t = 7:* 2.45		*in t = 5:* 0.2 *in t = 7:* 2	
discount rate		4 per cent			

Notes:

* Modified variable (all other *nominal* data changes are induced by multiplication with percentages)

† The lower bound of the investment estimation for each venue is represented by the official assessment of the stadium owners made in 2001 (see Table 8.1 in the text). Those data are deflated to 1996 prices in the model to keep the values consistent with the other estimations of the 1998 study. Since the true construction costs in most of the cases significantly exceed the initial assessment, the upper bound is estimated at 115 per cent of the lower bound.

‡ Both multipliers were computed by the *Rheinisch-Westfälisches Institut für Wirtschaftsforschung (RWI), Essen.* The investment multiplier is dynamic over three periods and was derived for public infrastructure investments from an econometric business cycle model. The multiplier of the tourist expenditure is a static one for the hotel and restaurant industry and had been calculated by an econometric input–output model.

§ The value of the multiplier is reduced by one in the first successive period after the investment to make sure that only *additionally* induced income from the impulse of investment *costs* (!) are counted as benefits.

*Table 8A.6　Total net benefit returns of venues per period by 1998
hypotheses (in million DM, basis 1996) (t = 6 to t = 15)*

	Hypothesis I		Hypothesis II		Hypothesis III	
	upper bound	lower bound	upper bound	lower bound	upper bound	lower bound
benefit returns	92.8	50.7	89.6	45.8	86.4	40.9
operating costs	64	96	64	96	64	96
capital charges	53.2	153.9	65.55	191.9	77.9	229.9
total costs	117.2	249.9	129.55	287.9	141.9	325.9
net benefit returns	−24.4	−199.2	−39.95	−242.1	−55.5	−285

Table 8A.7 Total net benefit returns of venues per period by modified hypotheses (in million DM, basis 1996) (t = 6 to t = 15)

	OH		HA		HB		A12		B12	
	upper bound	lower bound	upper bound	lower bound	upper bound	lower bound	upper bound	lower bound	upper bound	lower bound
benefit returns	96	55.6	92.8	50.7	89.6	45.8	112	60.7	108.8	55.8
operating costs	64	96	64	96	64	96	76.8	115.2	76.8	115.2
capital charges	134.5	154.7	170.5	196.0	216.4	248.8	203.7	234.3	236.0	271.4
total costs	198.5	250.7	234.5	292.0	280.4	344.8	280.5	349.5	312.8	386.6
net benefit returns	−102.5	−195.1	−141.7	−241.3	−190.8	−299.0	−168.5	−288.8	−204.0	−330.8

Table 8A.8   Selected net present values of the 1998 CBA (in million DM, basis 1996)

Time hori-zon	Hypothesis I		Hypothesis II		Hypothesis III	
	upper bound	lower bound	upper bound	lower bound	upper bound	lower bound
4	−149.99	−757.02	−184.81	−943.93	−219.63	−1130.85
5	18.78	−934.55	23.14	−1165.30	27.50	−1396.06
6	1702.55	−107.97	1793.93	−288.33	1885.32	−468.69
7	4664.21	1140.56	4803.05	968.13	4941.89	795.70
8	4755.49	1073.92	4908.31	889.63	5061.12	705.34
12	4690.78	545.58	4802.35	247.50	4913.91	−50.58
13	4676.12	425.94	4778.35	102.10	4880.58	−221.74
14	4662.03	310.91	4755.28	−37.71	4848.53	−386.32
15	4648.48	200.30	4733.10	−172.13	4817.71	−544.57

Table 8A.9 Selected net present values of the modified CBA (in million DM, basis 1996)

Time horizon	OH		HA		HB		A12		B12	
	upper bound	lower bound	upper bound	lower bound	upper bound	lower bound	upper bound	lower bound	upper bound	lower bound
4	-379.31	-761.04	-480.58	-964.22	-610.02	-1223.9	-574.32	-1152.3	-665.28	-1334.8
5	47.49	-939.52	60.17	-1190.4	76.38	-1511.0	71.91	-1422.6	83.30	-1647.9
6	2214.63	-168.44	2585.01	-308.73	2915.71	-566.66	2821.05	-505.74	3047.28	-691.13
7	5250.57	967.65	5998.63	942.89	6474.89	680.42	6322.33	727.23	6637.40	531.79
8	5451.59	904.41	6244.74	867.07	6779.29	589.52	6617.02	636.36	6972.35	429.25
9	5379.55	767.32	6145.22	697.51	6645.25	379.43	6498.63	433.47	6829.04	196.86
10	5310.28	635.51	6049.52	534.48	6516.38	177.42	6384.79	238.40	6691.25	-26.59
11	5243.67	508.76	5957.50	377.72	6392.46	-16.82	6275.33	50.82	6558.76	-241.45
12	5179.62	386.89	5869.02	226.99	6273.30	-203.59	6170.08	-129.54	6431.36	-448.04
13	5118.04	269.71	5783.95	82.06	6158.73	-383.18	6068.88	-302.97	6308.86	-646.69
14	5058.83	157.03	5702.14	-57.30	6048.57	-555.86	5971.57	-469.72	6191.07	-837.70
15	5001.89	48.69	5623.49	-191.30	5942.64	-721.90	5878.00	-630.06	6077.82	-1021.4

9. Sports policy at regional level: estimating the economic value of amateur sports managers

Carlos Pestana Barros and Jaime Lucas

1. INTRODUCTION

The provision to the community of sport, which constitutes an imperfect public good, is made mainly through clubs. These are, for the most part, non-profit oriented organisations, which provide attendance events for individuals as well as participation for professional and non-professional sportsmen and women.

Sloane (1971), in asserting that sports managers maximise the utility of winning competitions, proposes the non-profit nature of the sport clubs. This proposition is supported in Europe, where the clubs frequently operate with deficits. In the USA, Quirk and El-Hodiri (1974) consider that sports clubs are profit maximisers, while more recently, Vrooman (2000) posited an intermediate position in which the sports managers maximise both profit and the utility of winning.

We observe that, on one hand, profit-oriented organisations are always managed by professionals, while on the other hand, the non-profit-oriented clubs are managed either by professionals or amateurs. In Portugal, a recent development has seen the shares of the three largest professional football clubs listed on the stock market. However, up till now, the remainder of the country's clubs of all sports have shown no indication of following this trend. The latter clubs are currently managed by amateurs, who usually do not receive any payment for their efforts and who are commonly obliged to fund any occasional deficit.

The non-profit nature of these sports managers' work reveals a perception of appropriateness in supporting the sporting life of their communities. Since this work is not registered for economic purposes, the IDRAM, Madeira's regional sports controlling body,[1] undertook the task of evaluating the economic value of the managers' voluntary work in order for this to be included in an estimation of the aggregated economic value of sports in Madeira.

A means of estimating the value of an imperfect public good which is traded in the market with unobserved prices is through indirect demand, asking a sample of consumers about their willingness-to-pay (wtp) and their willingness-to-accept (wta) for the good. A technique used to estimate the wtp and wta is the contingent valuation method, which is adopted in this chapter.

In this chapter, we estimate a wta for the role of amateur sports organisation manager, using data from a questionnaire distributed among sports club managers on the island of Madeira in late 1999 and early 2000. We consider that such managers reflect a sense of appropriateness in supporting the sporting life of a community, blended with their own personal motives, in terms of the prestige and influence associated with the role. In this context, the sports manager will work in a voluntary capacity, and the work and time devoted to the club will define the opportunity cost which, in turn, defines the willingness-to-accept for the role.

The chapter is organised as follows: in Section 2, we describe the institutional setting. Section 3 contains a brief review of the literature on this area of research. In Section 4, the model is considered, and in Section 5, the hypotheses are discussed. In Section 6, we detail the empirical study and give the results in Section 7. In Section 8, we present the policy implications, followed, in Section 9, by the conclusion.

2. INSTITUTIONAL SETTING

The island of Madeira is an autonomous Portuguese region with its own regional government. Sports policy is implemented by a public agency, the Instituto para o Desporto da Região Autónoma da Madeira (IDRAM). The IDRAM promotes school and amateur sports, as well as financing professional sports. About 80 per cent of IDRAM funds are allocated to professional clubs through subsidies. As such, Madeira is representative of Portugal as a whole, in terms both of organisational structure and sports policy.

The European Union Maastricht Treaty of 1992 altered the philosophy of public spending at the European level, inaugurating an age of retrenchment. Today, the restructuring of the responsibilities of government is being put into effect through privatisation and subsidy shrinkage. This policy change is putting stress on amateur sports clubs, which are increasingly obliged to look to the market to finance their activities. With regard to its current state and regional sports funding policy and practice, Portugal might be considered to be acting counter to the spirit of the European Union's directives. However, if sports are imperfect public goods, then they would seem to deserve Government support.

The IDRAM policy is established by the Regional Government pro-gramme and its present thrust can be characterised as a Keynesian sports policy, supported by heavy public expenditure. In late 1999 and early 2000, the IDRAM undertook an analysis of the economic value of the sports. Within this mission, a sub-project was designed to evaluate the economic worth of the work of sports managers by means of a standard contingent valuation questionnaire. We assumed that amateur sports managers reflect a public perception of appropriateness in supporting the sporting life of a community, blended with their own personal motives, in terms of the pres-tige and influence associated with the position. They are consequently con-fronted with the opportunity cost of the work which they devote voluntarily to the clubs.

We can consider that the government subsidises sport because its posi-tive consumption externalities are derived from sport's public-good nature, namely, local identity, local unity around sports clubs, fan loyalty, civic pride, local pride and prestige. These issues are nonrivalrous and nonex-cludable, conferring on sports the nature of public goods meriting subsid-isation. This situation is recognised by sports economists, Noll and Zimbalist (1997, p. 56), Quirk and Fort (1992, p. 176) and Siegfried and Zimbalist (2000). A response to the question as to what should be the eco-nomic value of sports subsidies is that this value should be equal to the non-market value of sport. This leads in turn to the question, what is the non-market value of sport?

The demand for sports events has three elements. First, there is the direct demand for sports events, either in terms of attendance, or of participation. However, if the demand for attendance at sports events is inelastic, as applies in the case of fanatical supporters, then the consumer surplus can be substantial, though this benefit cannot be reaped directly by a club through conventional revenue channels.

The second element is the indirect demand for sports events by those who never attend nor participate in them. This is evident in the form of daily conversations on sport at work and in social meeting places, the nurturing of local identity and unity around clubs, personalities and events, fan loyalty, local civic pride and prestige. These effects are external conse-quences of sports and, as such, also fail to yield direct benefits to clubs.

The third element is the value of an enhanced community image. This indirect element of demand gives to sport the nature of a public good, because it is impossible to exclude beneficiaries from enjoying it. Image enhancement will be underprovided in the private sector, but if it is large enough, it will provide a broad political support for a public subsidy.

None of the above-mentioned non-market benefits – consumer surplus, externalities and the public-good nature of image enhancement – can be gained by clubs through conventional revenue channels while, on the other hand, externalities and image enhancement at least establish the basis for the public subsidisation of sports. To the above non-market value of sports, we must add the economic value of amateur sports managers, the investigation into which is the objective of this chapter.

3. LITERATURE REVIEW

The use in economics of the contingent valuation method to obtain the willingness to pay and willingness to accept is widespread, particularly in the field of environmental economics. For a recent survey applied to the latter, see Kerry Smith (2000). For a primer on contingent valuation modelling, see http://www.csba.uncwil.edu/people/whiteheadj/research/papers/CVM%20and%20BCA5.pdf. This research is always demand-oriented, from the consumer perspective and sometimes enclosed in an impact analysis.

Within the ambit of sports economics, this method has rarely been used and the impact analyses currently carried out in this field usually apply cost–benefit analysis with the benefit estimated as employment (Baade, 1996), income and employment (Barget and Gouguet, 2000).

Among the scarce applications in sport, Johnson and Whitehead (2000) analysed the value of a basketball arena and a baseball stadium in the USA, concluding that neither project would generate sufficiently valuable public goods to justify public finance. In a related paper, Johnson et al. (2001) measured the value of the public goods generated by sports teams (Pittsburgh Penguins of the National Hockey League in the USA), concluding that, in one case, the value of public goods generated by the team was far less than the cost of building a new arena.

4. THE MODEL

Let us consider a sports club manager who consumes private goods (x), and public goods (z) and produces work (l). The public good in discussion is the role of an amateur sports club manager in a heavily subsidy-dependent club. The utility derived from the role is in terms of the prestige and influence associated with it, and which is defined by the following utility function, which may be separated in time:

$$W = \Sigma(1 + \gamma)^{-t}u(x_i, z_i, l_i)$$

in which $\gamma < 1$ is the discount rate and t the time. The cardinal sub-utility function is to be strictly increased in each of its arguments, and to possess all the other properties, such as that of being quasi-concave, which are usually employed in micro-economics. With regard to the social role of the sports club manager, it is assumed that $z > 0$ represents the status gained from the role and that $u = 0$, when $z = 0$.

From the dual-consumer approach: min $\Sigma p_i z_i$, st. $W(u) = w$, one obtains the expenditure function $e(p,u)$, where p is the price level. The period t aggregated expenditure function $e_t(p,u)$ may be used to analyse the adjustment of sports club managers to marginal variations in prices and income.

Let us assume that the sports club manager is asked about his willingness-to-accept for his role, in the form of a predetermined sum of money. Willingness-to-accept is expressed in welfare measures: compensation and equivalent variations.

The compensation variation arising from the conceptualisation of the sports club manager is the result of the variation of the state of being a sports club manager, z_1 to the state of not being a sports club manager, z_2, which alters the level of prices and utility from (p_1, u_1) to (p_2, u_2) where $u_2 > u_1$, and is defined as:

Compensation variation $= y_2 - e(p_2, u_1)$

And the equivalent variation $= e(p_2, u_1) - y_1$

5.   HYPOTHESES

The contingent valuation method allows wta to be estimated directly and the determinants of wta to be estimated through a regression. In this section, we discuss the determinants of wta.

The literature on sports economics identifies four reasons why people value sports, these reasons also being applicable to sports club managers: consumption value, option value, existence value (prestige) and endowment value. We assume that sports club managers are voluntary workers, since, for the most part, the sports clubs are non-profit organisations. The higher the individual's valuation, the more likely he is to support the sports and to value his work, asking for a higher wta for his role as amateur sports manager.

The consumption and option values are determined by the same parameters that determine actual demand. Those variables that induce an individual to actually consume sports will also induce him to value the option to potentially consume sports in the future. Income and education are two variables that explain most sports consumption.

Hypothesis 1: The wta varies positively with the average income of sports club managers.

Hypothesis 2: The wta varies positively with the level of education of sports club managers

A formal degree of education, however, may not entirely express the actual education level, since it relates to the individual's past. Human capital could have depreciated or conversely, appreciated over time. In addition, the kind of education that colleges impart may not be precisely the education that a person requires in order to be a sports club manager. It is therefore appropriate to include some measure of the interest an individual currently takes in politics in general. This interest will presumably reflect a higher consumption value, in addition to a higher prestige value, since individuals who wish to take part in public affairs also tend to care more about their political and social environment. We have chosen proxy variables to account for this. First, to vote for the incumbent political party, which serves as a measure of responsiveness to political issues. Secondly, to manage a club with a large membership, which serves as a measure of prestige value. We summarise this in the following two hypotheses:

Hypothesis 3: The greater the awareness and responsiveness concerning political issues as measured by voting for the incumbent political party, the greater the wta.

Hypothesis 4: The greater the prestige value, measured by the number of club members, the higher the wta.

The opportunity cost of being a sports club manager (a non-remunerated voluntary job) is the main cost in this framework. Opportunity costs per-unit-of-time may vary across different professions. Typically, the self-employed have higher opportunity costs of leisure than individuals with fixed working hours. Retirees should have very low opportunity costs. Thus, we can formulate the fifth hypothesis:

Hypothesis 5: The wta declines with professional activity, as measured by a dummy variable, which is 1 if the individual has fixed working hours and is zero if not.

When valuing the utility derived from sports activity, the managers might also take endowment value into account. It is reasonable to consider that sports club managers wish to maintain the sporting heritage for future generations. It is, moreover, most likely that this motivation will be stronger for individuals with young children. As we did not gather data on children of school age or younger, we approximated this with the number of offspring. Furthermore, the older the manager, the lower he may value sporting heritage, since older adults do not have young children, their offspring already being integrated into the labour market. Thus, we have:

Hypothesis 6: The stronger the endowment value, as measured by the number of offspring, the greater the wta.

Hypothesis 7: The higher the age of the individual, the less the wta.

In order to test these hypotheses, we regressed wta on the independent variable referred to above.

All parameters were expected to be positive, with the exception of professional activity and age.

6. EMPIRICAL STUDY

The empirical study was carried out by means of the previously-mentioned questionnaire, with the central aim of determining the extent of the manager's willingness-to-accept for his role as a sports manager, this estimate denoting an economic value for amateur sports managers. Our objective was to inquire into the wta of sports club managers as an estimate of their economic worth.

The sample was stratified by region, using an IDRAM database of all Madeira's sports club managers. Because of budgetary restrictions and the limited time available, it was decided to collect data from 100 sports club managers out of a total of 600 on the database. The IDRAM sent out 100 questionnaires and received 62 returns, which gives a response rate of 62 per cent.

Various types of managers were considered for the present analysis, representing all of the different types of sports clubs to be found in Madeira. Traditionally, the sports clubs are managed by an administrative council, headed by a president. For the purposes of our analysis, no distinction was made between the councils of league and non-league clubs. The study included sports clubs participating in a Portuguese (national) league, as well as clubs only competing within the regional confine.

The rate response does not differ significantly from the sample for age variable (chi-square $= 8.53$, $p = 0.05$), nor for gender (chi-square $= 7.55$,

$p = 0.05$). Hence, we can assert that the 62 managers that answered the questionnaire are representative of all Madeira's sports club managers, that is there is no suggestion that those who failed to respond were significantly different from those who did respond.

The general characteristics of these respondents were male (98.4 per cent), with an average age of 42, with a college degree and with an average monthly income of 1 404.6 euros. This profile leads to an overall definition of the responding managers as Portuguese male, middle-aged and middle-class.

The questionnaire was presented to all sports club managers at their club headquarters after they had been approached, first by phone and then personally. The questionnaire was pre-tested on students of sports economics at the Faculdade de Motricidade Humana de Lisboa (the Sports Department of the Technical University of Lisbon).

The managers were asked to complete a standard questionnaire, including questions on socio-economics and other issues. We fitted regression with the willingness-to-accept (wta) as the dependent variables and the variables referred to in the previous section as explanatory variables. The generic model is the following:

$$wta = \alpha_0 + \alpha_1 . inc + \alpha_2 . educ + \alpha_3 . incumb + \alpha_4 . memb + \alpha_5 . acti + \alpha_6 . offsprings + \alpha_7 . age + \varepsilon$$

Table 9.1 summarises the variables. The respondents were asked to determine their wta by answering several bid values – defined as a percentage of the club budget – designed to produce information on the variability of wta.

The wta variable is censored at zero (there are no negative wta values) and is defined at intervals, not continuous data (Greene, 2000). Under these conditions, the OLS are not efficient, and Tobit is an alternative.

7. RESULTS

Table 9.2 presents the results estimated with OLS (the endogenous variable wta is estimated as the percentage of club budget to be allocated to the manager income). However several wta values are zero and for that reason we recoded the endogenous variable and estimated a censored Tobit model. Both models, OLS and Tobit, are presented for comparative purposes.

In order to test this hypothesis with logit, we assumed that the probability of wta could be described by a cumulative logit-probability function of the exogenous variables X_i:

Table 9.1   Characterisation of the variables

Variables	Variable description	Range	Mean	Std. Dev	Testing the influence of:
Wta	Willingness to accept	0–1	0.09	0.060	Endogenous variable
Inc	The median income of the individual	100–950	258	193	Income
Educ	The education level of the respondent	1–6	2.96	0.81	Education
Incumb	Dummy variable (1 if the individual votes for the incumbent party and zero, if not)	0–1	0.74	0.44	Political awareness
Memb	The median number of club members	100–7500	1395	1834	Prestige
Acti	Dummy variable (1 if the individual has fixed working hours and zero, if not)	0–1	0.27	0.44	Opportunity cost
Offspring	Dummy variable (1 if the individual has offspring and zero, if not)	0–1	0.75	0.46	Endowment value
Age	The age of the individual	28–71	42	8.84	Endowment value

$$P_i = F(\alpha + \beta.X_i) = \frac{1}{1 + e^{-(\alpha+\beta.X_i)}} \tag{9.1}$$

Thus,

$$P_i/(1 - P_i) = e^{\alpha+\beta.X_i} \tag{9.2}$$

and taking natural logarithms results in:

$$\text{Log}\frac{P_i}{1 - P_i} = \alpha + \beta.X_i + \mu \tag{9.3}$$

The dependent variable is known as the log odds ratio and is specified as natural logs and transformed into a log ratio for wta. Thus we measure P_i by the probability that the sports manager declares his wta (wta $>0=1$, wta $=0=0$), we measure X_i as observed characteristics and μ is the residual variable.

The OLS model fits the data well with an R^2 of 23 per cent, suggesting

Table 9.2 *Regression results*

Variable	OLS estimates of wta	Tobit estimation of wta
Constant	0.642*	0.639
	(5.004)	(0.148)
Income	0.00003	0.659*
	(0.273)	(0.784)
Education	0.521	0.004
	(0.274)	(0.307)
Incumbent Party	0.1611*	0.203*
	(2.862)	(3.374)
Members	0.3848*	0.036*
	(2.814)	(2.78)
Activity	0.075*	0.0862*
	(2.567)	(2.973)
Offspring	0.1031	1.330
	(1.756)	(1.576)
Age	*−0.0063**	*−0.559**
	(−2.540)	*(−3.647)*
F-statistic	2.76	–
	(0.02)[a]	
R^2	0.23	–
R^2 adjusted	0.14	–
Log likelihood	−21.012	−39.894
Sigma	–	0.60
Chi-Square		45.36
		(0.000)[a]

Notes:
Number of observations: 62 in all cases; t–ratio in parentheses.
[a] probability value
* significant of the 5 per cent confidence level.

that this set of variables can 'explain' as much as 23 per cent of the variance, which is reasonable for cross-data. The F statistic allows us to accept that the fitted regression is not the result of chance.

Assuming that the lack of independence appears to be the rule rather than the exception in survey data, we estimated the White's test of heteroscedasticity. The tests strongly reject the heteroscedasticity of the residuals (the White test is 75.185 and the 95 per cent critical value is 14.7) .

Regarding the signs of the explanatory variables, as previously mentioned, all parameters were expected to be positive, with the exception of age. The wta regression coefficients correspond to the expectations.

The Tobit model also fits the data well. The homoscedasticity of the error process is supported by the likelihood test. The Chi-square test rejects the hypothesis that the set of coefficients are not statistically different from zero at the 1 per cent level of significance. The t-ratios below the parameter values, in parenthesis, measure the statistical significance of the parameters.

Regarding the signs of the explanatory variables, all variables are in accordance with the hypothesis. The marginal effect associated with the estimated parameters measures the partial impact of changes in the corresponding variables on the likelihood of sport managers revealing a wta, all other factors being constant.

8.   POLICY IMPLICATIONS

To estimate the individual mean wta (the mean economic wage of amateur sports managers), we multiplied the mean wta estimates by the average budget of clubs whose managers responded to the questionnaire. In the year 2000, the average club budget was 299 919 euros which gives the year average individual wta of 26 992 euros.

The aggregated wta upper bound figures were calculated by multiplying the individual mean wta estimates by the number of sports managers. There are 120 sports clubs in Madeira, each with 5 managers on the administrative council, giving a total number of 600 managers.

The lower bound figures are 62 per cent of the upper bound: 62 per cent of the questionnaires were completed; the remaining 38 per cent who failed to return them are assumed to have no interest or to be only minor participants in sports organisations and, following the practice recommended by Mitchell and Carson (1989, p. 282), they are assumed to have zero wta in order to avoid sample-selection bias.

Table 9.3   Aggregated value estimates for the economic value of sports managers

	Mean value	Upper bound	Lower bound
Aggregated wta (euros)	8 146 400	16 195 627	97 173

The aggregated mean value is the mean between the upper and lower bounds. Table 9.3 presents the estimates. We verify that values estimated are similar to a market salary for a graduate working in the private sector, and thus we conclude that the wta are overvalued for managers working in the public sector. This estimated economic worth is an estimation of the remuneration for a voluntary sports manager's work which would be paid in addition to the salary earned in his full-time (non-sport) occupation.

9. CONCLUSION

We have arrived at an estimation of the wta of Madeira's sports managers for their voluntary work using the OLS and Tobit estimators, which demonstrate that, despite different values for the parameters, the signs of these parameters are the same for all of the variables.

We verify that the signs of the variables are in accordance with the hypotheses. We conclude that the wta increases in relation to the size of the club and to voting preference, that is the larger the club (measured by the number of members), combined with voting for the incumbent political party, the higher the wta. On the other hand, the higher the age and having fixed working hours, the lower the wta.

What is the meaning of these results? These results are varied and difficult to interpret, but we can characterise the determinants of wta of the sports managers for their role in sport and say that the willingness-to-accept for their voluntary work (the probability in the Tobit model) is positively correlated with the club's dimensions, measured by the number of members. Possibly, this is because larger clubs require more effort to manage. Consequently, amateur managers may require a fee linked to the prestige of the club. Moreover, the wta is positively linked to the preference for voting for the incumbent political party, possibly signifying that sports managers seek to be compensated for their political preferences.

Wta is negatively related to occupation (the manager who has fixed working hours), denoting that the managers do not wish to be compensated by the opportunity cost associated with performing managerial tasks in sport. Finally, the wta is negatively related to age, meaning that older sports managers have no endowment value.

The policy implication of these results is that the annual individual economic salary for sports managers should be 26992 euros which is a high remuneration for a managerial position when compared with the revealed average year market wage of 19656 euros. The aggregated value of this economic salary is to be added to the aggregate non-market value of sports, which is a benchmark for the subsidy to be allocated to sports clubs.

Additional research is needed in order to confirm these results.

NOTE

1. An outline description of the IDRAM follows in Section 2 below

REFERENCES

Baade, R.A. (1996), 'Professional sports as a catalyst for metropolitan economic development', *Journal of Urban Affairs*, **18** (1), 1–17.

Barget, E. and J.J. Gouguet (2000), 'Impacte économique du spectacle sportif', *Revue Critique de la Littérature. Reflects et Perspectives de la Vie Économique*, Special edition, Bruxelles, 17–33.

Greene, W. (2000), *Econometric Analysis*. 4th edn, London: Prentice Hall.

Johnson, B.K. and J.C Whitehead (2000), 'The value of public goods from sports stadiums: the CVM approach', *Contemporary Economic Policy*, **18** (1), 48–58.

Johnson, B.K., P.A. Groothuis and J.C. Whitehead (2001), 'The value of public goods generated by a major league sports team: the CVM approach', *Journal of Sport Economics*, **21** (1), 6–21.

Mitchell, R.C. and R.T Carson (1989), *Using Surveys to Value Public Goods: Contingent Valuation Method*, Washington, DC: Resources for the Future.

Kerry Smith, V. (2000), 'JEEM and non-market valuation: 1974–1998', *Journal of Environmental Economics and Management*, **39**, 351–74.

Noll, R.G. and A. Zimbalist (eds) (1997), *Sports, Jobs and Taxes: The economic impact of sport teams and stadiums*, Washington, DC: Brookings Institution.

Quirk, J. and M. El-Hodiri (1974), 'The Economic Theory of Professional Sports Leagues', in Roger Noll (ed.), *Government and Sports Business*, Washington, DC: Brookings Institution.

Quirk, J. and R.D. Fort (1992), *Pay Dirt: The business of professional team sports*, Princeton, NJ: Princeton University Press.

Siegfried, J. and A. Zimbalist (2000), 'The economics of sports facilities and their communities', *Journal of Economic Perspectives*, **14** (3), 95–114.

Sloane, P. (1971), 'The economics of professional football: the football club as a utility maximizer', *Scottish Journal of Political Economy*, **17** (2), 121–45.

Vrooman, J. (2000), 'The economics of American sports leagues', *Scottish Journal of Political Economy*, **47** (4), 364–98.

Index